"I consider *Keeping Your Kids on God's Side* to be an important, eye-opening 'gateway' book. Natasha has done a wonderful job of quickly introducing the important issues and evidences from the perspective of a parent. She's engaging, thoughtful, and she knows how to throw the ball so you can catch it. Let *Keeping Your Kids on God's Side* serve as an introduction to the most important work you will ever do as a parent."

J. Warner Wallace
author of *Cold-Case Christianity* and *God's Crime Scene*
international speaker, professor at Biola University

"I almost wish my children were young again so I could use Natasha Crain's book with them. Through her parenting blog, Crain has access to the most important questions and challenges parents are hearing from their children today. She writes in strong, vigorous prose and does a great job of pitching her answers at a level that parents can understand—and, even more importantly, that they can use."

Nancy Pearcey
author of *Total Truth* and *Finding Truth*
apologetics professor, Houston Baptist University

"*Keeping Your Kids on God's Side* is a timely and much-needed book. Natasha provides a road map so parents feel equipped to have the critical (and difficult) faith conversations with their kids. If you want to see your kids have a vibrant faith, then get this book and start having these conversations with your kids today!"

Sean McDowell
author of more than 15 books, including *A New Kind of Apologist*
international speaker, professor at Biola University

"*Keeping Your Kids on God's Side* is an outstanding resource *every* Christian parent should have in their home library…this book is the most accessible, non-intimidating treatment of key apologetics issues I've seen to date, and I will be recommending it to every parent I encounter!"

Melissa Cain Travis
Assistant Professor of Apologetics, Houston Baptist University
author of Young Defenders series of apologetics books for kids

"Parents, wake up. The secular culture is challenging our kids like never before and we've got to prepare them for the barrage of false ideas they will most certainly face. Apologetic conversations are no longer optional; they're a necessary part of our kids' discipleship. Thankfully, *Keeping Your Kids on God's Side* is the resource we all need. It's accessible and comprehensive, and it will equip you to engage your kids in conversations that count, big time."

Brett Kunkle
Student Impact Director
Stand to Reason

"Many well-intentioned, godly parents unknowingly send their children out into the world malnourished by an insufficient diet of evidence for their faith…We know. Ratio Christi sees it every day in our chapters on high school and college campuses. Students come to us starving for ways to defend their faith from intellectual assault. As the director of parent outreach at Ratio Christi, I've been looking for a tool to recommend to parents so they can start this training early at home. This is it. Start feeding your family a steady diet of *Keeping Your Kids on God's Side* to strengthen their hearts and minds for the battles against the secular smorgasbord they will face."

Julie Loos
Director, Ratio Christi Boosters

"As a youth pastor, I'm thrilled to see an apologetics book written with parents in mind! It is not a matter of *if* your children or students will encounter arguments against Christianity, but *when*. Questions will come, and when they do, where will your kids find answers? The Internet? Their college professors? Atheist friends? We need to take responsibility to equip ourselves to be that resource…this book will help you do just that!"

Patrick Brown
Student Ministries Director
Whitehaven Road Baptist Church

"As a pastor over family ministries, I am very excited about this book! It answers many of the strong objections against Christianity in amazing depth, yet in such a clear manner that even someone new to apologetics can easily understand it."

Jared Novak
Family Pastor
New Life Church Bonita Springs

"I strongly recommend *Keeping Your Kids on God's Side* for parents who need brief but trustworthy answers to the skeptical objections their kids are likely to encounter…It is rare that so much solid information is found in one accessible resource!"

Douglas Beaumont
Professor of Theology, Belmont Abbey College

"Aside from the Bible, *Keeping Your Kids on God's Side* has just become the most important book in our house. Natasha walks you through all the 'tough' questions in such a way that it makes conversations with your kids easy…To be honest, this book has helped me with things I've wrestled with myself! I will be buying a copy for every parent I know and care about."

Mirinda
mom of 3

Keeping Your Kids on

GOD'S SIDE

NATASHA CRAIN

HARVEST HOUSE PUBLISHERS
EUGENE, OREGON

Cover by Koechel Peterson & Associates, Minneapolis, Minnesota

Cover photo © Sunny studio / Shutterstock

Dedication

To my wonderful husband, Bryan,
and our three dear children.
May we continually grow strong
in the Lord together.

KEEPING YOUR KIDS ON GOD'S SIDE

Copyright © 2016 Natasha Crain
Published by Harvest House Publishers
Eugene, Oregon 97402
www.harvesthousepublishers.com

Library of Congress Cataloging-in-Publication Data
   Crain, Natasha, 1976-
   Keeping your kids on God's side / Natasha Crain.
      pages cm
   ISBN 978-0-7369-6508-8 (pbk.)
   ISBN 978-0-7369-6509-5 (eBook)
   1. Christian education of children. 2. Christian education—Home training 3. Apologetics.
   I. Title.
   BV1475.3.C73 2016
   248.8'45—dc23

                       2015017112

Printed in the United States of America

16 17 18 19 20 21 22 23 24 / BP-JH / 10 9 8 7 6 5 4 3 2

Contents

Foreword

As a youth pastor, my first class of graduating seniors proved how difficult it can be to keep your kids on God's side. By the time they first returned from university (at Christmas break in their freshman year), most were no longer Christians. I couldn't believe it, and I felt like a terrible pastor. I had these students for their entire senior year of high school, yet nothing I taught them seemed to make an impact on the decisions they made in the first ten weeks at university. It was then that I realized the error of my inaugural year as a youth pastor. I had entertained them, helped them to form friendships in our youth group, and maybe even inspired them to be better human beings. But I hadn't given them sufficient reason to believe Christianity was true.

I quickly shifted gears. I was a part-time pastor and full-time homicide detective; my journey to faith was characterized by a careful examination of the evidence related to the existence of God and the reliability of the New Testament. Why hadn't I taken this approach with the students in my youth group? In many ways I simply got caught up in what has become the norm for many youth ministries. I wanted my group to grow, I wanted my students to like me, and I placed the bar very low in terms of what I required from them. After that first year, I decided my students' future certainty was far more important than their present entertainment.

That's why I love what Natasha Crain has done in her first book. As a parent, she gets it. Youth pastors simply can't do what each of us, as parents, must. The spiritual growth of our kids is our responsibility; we can't assign it to someone else. If you want to keep your kids in the truth, you're going to have to teach them why Christianity is true, and you're not going to be able to teach them unless you are willing to learn. Most of us, if pressed to defend what we believe as Christians, find ourselves woefully ill-equipped. How are we ever going to prepare our kids if we aren't first prepared?

If you're a Christian parent but you haven't yet mastered the rich case for God's existence and the truth of the Christian worldview, this book is an excellent place to start. In fact, I consider *Keeping Your Kids on God's Side* to be an important, eye-opening "gateway" book. Natasha has done a wonderful job of quickly introducing the important issues and evidences from the perspective of a parent. She's engaging, thoughtful, and she knows how to throw the ball so you can catch it. Take the time to read this book and absorb the evidence Natasha presents; then visit Natasha's website to see her recommendations for additional reading. Let *Keeping Your Kids on God's Side* serve as an introduction to the most important work you will ever do as a parent. Learn the case so you can give your kids reasons to believe.

J. Warner Wallace
Cold-Case Detective and
author of *Cold-Case Christianity* and
God's Crime Scene

What Your Kids Need for a Confident Faith

I remember the exact day I realized I had no idea what I was doing as a parent.

My twins were four months old and were lying on a blanket in the living room. From birth until that moment, I confidently thrived as a new parent. I had two little humans who had predictable needs that I could manage and fulfill in my controlled home environment. I was one of *those* people who piled the books high on various philosophies of infant sleep scheduling, feeding, and development. I wanted to do everything *perfectly*. My twins were sleeping 12 hours per night by 10 weeks old, with 3 precisely scheduled naps and 8 precisely scheduled mealtimes during the day. As a true type A person who gets excited about taking charge, I was totally in my zone.

Then came that day when I stared down at the two four-month-olds lying on the floor. Their eyes expectantly searched mine, as if waiting for me to do something. I ran through my mental checklist of daily baby activities, but it wasn't time to eat, sleep, or poop. (Yes, I even documented every bowel movement for weeks to ensure my kids were within the expected range.) It wasn't until that moment that I realized my knowledge wasn't going to be sufficient for the job much longer. A palpable wave of fear suddenly washed over me: *Now what?*

I had no idea what to do next. My babies were ready for more, but "more" involved a never-ending sea of child development possibilities. It was no longer enough to keep them alive via my poop journal and sleep schedules (gasp!). Now I would have to help them *thrive*. I suddenly realized that day that what I had mastered so far wouldn't be enough.

When our twins were toddlers, my husband and I started thinking about new areas of parenting with seemingly endless possibilities: how to raise our kids to learn about, love, and follow Jesus. Frankly, I had no idea how to do that beyond taking them to church each week. As someone who was raised in a Christian home yet later spent years fighting spiritual apathy and doubt, I was all too familiar with the complexities of faith. If I had so much trouble figuring out my *own* faith, how on Earth was I going to help my kids figure out *theirs*?

To help me in the process, I casually decided to start a Christian parenting blog (NatashaCrain.com) so I could connect with other parents and share ideas for building a Christ-centered home. That turned out to be a fateful decision. My blog did introduce me to other Christian parents...but it also introduced me to a world of skeptics.

Portrait of a Hostile World

After I had been blogging for several months, I became interested in learning about the creation-versus-evolution debate and spent time studying it in-depth. I wanted to share what I had learned with other Christian parents, so I created and posted a flowchart showing the six major views people have on the subject (see chapter 33).

The post went viral—amongst atheist groups.

Within a few hours, it reached over 26,000 people and received almost 300 comments, most of which were personal attacks against me or the intelligence of Christians in general. Here's a sampling of the responses to my post:

"Yeah, facts and rational thought aren't very important for these crazies."

"Intelligent and religious are mutually exclusive. There is no god. End of debate."

"Please, don't tell me people actually believe this."

"Debating a Christian is impossible. They rely on 'faith' (fantasy) where an atheist relies on evidence."

"If your children are smart, they will ask for proof...unless you already brainwashed them to the point they won't DARE ask why out of fear that some imaginary sky being will torture them for eternity for asking such a simple question."

"Remember, folks, these people are breeding!"

I have to admit, I was *shocked* by these attacks. I grew up in a Christian home and, as an adult, rarely had friends or co-workers who were antagonistic to faith. Once I had kids, my world got even smaller. Without the luxury of significant free time, I found myself limiting friendships to a handful of people who were like me—in the same life stage and sharing the same values. I simply had never been so challenged in my faith as I was the day I received those scathing comments. I'm grateful now, because that day changed my life.

It was then that I realized how utterly unprepared I was to explain to nonbelievers—and, ultimately, my kids—why I believe in Jesus.

I knew that had to change.

I immersed myself nearly nonstop in learning how to make a case for and defend Christianity—a discipline called *Christian apologetics.* Although my passion for apologetics started because of my role as a blogger, I discovered in the process why an understanding of apologetics is even more important for my role as a *parent.* I learned that attacks on Christianity—like those I experienced on my blog—are driving young people away from faith in droves.

Our kids desperately need our help. Here's what's happening.

Outcomes of a Hostile World

> 61% of kids who were involved in church as recently as their teenage years become spiritually disengaged by their 20s—not actively praying, reading the Bible or attending church.[1]

This finding, based on the extensive surveys of researcher George Barna, is the alarm that has sent pastors, youth leaders, and young adult ministries desperately searching for answers. Multiple independent groups have since conducted their own studies and have identified the same trend—with some estimates of those turning away from Christianity as high as 88 percent.[2]

Why is this happening? Having studied the various survey results in depth, I think it's fair to summarize the collective problem in one sentence: *A lack of robust spiritual training has resulted in a featherweight faith for many of today's young adults, and that faith is being blown away by attacks from our secular culture.*

Young people are turning away from faith because they've accepted the popular claims that Christianity is irrational, antiscience, intolerant, and based on an irrelevant ancient book. These claims have compelling answers from a Christian worldview, but young people aren't leaving home *equipped* with those answers. For example, fewer than 1 in 10 Christian families read the Bible together during a typical week, and a study of 11,000 teenagers showed that only 12 percent of youth have regular conversations with their mom on faith issues.[3/4] Most kids growing up in Christian homes aren't receiving anything *remotely* resembling the spiritual training they need to have a lasting faith.

After young adults turn *away* from Christianity, they're turning *to* atheism or agnosticism. The percent of Americans identifying as Protestant, Catholic, or Orthodox has decreased 6 percent *just since 2007*.[5] Meanwhile, the percentage who identify as atheist, agnostic, or "nothing in particular" has grown by 4.3 percent. This trend is even more striking among young adults. Thirty-eight percent of atheists are now 18 to 29 years old, compared with 29 percent of the general public. The decline in Christians clearly corresponds to the increase in these groups.

Even with steadily rising numbers, the total percent of atheists and agnostics is currently only 5 percent in America. That number is highly misleading, however, when it comes to quantifying their *spiritual impact*. Atheists and agnostics represent much more than 5 percent of the voices kids will hear in the media and see online because so many of them are passionately engaged in advocating their worldview. There's nothing wrong with that, of course. They're as free to share their beliefs as we are. But it does mean young Christians are actively being drawn into a worldview battle that wasn't so prominent even 10 years ago. Unfortunately, they're losing their faith in that battle because they haven't been equipped for the fight. If you want to keep your kids on God's side, you'll have to make sure they're armed.

Solutions for a Hostile World

So what should Christian parents do? We need to raise our kids with a faith that's *specifically prepared* for the challenges they'll face. Let me explain.

We take this idea of *specific preparation* for granted in our everyday lives. If we're going to the beach, we bring a beach ball. If we're going out in the rain, we bring an umbrella. If we're going camping, we bring a tent. And if we're aiming to do something highly challenging, we make *extra* sure we're prepared. For example, imagine you want to climb Mount Everest. If you don't know and physically prepare for the specific challenges you'll face—for example, the temperatures, the oxygen level, and the elevation gain—there's no way you'll make it to the top. *No one* would blindly show up at the mountain having done a few jumping jacks.

How much more important is the goal of raising kids to know and love Jesus? Yet most Christian parents are doing the spiritual equivalent of a few jumping jacks at the mountain of their kids' faith development. They have little idea of the spiritual challenges their children will face, and consequently aren't doing what is *specifically needed* to prepare them for those encounters. Simply taking them to church each Sunday isn't going to cut it (nor should it).

Here's my call to action: We have to stop winging our Christian parenting and start getting in shape to prepare our kids for what's ahead.

Consider this book your personal trainer.

How This Book Will Help You

Based on my experience engaging with skeptics of Christianity, I've selected what I believe are the 40 faith conversations parents most urgently need to have with their kids (over time, of course—I'm not suggesting that "urgently" means in the next couple of weeks!). This "training plan" will (1) introduce you to today's hot-button topics of faith, and (2) give you concise, easy-to-understand answers that will prepare you for these discussions with your kids.

What this book does *not* do is actually script the conversations you should have. But there's a good reason for that: Every family has a unique set of personalities, ages, interests, relationships, and spiritual histories, so an *effective* one-size-fits-all conversation plan would be impossible to create. In order for dialogue to be meaningful, you'll need to tailor your discussions for your own family.

Although the chapters are somewhat independent of one another, I recommend that you read them sequentially, from chapter 1 to 40. The conversations have been arranged in a framework that will help you build your knowledge in the most logical and impactful way.

On a final note, in case you're wondering how you would ever have time to talk with your kids about the subjects in this book, rest assured that I completely understand how you're feeling. I have three young children. My time is also sucked away by explaining for the one-millionth time why sharing is important, shuttling kids to sports events, and figuring out how to get my kids to (please, please) stop fighting. I get it. The thought of talking with your children about challenging issues of faith in the midst of all that can sound unrealistic or flat-out impossible. But it's not. It's *really* not. You'll be surprised at how often opportunities arise to talk about faith once you're on the lookout for them.

So let's get to it! First up: What evidence is there for God's existence?

PART 1:

Conversations About
GOD

1. What evidence is there for God's existence?

A pastor I know asked his Facebook friends one day, "How do you find God?" Here's a representative sampling of the 70-plus responses:

"I find Him through worship music."

"In my husband and children."

"In the everyday moments of life."

"That still, small voice within."

"By being quiet."

"I just know He's there."

Not one of the people who responded mentioned finding God in any objective sense. Why does it matter? Personal experience, while meaningful to a Christian, is of limited value for discussing God's existence with nonbelievers—or with kids who are being challenged in their faith. To understand why, consider how easily a skeptic could counter each of the answers above.

"How you feel while listening to music has nothing to do with God's existence."

"Science shows that your husband and children are a product of blind evolutionary forces, not a loving God."

"The everyday moments of life are filled with horrible events for some people. That's evidence against a god, not for one."

"That still, small voice within is just you talking to yourself."

"When I'm quiet, I *don't* find God. So how do you know you're right?"

"I just know He's *not* there based on scientific evidence."

Consider how you would respond if *your kids* made statements like these. Would you be able to offer evidence for God's existence outside of your personal experience?

Melanie, one of my blog readers, faced that situation with her teenage son. She emailed me one day about his conversion to atheism:

> A year ago, when my son was 17, he told me that Christianity is the dumbest, lamest, and most ridiculous religion there is! He turned into a full atheist who has a scientific or philosophical answer to everything. All I had was a faith

that I knew was real and true because I felt it and I believed it. That's it! I had nothing to offer him—no knowledge of the answers he needed. The atheist worldview and philosophies won the battle. I didn't have the answers for my son. They did.

As Melanie said, if we don't have the answers our kids need, atheists will be happy to fill in the gaps.

This chapter will introduce you to three major arguments that provide compelling, objective evidence for God's existence: the cosmological argument, the design argument, and the moral argument. Chances are, your kids won't hear about this kind of evidence in church. *It will be up to you to share it with them.*

The Cosmological Argument

The cosmological argument states that the universe couldn't have just popped into existence on its own—its existence had to have been *caused* by something else. More formally stated:

1. The universe had a beginning.
2. Anything that had a beginning must have been caused by something else.
3. Therefore, the universe was caused by something else, which we call God.

Let's briefly look at each part of this argument.

Part 1: The universe had a beginning.

I know that sounds like a no-brainer: "Of course the universe had a beginning. How else would it have gotten here?" That's the logic of our everyday experience. We know everything around us had a beginning and hasn't just existed forever. But scientists for many years believed the universe *itself* was eternal.

Everything changed in the 1920s, however. Astronomer Edwin Hubble discovered that the universe is expanding. He observed that other galaxies are moving away from us, like spots on an inflating balloon. *If the universe is expanding, it implies a beginning.* Why? If you rewind the process of a thing expanding (think of *deflating* the balloon), you eventually get back to a single point—the moment that thing *began*. Hubble's findings had huge significance. They provided scientific evidence that the universe had a beginning after all.

Part 2: Anything that had a beginning must have been caused by something else.

The second part of this argument is somewhat less debated than the first. Almost everyone agrees that things with a beginning are caused by something or someone else; things don't pop into existence out of thin air. This premise is constantly confirmed by our experience in the natural world.

Part 3: Therefore, the universe was caused by something else, which we call God.

Let's recap what we have so far: (1) widely accepted scientific evidence that the universe had a beginning, and (2) knowledge that anything with a beginning is caused by something else. That leads us to the conclusion that the *universe* had to have been caused by something else. The million-dollar question: What could that have been?

A skeptic can't dismissively state, "It could have been anything." Knowing the capabilities it would take to create our known universe greatly narrows what kind of cause it could have been—for example, it *couldn't* have been a dog!

Dr. William Lane Craig, a leading Christian philosopher, concludes that the cause of the universe would have to match the following profile: personal (that is, able to choose to create), uncaused, beginningless, changeless, immaterial, timeless, spaceless, and enormously powerful.[1] That's consistent with what many people call *God*.

But if everything needs a cause, what caused God?

It's important to understand that the cosmological argument doesn't say *everything* has a cause. Rather, it says everything *that has a beginning* has a cause. In order for a cause to create a universe of space and time, that cause has to be *outside* of space and time (eternal). Whether you call that God or anything else, it cannot have had a beginning itself. It has to have been the original "uncaused cause."

In a nutshell, the cosmological argument provides evidence for God based on the need for a cause of the universe. Now we'll look at evidence for God based on the *design* of the universe and the life it hosts.

The Design Argument

Generally speaking, the design argument states that a designer (for example, God) must exist because the universe and living things show evidence of design by an intelligent agent. The most famous explanation of this is the watchmaker analogy given by theologian William Paley in 1802. Paley stated that if you were to find a watch in an empty field, you would instinctively conclude that it was designed and not just the result of accidental formation in nature. Similarly, when we look at the universe and life, it's natural to conclude that there's a designer because they appear to be so intentionally formed.

Almost all scientists—atheists and theists alike—acknowledge that the universe and life at least have the *appearance* of design rather than the appearance of formation by chance. The question is whether they demonstrate *actual* design attributable to a *designer* (such as God). More specifically, this question is debated in the context of certain areas of biology and physics. We'll now look briefly at those subjects.

Design in Biology: The Language of DNA

Our bodies are made up of trillions of cells (the basic biological unit in living organisms). Each cell contains DNA, which carries all the information needed to direct the functioning of the human body. The volume of information in human DNA is staggering: It's roughly equivalent to 12 sets of *The Encyclopedia Britannica*—384 volumes![2]

This complex information works amazingly like a computer code or language. *That's significant because all known codes and languages were created by an intelligent agent and not by chance.* This strongly suggests that the information in human DNA *also* came from an intelligent agent—a "designer" such as God (see chapter 40 for more on this).

Design in Physics: The "Fine-Tuning" of the Earth and Universe

To understand the meaning of "fine-tuning," Christian apologist and author Sean McDowell suggests imagining that you just stumbled upon a cabin in the woods.[3] When you enter it, you discover that your favorite music is playing, your favorite video game is on the television, and your favorite drinks are in the refrigerator. Would you think a cabin like that existed by chance, or would you assume someone prepared it for *you*? It would be hard to imagine that a place so perfectly tailored to your personal needs would have formed that way by chance.

In many ways, our Earth is like this cabin. It appears to have been uniquely designed to support human life—it's as if the Earth knew we were coming. A planet, its planetary companions, its moon, its star, and its galaxy have dozens of parameters requiring precise values in order for physical life to exist.[4] For example, if the Earth were tilted a little more or a little less, its surface temperatures would vary too much to support life. Similarly, the physical constants of nature (things like the strength of gravity) have extraordinarily precise values. If they were just a *hair* different, life couldn't exist.

The two arguments we've looked at so far—the cosmological and design arguments—are based on the nature of the physical world around us. The third and final argument is quite different: It considers the knowledge *within* us.

The Moral Argument

The moral argument states that (1) objective moral standards exist outside of personal opinion, and (2) the best explanation for the existence of those standards is the existence of a moral law giver (such as God). Again, let's look at each part of the argument.

1. Objective moral standards exist.

We all have a moral intuition that immediately tells us certain things are wrong regardless of opinion—for example, torturing someone for fun. It seems obvious we're born with that moral understanding. However, there are two major objections to the claim that objective standards actually exist.

Objection 1: Cultures have different ideas of right and wrong, so there must not be an objective morality. This sounds reasonable at first, but it's actually a weak objection. To see why, imagine ten people counting how many marbles are in a jar. If four people give the wrong number, does that mean there is no correct answer? Of course not. Similarly, it doesn't logically follow that there's no objectively correct morality just because cultures sometimes disagree over what's right and wrong.

Objection 2: Morals are just a matter of personal opinion. Some people would object to the marbles example because they claim morals are just a matter of personal opinion and don't *have* correct answers. This idea is pervasive in our culture, but it's easy to see the contradiction in such a belief. If morals are just a matter of opinion, you can never legitimately say anything or anyone is objectively wrong. But if you steal a car from a person who claims that morals are just a matter of opinion, you can bet they'll still say you did something bad. Telling them that, in your opinion, stealing is just fine won't go over very well. While it may be convenient to claim morals are just a matter of opinion, no one actually lives as if they believe that's true. The fact that at least *some* objective moral standards exist is hard to deny.[5]

2. The best explanation for the existence of objective moral standards is the existence of a moral lawgiver.

If there's an objective set of moral laws that, to some degree, guide all humans, where do those laws come from? *Laws imply a lawgiver.* Therefore, the existence of objective morality is best explained by the existence of a lawgiving God.

Before we conclude, it's important to note what the moral argument does *not* suggest. Many people erroneously believe Christians think non-Christians can't be "good" without God. Not so. The Bible says God gave *everyone* a moral compass (Romans 1:18-23). Anyone can exhibit good behavior in relation to those objective standards, whether they choose to acknowledge the Source of those standards or not. The question is not whether people can be good without believing in God, but whether anything can legitimately be *called* good without a God who defines objective standards.

Three Powerful Lines of Evidence for God's Existence

Contrary to the popular claims of atheists, there *is* powerful objective evidence for God's existence (see chapters 8 and 11 for more on this). In this chapter, we looked at the three most frequently discussed arguments that provide this evidence: the cosmological argument, the design argument, and the moral argument.

To be clear, these arguments don't show that the creating, designing, and moral lawgiving God is the same as the biblical God. In fact, some people have come to believe there's a supreme being based on this evidence but continue to reject any revealed religion.[6] That means this kind of evidence is *necessary* but not *sufficient* for demonstrating the truth of Christianity. It should be valued for what it is: the critical starting point that opens the door to discussing the topics covered in the rest of this book.

2. How could a good God allow evil and suffering?

My daughters are both strong-willed. As parents of strong-willed children know, that's a euphemism for "they can quickly drag me to the very edge of my sanity." The good side of this challenge (or so I tell myself) is that it gives me plenty of opportunities to talk to them about how we can work with God daily to have a "good heart" and to "want the things that God wants."

One night, I was tucking my oldest daughter into bed after a particularly difficult day. I didn't have to tell her just how hard it had been. Unsolicited, she cried, "Mommy, I tried soooo hard to be good today. But I just kept messing up. I don't know how to be better like God wants!"

I empathetically smiled at her, thinking of how the apostle Paul felt the same frustration of not being fully transformed in this life (Romans 7:15-20). But before I could dispense my motherly wisdom on why we'll never be perfect, she took the conversation in another direction.

"Why doesn't God just stop me from being mean before it happens? Like, right before I'm mean, why doesn't He just make me be nice?"

My son, listening with interest from the other room, yelled over, "Yeah, like I don't understand why He doesn't just stop bad guys before they do bad stuff. Why wouldn't He just want good things to happen?"

There it was. My young twins had already sniffed out a perceived contradiction in their budding faith: If God is perfectly good, how can there be evil in the world He created? My kids were in good company by identifying the issue. It's a question that's been asked for thousands of years and continues to be one of the most significant challenges to Christianity today.

Millions of pages have been written on the problem of evil. This chapter will introduce you to *one* major framework Christians use to address the issue. If you'd like to do further reading, I highly recommend the resource in this chapter's endnotes as a starting point.[1]

Defining the Problem of Evil

In chapter 1, we looked at the claim that there's no evidence *for* God. Here, we're looking at a very different kind of problem. We're looking at what atheists assert is evidence *against* God: the existence of evil.

Why is the existence of evil such a difficult problem for Christianity? The heart of the issue is this: If God is all-good, He *would* eliminate evil. If God is all-powerful, He *could* eliminate evil. But evil exists. How, then, can the existence of evil be reconciled with the existence of God?

Christians often run straight to Genesis 3 to answer any and all questions of this nature. This is the passage that describes what is often called "the fall of man." When Adam disobeyed God by eating from the tree of knowledge of good and evil, God said:

> Because you listened to your wife and ate fruit from the tree about which I commanded you, "You must not eat from it," cursed is the ground because of you; through painful toil you will eat food from it all the days of your life. It will produce thorns and thistles for you, and you will eat the plants of the field. By the sweat of your brow you will eat your food until you return to the ground, since from it you were taken; for dust you are and to dust you will return (Genesis 3:17-19).

Many Christians believe all evil and suffering in the world can be traced back to this "fall."[2] That said, there are a couple reasons why we need to address the problem of evil beyond a pat response of, "The Bible tells us we're a fallen people in a fallen world."

First, when the problem of evil is raised by an atheist, keep in mind that person doesn't believe in the truth of the Bible. In order for our kids to engage with nonbelievers on this issue, they need an understanding of how it can *logically* be possible for God and evil to coexist.

The second reason is that the problem of evil can be a very emotional one—one that's often tied to a tragic personal experience. It can be difficult even for Christians to understand how the bad choice of one person—Adam—led to all the evil and suffering in our world. It's all the more impossible to imagine for nonbelievers who have experienced tragedy closely. Gaining a deeper understanding of how God and evil can coexist helps everyone—believer *and* nonbeliever—make further sense of this difficult problem.

Let's look now at one framework many Christians use to address the problem of evil.

Did God Create Evil?

There are many aspects of the problem of evil, but the starting point for discussion is typically this: If God created everything, and evil is something, doesn't that mean God created evil? Because Christians believe God is perfectly good, and that God created only good things (Genesis 1:31), it can seem impossible to answer this question without admitting to a major contradiction. But the premises of the argument aren't quite right. Let's see why.

There's no doubt from the Christian perspective that God created everything (Genesis 1:1; John 1:3; Colossians 1:16). Christians also believe that evil is very real. (The reason it's important to state that seemingly obvious point is that there are some religions, like Christian Science, which claim evil is *not* real.) The tricky part is what we mean when we say that evil is "something." *We need to understand that evil is real, but it doesn't exist as a "something" by itself.* Instead, evil is the *corruption* of a *good* thing.

That's not as hard to understand as it might seem at first. Think of rot in a tree, for example. Rot doesn't exist by itself—it only exists as a corruption of the formerly good tree. Another example would be a wound on your body. Thinking about evil in this way means that God created only good things, but evil is the corruption of His good creation.

So Where Does Corruption Come From?

So far we've established that God didn't create evil, but evil (the corruption of a good thing) does happen, and God obviously *allows* it to happen. So where does corruption come from? First, let's consider human corruption, or moral evil. Later in this chapter we'll consider corruption in nature, or natural evil (for example, tornadoes and hurricanes).

Why didn't God make perfect humans who *can't* be corrupted? The traditional answer is free will, which is our ability to make choices without external coercion. It's one of the good things God created. God made moral evil *possible* by giving us free will, but we are the ones responsible for making it *actual*.

In *Mere Christianity*, C.S. Lewis took this a step further and proposed why free will might be so important to God that He would choose to make free creatures despite knowing the evil that would inevitably result from their choices:

> Why, then, did God give them free will? Because free will, though it makes evil possible, is also the only thing that makes possible any love or goodness or joy worth having. A world of automata—of creatures that worked like machines—would hardly be worth creating...Of course God knew what would happen if they used their freedom the wrong way: apparently He thought it worth the risk.[3]

In other words, God wanted us to *freely* love Him. A forced love is no love at all.

But Why Doesn't God Just *Stop* Moral Evil?

At this point, many people ask why an all-good and all-powerful God doesn't just stop the moral evil that's *possible* before it *happens* (this is what my twins effectively asked). To answer this, we need to be careful about how we define *all-powerful*. Christians often say, "God can do anything!" But that's actually not true. For example, it's impossible for God to lie (Hebrews 6:18). Lying would be contrary to God's very nature. In addition, God can't do anything contradictory, like make a square circle or a stone so heavy He can't lift it.

Given that God chose to create us with free will, is it possible to destroy moral evil without destroying our present world? Actually, no. This is one of those contradictions—like creating a square circle—that makes something impossible: God can't *force* us to *freely* make good choices. The only way God could destroy evil would be to destroy our freedom.

To conclude our discussion of moral evil, it's important to note that Christians believe the story doesn't stop there. Christians acknowledge that this is the current state of affairs, but that one day God will defeat evil by bringing this world to an end and creating a new Earth (Revelation 21–22). This new Earth will be free from evil, suffering, and death.

What About Natural Evil?

Let's return now to the question of where corruption *in nature* comes from. Most theologians agree that natural evil is more difficult to address than moral evil. While skeptics might admit that God need not be responsible for the free will actions of humans, they are quick to point out that humans don't choose devastating natural disasters.

The most common response to the problem of natural evil is that it's actually the *byproduct* of good processes. For example, earthquakes are the consequence of plate tectonics, or the movement of giant plates under the ocean floor. Without these plates, we would have no continents. They're a necessary prerequisite to human survival on the only planet known to have life. Occasionally, however, these same processes hurt or kill people. Author Dinesh D'Souza notes, "Our planet requires oxygen and a warming sun and water in order for us to live here, and we appreciate this, even though we recognize that people can get sunstroke and drown in the ocean. So, too, it seems that plate tectonics are...a 'central requirement for life' as we know it."[4]

In other cases, things that appear to be natural evils are actually the result of moral evils. For example, millions of Africans die of starvation because their corrupt governments don't allow the necessary food to reach them—*not* because the Earth doesn't produce enough food. In such cases, the problem circles right back to individual free will.

Ultimately, we can't explain every instance of natural evil. What we *can* say is that God must have *morally sufficient reasons* for permitting the natural evil we do see.

The Problem of Evil Is Tough but Not Insurmountable

While the problem of evil is undoubtedly a difficult challenge to Christianity, that doesn't mean there are no answers we can offer. As we just saw, moral and natural evil can both be viewed as byproducts of God's perfectly good creation. We can best help our kids in this area by honestly acknowledging the enormous difficulty of the issue, introducing them to thoughtful answers like those discussed here, and pointing them back to the overwhelming evidence for God discussed in chapter 1.

3. Why would God command the genocide of the Canaanites?

When I was a kid, my favorite church song was "Joshua Fought the Battle of Jericho." If you grew up in a Protestant church, you can probably hear the tune in your head right now. I was fascinated by the thought of how the "walls came a-tumblin' down" after the Israelites marched around the city of Jericho seven times. And I *loved* falling to the ground with my friends when we shouted the last "down" in the song together.

We would laugh hysterically and ask the teacher if we could please sing it just one more time.

Today I can't hear that song without thinking of how disturbing many skeptics would find this scene of children joyfully singing about the first battle of what is popularly called the Canaanite genocide...arguably the most morally controversial event in the Bible.

In case you're a little fuzzy on Old Testament history, the Canaanite genocide refers to God's command to utterly destroy the people of Canaan so the Israelites could take over their land and build a nation. The books of Joshua and Judges are devoted to describing the long sequence of wars and the aftermath that ensued as the Israelites carried out God's instructions.

The idea that God ordered an entire nation of men, women, and children to be wiped out in this manner is no small moral issue from the skeptics' perspective. They argue that if a good God exists, He clearly wouldn't command something immoral like genocide. They conclude that God must not exist or the Bible must be wrong in attributing these events to His command.

This issue has impacted the faith of many people. As one example, here's a comment from my blog, written by an atheist who lost her faith due in large part to Old Testament difficulties. She explained:

> The kicker for me, ultimately, was the problem of evil, or as I would put it more personally, the problem of indignity and horror. Yes, *maybe* God has a "morally sufficient reason" for allowing horror and commanding horrific acts, but...if there is a single moral standard that applies universally across all responsible agents, then it is just as wrong for God to stand by and watch evil being done as it would be for us to do so.

This is a topic that Christians often don't think about until adulthood—long after they stop singing "Joshua Fought the Battle of Jericho" in Sunday school. But it can eventually become extremely concerning, as it did for this commenter. Today's atheists are placing a significant emphasis on bringing Old Testament concerns to everyone's attention, so this is a conversation we really need to have with our kids (see also chapters 30, 31, and 32).

In this chapter, we'll look at the biblical background for the "Canaanite genocide," then consider the big question: Was God's command immoral?

A Promise of Land...and an Execution of Judgment

In order to better understand the Canaanite invasion, we need to back up to a key event that happened more than 400 years earlier.

In Genesis 12:1-3, God promised Abraham that He would bless all the families of the Earth through his descendants. As a result, Abraham was to become the ancestral father of God's chosen people, the Israelites, and ultimately of Jesus Himself. Part of this blessing included the Israelites' eventual inheritance of the land of Canaan (Genesis 15:18-21).

When the time came for the Israelites to inherit the land, however, they couldn't just pack their bags and move in. *The land was already inhabited by the Canaanite people.*

Why was that such a big deal? Well, the Canaanites were very depraved. In Leviticus 18:20-30, God said they were guilty of multiple abominations, including adultery, child sacrifice, homosexuality, and beastiality. In addition, they practiced idolatry, witchcraft, fortune-telling, and sorcery (Deuteronomy 18:9-14). They weren't necessarily the worst people who ever lived, but the Bible makes it clear that they were extremely corrupt.

God didn't want the Israelites to settle amongst the highly immoral Canaanites because this was a particularly crucial time in the history of salvation. He sought to establish Israel in the Promised Land to facilitate His longer-term plan of bringing redemption to mankind through Jesus. He wanted the Israelites to be physically, morally, and theologically set apart to carry His message forward hundreds of years to the time of the Savior. Otherwise, Israel could have been permanently led astray by false teachings.

If (1) God promised the Israelites the land of Canaan, (2) the

Canaanites were already living there, and (3) the Israelites and Canaanites couldn't live in the land together given the potentially devastating influence of the Canaanites' immorality, *the Canaanites had to go.*

We have no idea how God would have made the Canaanites go if they weren't such a depraved people (or if they would have needed to go in the first place). But, given their level of wickedness, God chose to execute judgment on them and issued the command that troubles so many people today:

> In the cities of these peoples that the LORD your God is giving you for an inheritance, you shall save alive nothing that breathes, but you shall devote them to complete destruction, the Hittites and the Amorites, the Canaanites and the Perizzites, the Hivites and the Jebusites, as the LORD your God has commanded, that they may not teach you to do according to all their abominable practices that they have done for their gods, and so you sin against the LORD your God (Deuteronomy 20:16-18).

Skeptics, of course, focus on the difficult command here to destroy every single Canaanite. But it's clear from the wider context that God wasn't ordering some kind of indiscriminate massacre so His favored people could move in. This was a *judgment.* In fact, God explicitly stated as much in Deuteronomy 9:5:

> Not because of your righteousness or the uprightness of your heart are you going in to possess their land, but because of the wickedness of these nations the LORD your God is driving them out from before you, and that he may confirm the word that the LORD swore to your fathers, to Abraham, to Isaac, and to Jacob.

What we've seen here is that the time for the fulfillment of God's land promise to Abraham converged with the time when God was ready to execute judgment upon that land's inhabitants. This is the essential background we need in order to answer the next big question:

Was God's Command Immoral?

As I mentioned earlier, skeptics often refer to God's command as an order of genocide. *Genocide* is "the deliberate and systematic extermination of a national, racial, political, or cultural group."[1] Many Christians bristle at that label because genocide evokes horrendous images of events like the Holocaust, carried out by deplorable dictators. A war of terminology then ensues. But assigning a label is far less important than getting to the crux of the skeptics' concern: Was God's command to exterminate a cultural group immoral or not?[2] To address this, we need to establish one key point: *God commanding "genocide" is in no way morally comparable to* humans *commanding genocide.*

Most people accept that earthly judges have the authority to sentence depraved criminals to death. If the perfectly good and just God of the Bible exists, we have to acknowledge that He would similarly have the authority to execute judgment on sinners—anyone from individual sinners to entire cultural groups (see chapter 4 for more on the nature of sin and God's just character). As we saw earlier, God said His command was indeed an *act of judgment* on guilty people—something in a completely different moral category than an unmerited massacre of innocent life, as is always the case when humans command genocide.

Frankly, skeptics hate this logic. They find it revolting that someone would suggest genocide could be anything *but* immoral, regardless of *who* commanded it. But when we're making a moral distinction based on the source of the command, we're not splitting fine hairs and uncomfortably tiptoeing away—the source of the command makes all the difference in the world. It's the difference between a perfectly good God who can never choose to do evil and sinful humans who can choose to do evil at any time; between a God who has the *authority* to execute judgment and humans who have *no* authority to execute judgment; and between a God who has the *ability* to judge fairly and humans who have *no* ability to judge fairly because they lack the necessary perspective to do so. In other words, this isn't the difference between John Doe and Mary Smith. This is the difference between humans and *God*.

Many arguments have been raised to challenge this notion that the Canaanite genocide could have been the fair judgment of a perfect God. For example, skeptics say it doesn't sound like the Canaanites were bad *enough* to warrant such severe judgment; that they shouldn't have been held morally responsible for their sin because they were simply following the practices of their parents; that a fair God would have given them more opportunities to repent; or that even if the parents were bad, the children were innocent.

Christians have offered extensive responses to each of these (and many related) objections. I've listed resources in the endnotes if you'd like to read more.[3] But ultimately they all come back to this: *Only God knows the depth of people's depravity and whether or not they will repent in any given circumstance.* The Bible even hints at how precisely God knows people's depravity: In Genesis 15:16, He told Abraham that He would wait several generations to bring the Israelites into the Promised Land because the iniquity of the Amorites (one of the Canaanite groups) *was not yet complete.* In other words, God wasn't willing to execute judgment until their sinfulness had reached a very specific limit. It's simply not reasonable to think that humans are in a position to evaluate how fair a divine judgment was based on the limited perspective we have.

An Execution of God's Judgment...Not an Immoral Massacre

God's command to destroy the Canaanites was given in a unique historical and theological context; the time for the fulfillment of God's land promise to Abraham converged with the time when God was ready to execute judgment upon that land's inhabitants. While this event is undoubtedly difficult to understand, we have to acknowledge that God commanding "genocide" is in no way morally comparable to humans commanding genocide. God uniquely has the *authority* to judge people and the *ability* to do so fairly. That makes all the moral difference in the world. The Canaanite "genocide" was an execution of this judgment—not an immoral massacre.

4. How can a loving God send people to hell?

A friend once said to me, "I believe in Jesus and all He taught. But I can't believe in hell. I think of how much I adore my own kids, and no matter what they did, I would never want them to be severely punished. God must love us even *more* than that, so how could He create hell?"

I replied, "Well…if you believe all that Jesus taught, you'll have to believe in hell. Jesus Himself spoke of it as a reality many times."

My friend paused for a long moment, then concluded, "I just don't believe in hell."

There was absolutely nothing that could convince my friend that any kind of punishment after death was a plausible idea. Like my friend, many people see such punishment as being impossibly at odds with a loving God.

There's no denying that hell is a very difficult topic—one of the most difficult topics for Christians to discuss. Parents often avoid talking about hell with their kids because they're either worried it will scare them or they just don't know what to say. But the Bible undeniably speaks of hell as a harsh reality, so it's important that we don't just ignore it.

In addition, there are many very wrong ideas about hell floating around, and Christian parents have the responsibility of proactively giving their kids an *accurate* understanding of it. When young people lack this understanding, they're often quick to dismiss hell based on simple "gut reaction." But hell is too serious a topic to leave to the discretion of our kids' feelings. We need to guide their understanding from a biblical perspective.

In the next few pages, we'll look at three layers of questions about hell that people often unknowingly roll into one big objection: (1) Why does God need to punish *anyone*? (2) *Who* should be punished? And (3) what should the *nature* of punishment be?

Why does God need to punish *anyone*?

My friend's logic—that *any* punishment is at odds with God's love—is very common. There are two big problems with that thinking, however: (1) It ignores the problem of sin, and (2) it ignores the fact that God is both loving *and* just. Let's look at each of these issues.

First, the reality and seriousness of sin is ignored when we suggest there's no need for God to punish people. To see why that's such a problem, we need to better understand what sin is. The Bible tells us that God is perfectly good, and that He has written His moral laws on the human heart (Psalm 18:30; 1 John 1:5; Romans 2:14-15). *Sin is a transgression against those laws.* If God didn't exist, there would be no sin, because there would be no moral laws to sin against (see chapter 20 for more on this). But if a perfectly good God exists, and humans violate His moral laws, we have to ask, What should God do about it? We expect a penalty for breaking *human* laws, so why wouldn't we expect a penalty for breaking *divine* laws? This brings us to problem number two.

When people can't imagine God punishing anyone because He's perfectly *loving*, they're forgetting that He's likewise perfectly *just*. Justness is the quality of fairly conferring *deserved rewards and punishments* against a standard of right and wrong. There are numerous Bible verses on God's justness. Here are a few representative ones:

- "The Rock, his work is perfect, for all his ways are justice. A God of faithfulness and without iniquity, just and upright is he" (Deuteronomy 32:4).

- "The Lord sits enthroned forever; he has established his throne for justice, and he judges the world with righteousness; he judges the peoples with uprightness" (Psalm 9:7-8).

- "He loves righteousness and justice; the earth is full of the steadfast love of the Lord" (Psalm 33:5).

- "I the Lord love justice; I hate robbery and wrong" (Isaiah 61:8).

It's important to understand that God's justness doesn't contradict His lovingness. In fact, His justness and lovingness go hand-in-hand. Just as an earthly judge wouldn't be loving for setting free those who break human laws, God as a heavenly judge wouldn't be loving for setting free those who break divine laws.

The bottom line: If sin is real, and God is just, there must be a penalty for that sin.

Who should be punished?

If we're honest, most of us can get our heads around this idea of necessary punishment—for really bad people. Murderers, rapists, and child molesters quickly come to mind. I'm guessing that if I had asked my friend if he could imagine a place of punishment for those people, he would have found the idea more palatable. But garden-variety sinners? People who lie, lose their temper, and live more selfishly than they should? We think these people deserve something more like an extended time-out, not hell. In other words, it's not that we don't think God should punish people, but that we don't think He should punish people like us.

There are two key verses that address this (misguided) idea. First, the Bible says that "*all* have sinned and fall short of the glory of God" (Romans 3:23, emphasis mine). Did you catch the word "all"? Not one human is morally worthy of being in God's presence. As unflattering as we may find it, *the entire human race* is in the same boat of being separated from God by sin.

Second, the Bible plainly says that God's penalty for our sin is death (Romans 6:23). The combined picture of these verses is really quite simple, even if we don't like it: Every single person is guilty of breaking God's moral laws, and the penalty is death.

So *who* should be punished? All of us—in the absence of Jesus' sacrifice on the cross.

That said, many Christians believe the Bible suggests there will be different levels of punishment in hell—just as there are different levels of punishment on Earth, depending on the severity of the crime. There are two passages that may support this idea. First, Jesus said in Luke 12:47-48:

> That servant who knew his master's will but did not get
> ready or act according to his will, will receive a severe

beating. But the one who did not know, and did what deserved a beating, will receive a light beating. Everyone to whom much was given, of him much will be required, and from him to whom they entrusted much, they will demand the more.

Second, Revelation 20:12 says:

I saw the dead, great and small, standing before the throne, and books were opened. Then another book was opened, which is the book of life. And the dead were judged by what was written in the books, according to what they had done.

While these passages may suggest different levels of punishment, the overwhelming emphasis of the Bible is on avoiding hell altogether. When we discuss hell with our kids or nonbelievers, we should be careful to never make it out to be something less than what it is.

That, of course, prompts the question: What exactly *is* the nature of hell?

What should the *nature* of punishment be?

When you think of hell, the first thing that probably comes to mind is fire. If hell involved only 100 years in jail, we'd spend a lot less time talking about it. But the traditional view that hell is an eternity spent suffering in flames? That's where many people draw their line of "reasonableness."

The problem is, our human idea of what's reasonable has no necessary bearing on what's true. That's what makes hell such a difficult topic to discuss. People often assume that their ways of thinking are God's ways of thinking, but the Bible tells us that's not the case (Isaiah 55:8). We do know, however, that God is perfect, so His punishment *must* be just—even if we don't fully understand it. Because we can't use our own idea of what's reasonable to determine what's true about hell, we have to look at what God has revealed about it in the Bible.

Jesus referred to hell as a terrible place to be avoided at all costs—an unquenchable fire (Mark 9:48-49), an outer darkness (Matthew 22:13), a fiery furnace (Matthew 13:42), a place of weeping and gnashing of teeth (Matthew 8:12), and a place of spiritual and bodily destruction (Matthew 10:28). The severity of hell is something that all Christians agree on. There are different views, however, on what exactly hell is and how long it will last:

- Those who hold the *literal* view believe hell is a place of actual fire where those who reject Jesus' free gift of forgiveness will experience conscious, unending torment.

- Those who hold the *metaphorical* view believe hell is everlasting punishment of some kind, but not a literal fire; they say fire is merely a biblical symbol for judgment.

- Those who hold the *conditionalist* view believe those who are not saved will eventually cease to exist, rather than suffer unending torment; they say the many biblical references to eternal or everlasting punishment refer to the punishment's *finality*, not its *duration*.

It's beyond the scope of this chapter to lay out the biblical case for each of these views. If you're interested in reading more, I recommend the book *Four Views on Hell* by John F. Walvoord, William Crockett, Zachary J. Hayes, and Clark H. Pinnock.[1]

Though there's disagreement on what exactly hell is and how long it will last, we know that it's a very serious (and just) punishment of eternal separation from God.

Hell Is a Harsh Reality, But It's Also a Choice

Author C.S. Lewis famously said, "There are only two kinds of people—those who say 'Thy will be done' to God or those to whom God in the end says, '*Thy* will be done.' All that are in Hell choose it."[2] People who reject the idea of hell often ignore the fact we can avoid it if we accept Jesus' sacrifice on the cross as payment for our sins. That's the crucial other half of this picture. For the rest of this conversation, be sure to read chapter 20: Why did Jesus need to die on the cross for our sins?

5. How can God judge people who have never even heard about Jesus?

In the previous chapter, we looked at the difficult subject of hell. Here, we're looking at a related follow-up question that typically goes like this: "Okay, let's assume there really is a hell for people who don't accept Jesus. What happens to all the people who never even heard about Jesus? Sending people to hell because they didn't believe in someone they had never heard of isn't justifiable. God is either unfair, or people don't have to believe in Jesus to go to heaven."

People generally raise this question to challenge the idea of an exclusive Christian path to salvation. They're typically not really suggesting that God might be unfair—that's just a rhetorical device. The implied claim is really this: "If God exists, He must be fair. Therefore there must be multiple paths to salvation, since not everyone will hear about Jesus."

We'll look more closely at *religious pluralism*—this idea that all religions can point to the same truth—in chapter 10, but here's the spoiler: They can't. Religions differ in their claims of where we came from, why we're here, the problem of evil, the nature of reality, where we're eventually headed, and much more. These contradictory claims cannot logically all point to one truth. Legitimizing religious pluralism is *not* the answer to this chapter's question, though it's often the motivation for asking it in the first place.

What *is* the answer? It's actually straightforward: We don't know for sure. That's not a cop-out. It's just an acknowledgment that the Bible doesn't explicitly tell us. There are several passages, however, that are relevant to the topic and can help us more thoroughly respond to the question. In this chapter, we'll consider the important foundational concepts of general and special revelation, look at how people in Old Testament times were saved without knowing Jesus, and explore two key Christian views of how that may apply to people today who haven't heard of Jesus.

General Revelation: What God Reveals by *Natural* Means

God's *general revelation* is what He has revealed of Himself through the natural world and our moral conscience. The Bible says that *every* human is accountable for acknowledging this level of revelation. There are two key passages that speak to this truth. First, Romans 1:19-20 describes what God has revealed of Himself through the natural world:

> What can be known about God is plain to them, because God has shown it to them. For his invisible attributes, namely, his eternal power and divine nature, have been clearly perceived, ever since the creation of the world, in the things that have been made. So they are without excuse.

Second, Romans 2:14-15 describes what God has revealed of Himself through our moral conscience:

> When Gentiles, who do not have the law, by nature do what the law requires, they are a law to themselves, even though they do not have the law. They show that the work of the law is written on their hearts, while their conscience also bears witness, and their conflicting thoughts accuse or even excuse them.

In other words, the Bible says there are no people who are ignorant of God's existence and moral requirements. So when we talk about those who have "never heard," it's important to acknowledge that there's a sense in which everyone has at least "heard" of God. As you'll see later, this fact is the key to understanding the two main Christian views of what happens to those who have never heard of Jesus.

Special Revelation: What God Reveals by *Supernatural* Means

It's not possible to simply look at the splendor of creation and our moral conscience to deduce the specific truths that an all-powerful Creator had a Son who lived on Earth, was fully human and fully God, died for the forgiveness of our sins, and was resurrected. For us to learn about these truths, God had to reveal Himself in *supernatural* ways, such as through the Bible and Jesus. This is called His *special revelation*.

It's one particular aspect of God's special revelation that makes this chapter's question so weighty—the Bible clearly reveals that Jesus is the *exclusive* Savior of the world:

- "Whoever believes in [Jesus] is not condemned, but whoever does not believe is condemned already, because he has not believed in the name of the only Son of God" (John 3:18).

- "Jesus said to him, 'I am the way, and the truth, and the life. No one comes to the Father except through me'" (John 14:6).

- "If you confess with your mouth that Jesus is Lord and believe in your heart that God raised him from the dead, you will be saved" (Romans 10:9).

- "God gave us eternal life, and this life is in his Son. Whoever has the Son has life; whoever does not have the Son of God does not have life" (1 John 5:11-12).

The response to this chapter's question, therefore, isn't to add more paths to God—something the Bible clearly doesn't support—but to offer possible answers *given the knowledge that* (1) God is fair (see chapter 4), and (2) He's revealed that Jesus is the only path to salvation.

The Big Question: General Revelation Without Special Revelation

Now that we've defined God's two types of revelation, we can more specifically frame our question: What happens to those who have access to God's *general revelation* but not His *special revelation* of Jesus?

We actually know the answer to this question for one particular group of people—the Old Testament "heroes of faith." Clearly, those who lived before Jesus didn't have the opportunity to know about Him, yet the Bible makes it clear that at least some are now with God. Hebrews 11 commends the faith of several such individuals. "These all died in faith, not having received the things promised, but having seen them and greeted them from afar...God is not ashamed to be called their God, for he has prepared for them a city" (verses 13,16).

So how were these Old Testament people saved if the New Testament clearly says Jesus is the only way to God? The apostle Paul explains the answer in Romans 1–3. He emphasizes that no one is made righteous by observing the law; *every* human is unrighteous, whether Jew or Gentile. The only way anyone can be made righteous is by accepting God's gift of grace by faith—a gift made possible by Jesus' sacrifice on the cross (see chapter 20).

To demonstrate that it is faith, not the law, which makes a person right with God, Paul pointed to Abraham, who lived long before the law was even revealed. Paul said, "If Abraham was justified by works, he has something to boast about, but not before God. For what does the Scripture say? 'Abraham believed God, and it was counted to him as righteousness'" (Romans 4:2-3; see also Genesis 15:6). In other words, Abraham was made righteous because of his belief in God's promises, even if he didn't live to see them all fulfilled.

This doesn't mean Jesus' sacrifice on the cross was unnecessary for Abraham. To the contrary, the only reason anyone *ever* has the possibility of being saved is that Jesus died for the forgiveness of our sins. In the case of Old Testament believers, His sacrifice applied retroactively (something not problematic for God, who has a comprehensive view of time).

That brings us to the big question: How does this pertain to those who live *after* Jesus but don't know of Him? Christians have traditionally held one of two main positions: *restrictivism* or *inclusivism*.

Restrictivism

Restrictivists believe God does not provide salvation to those who don't hear about Jesus and come to faith in Him before they die. Christians holding this position do grant that there may be exceptions in the cases of children who die young or the mentally handicapped (for example, in 2 Samuel 12:15-23, David clearly believed his deceased baby was in heaven).

Restrictivists recognize that knowledge of Jesus was not a necessary condition for the salvation of the Old Testament faithful. However, they believe that these saved people were in a different spiritual situation than non-Christians today. They say those believers placed their faith in God according to how He had revealed Himself at the time, and were saved by trusting in the promises of a *future* Savior. As such, restrictivists say no analogy can be drawn between the salvation of those in the Old Testament and those who don't know about Jesus today. They maintain that those who live after Jesus must hear and accept the gospel to be saved, and that we can trust the results will be fair given what we know of God's perfect character.

Inclusivism

Inclusivists believe those who haven't heard about Jesus can be saved if they respond to God in faith based on His general revelation. They believe the only reason anyone can *ever* be saved is because of Jesus' sacrifice, but that His sacrifice can apply to people who don't know about it—just as it applied retroactively to those who lived in Old Testament times. Inclusivists believe that if general revelation is enough to condemn a person (Romans 1:19-20), it must also be enough to save a person.

It's important to understand that *inclusivism* is not the same as *pluralism*. Pluralism is the belief that there are many paths that lead to God and salvation. This implies a person could know about and reject Jesus, but ultimately be saved through another religion. By contrast, inclusivists believe that those who have heard about Jesus and reject Him will be lost, but those who have *never* heard may be saved based on their response to God's general revelation.

The Only Certain Answer: God Will Be Fair

Many Christians remain agnostic on the answer to this chapter's question. They say we just can't know what happens to those who have never heard of Jesus because the Bible doesn't tell us. That's an entirely reasonable answer. There are many questions about God, our lives, and eternity that we simply don't have clear answers to in the Bible. That's okay. The fact that there are questions we can't answer with certainty doesn't detract from the truth of what we do know: God is perfectly just, so we can be confident He'll do what is fair on judgment day.

6. Why would God need people to worship Him?

Over the last couple of years, I've received a lot of blog comments from atheists who want to challenge something I wrote or Christianity in general. Sometimes the comments are thoughtful and eloquent. I can tell the commenter has put a lot of thought into their view. Other times they're brash and uninformed. I wonder if they've ever truly considered what they believe.

Normally I throw those brash comments into my virtual trash bin without much additional consideration. One such comment, however, has always stuck with me: "You have to worship me or you'll go to hell! Mwah-ha-ha-ha. Love, God."

While at first glance that might appear to be a snarky comment thrown out in jest, it's actually succinctly representative of the common negative (and incorrect) view of worship that many skeptics have. They find it absurd and inexplicable that a supposedly perfect God would be needy of human adoration. For example, atheist author Daniel Dennett says, "Part of what makes [God] such a fascinating participant in stories of the Old Testament is His kinglike jealousy and pride, and His great appetite for praise and sacrifices."[1]

If we're honest, a lot of us as Christians don't fully embrace or understand the idea of worship either. My pastor once preached on the book of Revelation and the idea of an "eternal worship service." A friend of mine nervously confided in me after church, "I don't think an eternity of worshiping God sounds that exciting…" But that feeling, too, was rooted in a misunderstanding of what worship really is.

My favorite way to define worship is this: *Worship is responding to all that God is with all that we are.* In this chapter, we'll look at worship by studying the two parts of that statement: (1) all that God is, and (2) responding with all that we are.

All That God Is

For many people, the word *worship* has a negative connotation. Whether we realize it or not, we're used to thinking of it in terms of someone revering another human or thing to an inappropriate extreme.

For example, we think of fanatical fans who have plastic surgery to look like their favorite celebrity. We wonder how anyone could possibly value themselves so little that they would be willing to give up part of their identity to honor someone else in that way.

The problem when we think of worship like this is that we're thinking solely in human terms—what happens when humans worship other humans or things. We have a sense that that kind of worship is just not right. And that sense is correct. The Bible tells us that mankind was created in God's image, so every human is equal in value. No human or thing *deserves* worship because no human or thing is inherently more valuable than another.

Our view of worship must be significantly adjusted, however, when we appropriately recognize that God is unlike any human or earthly thing. *God is a perfect Being and the Creator of all.* God actually *deserves* worship. This kind of worship is not in error because we can't possibly assign too much greatness to God.

Recognizing that God uniquely deserves our worship is the crucial starting point for understanding what it means to respond to "all that God is." But even when skeptics grant that a hypothetical God might *deserve* worship, they often question why He would *need* or *want* it. After all, wouldn't a perfect God be so humble that He wouldn't need or want His creatures to worship Him—even if He deserves it?

Does God **Need** Our Worship?

Just because the Bible says we *should* worship God doesn't mean God *needs* us to worship Him. God doesn't actually need anything at all to complete His character or existence. Acts 17:24-25 says:

> The God who made the world and everything in it, being Lord of heaven and earth, does not live in temples made by man, nor is he served by human hands, as though he needed anything, since he himself gives to all mankind life and breath and everything.

In other words, God is perfectly self-sufficient. Any idea that God *needs* our worship is unbiblical and mistaken.

Does God **Want** Our Worship?

The answer to this question is an unequivocal yes! The Bible tells us, for example, "Ascribe to the LORD the glory due his name; bring an offering and come before him! Worship the LORD in the splendor of holiness" (1 Chronicles 16:29). John 4:23 says, "The hour is coming, and is now here, when the true worshipers will worship the Father in spirit and truth, for the Father is seeking such people to worship him." And in Romans 12:1, Paul calls readers to "present your bodies as a living sacrifice, holy and acceptable to God, which is your spiritual worship" (Romans 12:1).

Is it arrogant for God to want this kind of worship? Not at all. Arrogance involves having an inflated sense of self. A perfect God can't have an inflated sense of self. He has an accurate understanding of His immeasurable worth.

Rather than wanting us to worship because He's arrogant, God wants us to worship because He knows we'll be *fulfilled* by it. We were created to be in relationship with Him, so worshiping—responding to God with all that we are—realizes our very purpose. Of course God wants that for us. When we understand God's glory, we start to grasp that our deepest longings for meaning can only be satisfied by responding to Him with the complete devotion of our lives.

Worship is a natural response to an appropriate understanding of who God is, not an act of reluctant humility before an attention-seeking Creator.

In looking at "all that God is," we've answered the *why* of worship. That's the primary concern of skeptics. They're naturally far less interested in the *what* of worship—how it should look in a believer's life. However, it's important for our kids to also understand what it means to respond to God "with all that we are," so let's conclude by clarifying that now.

Responding with All That We Are

Until more recently than I'd like to admit, I associated the idea of worship solely with what happens before the sermon at church—singing, greeting other believers, and corporate prayer. Defined in that way, I've never liked "worship."

I can't sing a pleasant note to save my life, so I don't enjoy music. When the pastor says, "Shake hands with a neighbor," all I can think about is which person to turn to first to minimize the chance I'll be left awkwardly standing with an unnoticed outstretched hand. And if there is any chance the congregation will be praying out loud for one another that day, you'll find me in the bathroom (if you fear praying out loud, take heart—there are many of us).

I had a serious misconception of what it means to worship God. Sure, part of it involves the corporate expression of praise on Sunday morning. But that's just one part of it. To worship means to respond to God's glory with the humble devotion of our *whole lives*. For example, we worship God by praying, reading the Bible, singing, giving of our financial resources, serving others, striving to live a Christlike life, and attending church.

Of course, this doesn't mean worship is just going through those motions. *How* we worship matters. As we saw, Jesus specifically noted we must worship "in spirit and truth" (John 4:23). Theologian John Piper, in *Desiring God*, beautifully explains what that means:

> There must be spirit and there must be truth…Truth without emotion produces dead orthodoxy and a church full (or half-full) of artificial admirers…On the other hand, emotion without truth produces empty frenzy and cultivates shallow people who refuse the discipline of rigorous thought. But true worship comes from people who are deeply emotional and who love deep and sound doctrine. Strong affections for God rooted in truth are the bone and marrow of biblical worship.[2]

Clearly, worship is more than singing a few songs each Sunday morning. It is a *lifestyle*, not a weekly event.

Responding to All That God Is with All That We Are

Ironically, the human concern about God's desire for worship says more about our pride than His. We don't want to think we need to "bow down" to anyone…even if we're talking about the Creator of the universe. But that reluctance is rooted in our inability to fully grasp God's majesty. God, unlike any human or earthly thing, actually *deserves* our worship. He doesn't *need* it, but seeks it because He knows our complete devotion is the fulfillment of our very purpose. When we dedicate all that we are to Him—in spirit and in truth—it satisfies our deepest longings and gives God the glory He is due.

7. Why is God so hidden?

I'm part of several online groups dedicated to the discussion of apologetics (making a case for and defending the Christian faith). Participants in these groups passionately study topics like those in this book and are extremely knowledgeable of the evidence for Christianity. These people have given their faith a lot of thought.

Someone recently asked the members of one such group, "What is your biggest personal challenge to faith?" I was quite eager to see how people who are well-grounded in the reasons for Christianity would answer this. Hundreds of people replied. The most frequently cited challenge? The "deafening" silence of God.

If God exists, why doesn't He make Himself more obvious in our lives?

It's something almost every Christian struggles with at some point—regardless of how well-grounded they are in their faith.

Philosophers call this problem the "hiddenness of God." For Christians, the hiddenness of God hits home in our personal lives. We wonder why we sometimes don't feel His presence even though we're believers, why we sometimes feel like our prayers go into a black hole, and why we struggle to distinguish the Holy Spirit's leading from our own thoughts.

But for skeptics, the hiddenness of God is more than a personal challenge; it's considered universal evidence against God's existence (much like the problem of evil—see chapter 2). The logic basically goes like this:

- If God exists, He would make Himself more obvious to us.

- God has not made Himself obvious to us.

- God must not exist.

Far from being a philosophical topic that's discussed only in ivory towers, the question of God's hiddenness is one that even children ask about from an early age. In fact, it's the first question I remember my son asking when he was three: "Mommy, how do I know God is there if I can't see Him? Why doesn't He come to our house?" We need a better answer than the one I gave at the time: "Well, God's just invisible, like air!" (That hardly answers the question.)

Two Key Premises to Consider

Let's look now at the premises in the first two bullet points above to better understand whether the hiddenness of God should legitimately lead to the conclusion that He doesn't exist. This will provide a framework for addressing the question with your kids.

Premise 1: If God Exists, He Would Make Himself More Obvious to Us

I think we can all agree that it *seems* like, if God exists, He should want to make Himself a bit more obvious. But we have to acknowledge that we're not in a position to know anything about how God would act if He *were* to exist. An all-knowing deity would have infinitely more perspective than we do and may have perfectly good reasons for not acting in the ways we would expect or desire. In fact, God could choose to create the whole world and never touch it again. There's no necessary connection, therefore, between the mere existence of God and the obligation to make Himself known to us.

The question becomes more difficult in a Christian context, however. The Bible says God wants "all people to be saved and to come to the knowledge of the truth" (1 Timothy 2:4). It also tells us Jesus is the only path to salvation (John 14:6) and that those who fail to come to Him face eternal consequences (see chapter 4). If God wants everyone to be saved, and there are such dire consequences for not believing in

Him, is it not hard to understand why He wouldn't make His existence so obvious that no one could deny it?

This point was powerfully argued by German philosopher Friedrich Nietzsche:

> A god who is all-knowing and all powerful and who does not even make sure his creatures understand his intention—could that be a god of goodness? Who allows countless doubts and dubities to persist, for thousands of years, as though the salvation of mankind were unaffected by them, and who on the other hand holds out the prospect of frightful consequences if any mistake is made as to the nature of truth? Would he not be a cruel god if he possessed the truth and could behold mankind miserably tormenting itself over the truth?[1]

There is undeniable tension in that question. But philosophers have offered an answer that can help explain why God would *possibly* choose to remain somewhat hidden, even when our eternal destination depends on our understanding of His existence. That answer is rooted in the idea of free will.

Recall from chapter 2 that free will is our ability to make choices without external coercion. Many people believe human free will is necessary for us to genuinely love God; if God forced us to choose and love Him, that wouldn't be a meaningful love at all. We would simply be robots. Similarly, free will intersects with the problem of God's hiddenness: If God revealed Himself too much, He would take away our *freedom* to make morally significant decisions—decisions like choosing to love Him.[2] For example, if He were to show up in every person's living room and say, "Believe in me or you'll suffer eternal damnation," we would be *coerced* into belief. He would effectively be taking away our free will. By remaining somewhat hidden, He gives us space to either genuinely seek Him or avoid Him. And, very importantly, the Bible says that when we *do* diligently seek God, we *will* find Him (Deuteronomy 4:29).

Now let's consider the second statement: God has not made Himself obvious to us.

Premise 2: God Has Not Made Himself Obvious to Us

The statement that God has not made Himself obvious to us has two very different connotations. The first is that He hasn't made His existence so obvious that it's undeniable. That's the issue we just addressed. As we saw, there are good possible reasons why God wouldn't make Himself *that* obvious. But the second connotation is that He hasn't revealed Himself in *any* meaningful way. In my personal conversations with people, this tends to be the more frequent type of assertion. Atheists are quick to state there is absolutely no sign or evidence of God in the world. They say He is completely absent and therefore there is no reason to believe He exists.

Christians, however, believe God *has* revealed Himself to us—perhaps not in the overly obvious ways we might desire, but in ways that God has deemed *sufficient* for allowing us to find Him when we search. That's really the heart of the question. It's not whether God has made Himself obvious based on our subjective personal criteria, but whether He has revealed Himself *sufficiently* for all of mankind. In the Christian view, God has chosen to reveal Himself in several significant ways. For example, we see His revelation in...

- the existence of the universe (see the *cosmological argument* in chapter 1)

- the existence of objective moral values (see the *moral argument* in chapter 1)

- indications of intelligent design in biology (see chapter 40)

- the fine-tuning of the Earth and universe (see chapter 1)

- the authenticity of Scripture (see part 4)

- the life, death, and resurrection of Jesus (see part 3)

- the witness of the Holy Spirit (see chapter 12)

For some people, no amount of revelation is enough, short of God making a personal visit to their house. But what if God exists and doesn't choose to reveal Himself in that way? What if He says to us, "Look over here instead!"? Are we going to stomp our feet in protest and refuse to look where He points us because that's not what we deem sufficient? That's hardly a logical choice. God has clearly decided what is sufficient revelation for us to know Him. And that is exactly what we must have.

God Might Be Hidden, But He's Not Absent

Much like the problem of evil, the hiddenness of God is considered to be a significant piece of evidence against His existence. In particular, God's hiddenness is a challenge to a Christian worldview because Christians believe there are serious consequences for not believing in Him. Why wouldn't a good God want to make Himself so obvious that everyone chooses Him?

As we saw, one possible reason is that if God revealed Himself too much, it would actually take away our freedom to make morally significant decisions—decisions like choosing to love Him. Instead of coercing us into belief, He gives us sufficient revelation and promises that when we diligently seek, we will find. Helping our kids understand where to find (and how to evaluate) the revelation God *has* given is at the core of our Christian parenting responsibility.

8. Is faith in God the opposite of reason?

Our family went on a summer vacation when our twins were four and our youngest was two. Vacation with three young kids should really be called "that occasional week in your life when you take care of your kids in another location," but I digress. We soon realized how limited we were in the kinds of activities the kids could do at that age, so we spent most of the week at the hotel swimming pool trying to teach our twins how to swim.

My daughter quickly figured out how to make her way through the water independently, but things didn't go so smoothly for my son. He kept trying, but he was choking every time he came out of the water. He would pop up wailing, "I got water in my mouth and nose AGAIN!"

Each time, I reminded him, "You have to hold your breath! Don't open your mouth under water. Hold your breath." Then I would set him back on the edge of the pool to try again.

After a couple of days, I became exasperated. I couldn't figure out why he refused to hold his breath—such a simple thing! But then a light bulb went on in my mind. My eyes must have been as big as saucers when I realized the likely problem.

"Wait...do you know what breath is?! Do you know what it means to hold your breath?"

He burst into tears. "NO! I don't understand! WHAT is breath?"

I had practically beaten him over the head for two days with the words "hold your breath" and he didn't even know what that meant. He kept jumping in the water, hoping he would figure it out, but came up struggling every time.

That experience made me reflect on how easy it is to incorrectly assume our kids (both big and small) understand words and concepts that are foundational to what we teach them. One extremely important example of this is a word that almost every Christian parent uses but rarely stops to define: *faith*.

I heard it over and over again growing up in church, and I hear Christians say it all the time today: "Just have faith." But what does that mean? What exactly are we telling our kids to "just" have? Without further explanation, they can easily conclude over time that Christians are called to have a very simple, unexamined belief in God. That couldn't be further from the truth.

But that's not the only issue. The problem that Christians often use the word *faith* ambiguously has been exacerbated by the fact that atheists today are actively promoting their own definition—that *faith is the opposite of reason*. Even many Christians, unsure themselves of what biblical faith means, have started to buy this description. Without a strong footing in their own beliefs, they've retreated to an impenetrable spiritual fortress where they proudly respond that faith—not reason—is all they need.

Meanwhile, our kids eventually witness this cultural dialogue and feel the burden of shame for holding supposedly unreasonable beliefs. It has to stop.

Just as with my son's swimming experience, this is a problem of definitions. The definition of faith *and* the definition of reason matter greatly in the Christian life. In this chapter, we'll get to the bottom of what each word means.

What Is Reason?

Peter Grice, a contributing author to the excellent book *True Reason*, describes reason as "fundamentally the act of engaging the mind—whether done intuitively or rigorously, poorly or flawlessly. It is, ideally, a process of careful thinking, always involving logic, and often drawing upon evidence."[1]

I love this definition because it highlights a vital point often missed: Reason, at its core, is simply the process of thinking—a process that can be done well or poorly. There's nothing inherently praiseworthy about merely reasoning, though that's how atheists often make it sound. *Everyone* reasons. The more specific implied charge against Christians, therefore, is that they reason *poorly*.

So how, supposedly, do Christians reason poorly? I'll let four atheist authors tell you themselves. See if you can identify the theme:

- *Sam Harris:* "Tell a devout Christian that his wife is cheating on him, or that frozen yogurt can make a man invisible, and he is likely to require as much evidence as anyone else, and to be persuaded only to the extent that you give it. Tell him that the book he keeps by his bed was written by an invisible deity who will punish him with fire for eternity if he fails to accept its every incredible claim about the universe, and he seems to require no evidence whatsoever."[2]

- *Richard Dawkins:* "Faith is the great cop-out, the great excuse to evade the need to think and evaluate evidence. Faith is belief in spite of, even perhaps because of, the lack of evidence."[3]

- *William Harwood:* "The difference between faith and insanity is that faith is the ability to hold firmly to a conclusion that is incompatible with the evidence, whereas insanity is the ability to hold firmly to a conclusion that is incompatible with the evidence."[4]

- *Bertrand Russell:* "We may define 'faith' as the firm belief in something for which there is no evidence. Where there is evidence, no one speaks of 'faith.'"[5]

Did you catch the theme? No evidence, no evidence, no evidence. The pervasive claim that faith is opposed to reason is really shorthand for, "There's no evidence for God, so anyone who has faith in Him is necessarily using poor reasoning given that good reasoning is based on an intellectually honest response to evidence."

There are three essential things to note about this.

First, there *are* Christians who reason poorly, but that doesn't mean Christian belief is *necessarily* based on poor reasoning. Anyone, including atheists, can reason poorly. The ability to reason well cannot be claimed as the exclusive domain of those who have thoughtfully arrived at any particular worldview.

Second, the force of this entire implied statement rests on the assertion that there's no evidence for God. If I truly believed that, I would actually agree with the atheist's conclusion—believing in Him would be crazy! It would be like believing there's a unicorn in the other room when there's no reason to think as much. The reality is that neither Christians nor atheists are willing to believe in something without evidence; Christians believe there *is* evidence for God. It's dishonest for atheists to state as a given that there's *no* evidence and maintain that Christians are happy to believe anyway (see chapter 10 for a big-picture view of how the evidence for Christianity fits together). A more honest assessment would be that Christians and atheists disagree over what constitutes *legitimate* evidence for God.

Third, atheists label this ill-conceived idea of Christians believing in God without evidence "faith." As we discussed previously, they've used the word *faith* in this way so loudly and frequently that our culture has largely accepted that that's what it means. The Bible, however, gives a very different picture of what it means to have faith. Let's look at that now.

What Is Faith?

The Bible's most direct description of faith is found in Hebrews 11:1: "Faith is the assurance of things hoped for, the conviction of things not seen."

Many skeptics latch on to the words "hoped for" in this verse and claim that even the Bible says faith is just a matter of wishful thinking. But that completely ignores the other key words—"assurance" and "conviction." This verse doesn't say faith is the *hope* of things hoped for, but the *assurance* of things hoped for. Furthermore, the verse doesn't suggest that assurance is based on boundless fantasies, but on *conviction*. In other words, this doesn't portray faith as an irrational leap into the unknown. Rather, it *presupposes* that Christians have good reasons for belief, leading to assurance and conviction.

It's important to clarify here that faith itself isn't a belief. It's the *commitment* to a belief—a commitment that arises when you place your trust in something you have good reason to believe is true. All people—Christians and atheists alike—exercise faith. For example, you get on an airplane without checking the pilot's license, reviewing the mechanic's log, or checking the cargo for explosives. Do you know with absolute certainty that people have done those things for you and have done them correctly? No. Do you have good reason to trust that they have? Yes. That's faith.

Likewise, the Bible calls Christians to faithfully trust in Jesus because we've been given good reason to believe God sent Him to be the Savior of the world. Some key scriptures that speak to the importance of good reasoning in the Christian life include:

- "You shall love the Lord your God with all your heart and with all your soul and with *all your mind*" (Matthew 22:37, emphasis mine).

- "When I was a child, I spoke like a child, I thought like a child, I reasoned like a child. When I became a man, I gave up childish ways" (1 Corinthians 13:11).

- "Do not be children in your thinking. Be infants in evil, but in your thinking be mature" (1 Corinthians 14:20).

- "In your hearts honor Christ the Lord as holy, always being prepared to make a defense to anyone who asks you for a reason for the hope that is in you" (1 Peter 3:15).

Perhaps the ultimate testimony that God values evidence and good reasoning is Jesus' life. Jesus didn't run around making extraordinary claims without offering evidence to back them up. He substantiated His claims with miracles—actions no one could perform without the divine power He alleged He had. If God truly valued a blind, evidence-free faith, He could have sent Jesus unaccompanied by such proof. He could have delighted in seeing how many people would buy the astonishing claims of a first-century man from the unremarkable town of Nazareth. Instead, He offered evidence that Jesus was who He said He was—by the miracles performed during His life, and eventually through the greatest miracle of all, the resurrection (on the evidence for the truth of the resurrection, see chapters 21-24).

Biblical Faith and Reason Go Hand-in-Hand

As you'll see throughout this book, half our battle as Christian parents is just stopping to define words and concepts. We can't allow atheists to hijack the biblical meaning of faith and inappropriately redefine it in terms that leave our kids feeling ashamed of Christianity. Far from being the *opposite* of (good) reason, biblical faith is *rooted* in good reason. But your kids shouldn't just take your word for it. They need you to show them the evidence for Christianity (presented throughout this book) in order for that fact to become meaningful in their lives. So press on! It's time for part 2: Conversations About Truth and Worldviews.

PART 2:

Conversations About
TRUTH AND WORLDVIEWS

I was driving with my kids one morning when my son announced that he had seen a black, red, and yellow bird on his side of the car. My daughter immediately corrected him.

"You're totally wrong! The bird was black and red. It didn't have any yellow."

My son argued back, "No! I'm right! The bird *did* have yellow. It was on his back."

Tired parent syndrome kicked in, so I entered the fray with this disingenuous response: "Guys! It doesn't matter. Sometimes people see different things. You can both be right."

Fast-forward to the following week, when this came back to bite me in a big way. My younger daughter ran to me screaming, "Mommy! Sister hit me!"

In walked my older daughter with a casual shrug. "No I didn't. Stop talking about it. We can both be right. Sometimes people see different things."

Ouch. My lazy response from the week before had confused my older daughter's understanding of truth! I had given her the idea that everyone can be right at the same time, even when they're making contradictory claims.

As obvious as it may seem that there are many things which are either true or not true, this very basic understanding of truth—fundamental to Christianity—is under attack today. My daughter isn't the only one getting confused. In this chapter, we'll clarify the difference between *objective* and *subjective* truth and learn why it's so important for our kids to understand the distinction.

The Big Mix-Up: Objective and Subjective Truth

Whatever bird my kids saw was either (1) black, red, and yellow (as my son claimed); (2) only black and red (as my daughter claimed); or (3) something else altogether (if they were both wrong). But contrary to my lazy everyone-can-be-right response, the bird can't be all of those things at the same time.

The actual color of the bird is an example of *objective truth*. To say that something is objectively true means that it is independently true for all people, even if they don't know it or recognize it to be true.

A *subjective truth* is something that can be true for one person and not for another. If my daughter had said, "That bird is beautiful!" and my son had replied, "That bird is ugly!" they could have both been right, because aesthetic taste is a matter of opinion; it's a subjective truth.

Here's why this distinction matters. The secular world is increasingly claiming that all truth is subjective—a simple matter of each person's perspective and opinion. The idea that all truth is subjective, however, is in direct opposition to the claims of Christianity; Jesus clearly stated that His truth is objective. Quite directly, He said, "I am the way, the truth, and the life. No one comes to the Father except through me" (John 14:6). Christianity rests on a foundation of objective truth. If objective truth does not exist, that foundation crumbles and all of Christianity crumbles with it. This is no small issue.

While it may be fashionable for people to claim that all truth is subjective, no one actually lives as if that's the case (much like we discussed in chapter 1 that no one lives as if all *morality* is subjective). We make claims of objective truth every day: "It's raining outside." "My car is in the garage." "There are five houses on our street." These are all statements we recognize to be either true or false and not a matter of opinion. Everyone makes claims of objective truth, whether they realize it or not. Even when people say, "All truth is subjective," they're making a statement of objective truth—they're asserting that something is objectively true for all people.

The *existence* of objective truth cannot be consistently denied. How we can know *which* claim of objective truth is correct is another question. We'll look at that separately in chapter 11.

Two Common Attacks on the Existence of Objective Truth

There are two especially common attacks on Christianity that touch on this issue of objective versus subjective truth. Let's look at both, because you and your kids are sure to encounter them eventually if you haven't already.

1. Christians are intolerant of other beliefs.

By definition, *tolerance* simply means to bear with ideas other than your own. However, most people use the word as if it means to *accept* those (often conflicting) other ideas as equally true. Christians are then labeled intolerant simply because they don't accept that all ideas can be true at the same time. *But the fact that Christians believe objective truth exists doesn't mean they're intolerant.*

Consider this example. In an online religion forum, a poster asked the question, "Why are people intolerant of others' religions and beliefs?" One of the replies clearly demonstrates how people commonly equate intolerance with believing that ideas can be wrong:

> One reason is because those people genuinely believe that, "out of the kindness of their hearts," they should "help" others to convert to the right path. Others are simply just disrespectful of other religions with the belief that they are simply "wrong." These people have most likely not taken any time to understand these other religions and beliefs. Sometimes even a respectable argument can be intolerance if they are only putting the argument across to prove others wrong.[1]

Clearly, this commenter believes that tolerance requires a person to believe others aren't wrong. But, again, tolerance means bearing with ideas other than your own—*not* believing that those ideas are right. Our kids need to be prepared to explain that they believe Chrisitianity alone is true, but that a belief in a single truth doesn't make them—or anyone else—intolerant.

2. Christians indoctrinate their kids.

Here's another example where we need to get definitions straight. *Indoctrination* is teaching someone to accept the ideas, opinions, and beliefs of a particular group and to not consider other ideas, opinions, and beliefs. In other words, indoctrination is a problem with *how* a person teaches someone something. It's not inherently related to any particular belief system, though religion is one type of belief system where indoctrination is possible.

That said, a closer look at this claim shows that most people who accuse Christians of indoctrination aren't objecting to *how* we're teaching our kids. How would they know what's going on inside every Christian home? What they're really challenging (whether they realize it or not) is the fact that Christian parents teach the concept of objective truth. If Christian parents were teaching their kids that Christianity is a subjective truth that's no truer than any other belief system, you can bet there would be no claims of indoctrination flying around. This attack has nothing to do with indoctrination, but everything to do with an aversion to people teaching their kids that objective truth exists.

When kids hear that they've been "indoctrinated" because their parents have raised them with a Christian worldview, there can be a strong emotional impact if they don't understand the true meaning of the word. Who wants to feel like they're a mindless copy of their parents? Once again, let's look at an example of the kind of thinking they're likely to encounter. On a debate website, the following question was posed: "Is teaching children religion brainwashing?" (People frequently use the terms *brainwashing* and *indoctrinating* interchangeably.) The first response stated:

> Religion is a unique type of ideology. Religion is a particular type of ideology that does not allow for compromise. Within Christianity God does not "maybe" exist. It is a very absolutist stance that does not allow for much compromise; thus, yes religion is different from other "opinions" parents may impose.[2]

Here again, we encounter the prevalent idea that "absolutist [objective] stances" on truth are problematic. In this case, the idea is tied to the claim that Christians brainwash or indoctrinate their kids. And, once again, the commenter doesn't realize the self-refuting nature of what he's saying—he's advocating his own absolute (objective) stance that compromise is necessary! Help your kids remember that irony: People who claim that all truth is subjective are actually claiming their own objective truth.

Objective Truth: A Necessary Foundation of Christianity

If the terms *objective* and *subjective truth* are new to you, they may sound a bit philosophical at first. But, as you can see, these concepts have very practical and far-reaching implications. When we help our kids understand the meaning of objective truth and its importance for Christianity, we give them a much-needed foundation on which to build their faith. That foundation will help them understand, resist, and respond to the frequent claims that truth is just a matter of opinion. Most importantly, they'll understand that deciding on their spiritual beliefs shouldn't be a matter of simply picking what they like the best; they'll know it should be a matter of searching for what is *objectively* true.

10. Do all religions point to the same truth?

Once upon a time, there lived six blind men in a village. One day the villagers told them, "There's an elephant in the village today!" The blind men had no idea what an elephant was, but they decided to go find it. When they found it, each man touched a different part of the elephant. The first man, touching the leg, said, "The elephant is a pillar." The second man, touching the tail, said, "It's like a rope." The third man, touching the trunk, said, "It's like the thick branch of a tree." The fourth man, touching the ear, said, "It's like a big hand fan." The fifth man, touching the belly, said, "It's like a huge wall." The sixth man, touching the tusk, said, "It's like a solid pipe." The men were starting to argue about what the elephant really was when a wise man passed by. The wise man settled the matter by explaining, "You are each saying something different because you are each touching a different part of the elephant. The elephant has all of those features. You are all right."[1]

This Indian fable is often told today to illustrate that each religion is a part of the ultimate truth, and leads to that truth by different routes. The first time I heard it was from a friend over dinner. She was asking about my blog and why it's so important to me that my kids only believe that Christianity is true. She identifies herself as a Christian, but (in her own words) doesn't "buy into the idea that everyone else is wrong." When I asked my friend how all religions can be equally true, she recounted this story of the blind men and the elephant. She concluded that all religions can lead to God, who is ultimately bigger than them all.

This view—that multiple religions can be equally valid paths to God—is called *religious pluralism*, and it's a common idea our kids will encounter. One of the most well-known advocates of religious pluralism is Oprah Winfrey. Winfrey has said, "While Christianity is a valid way to achieve high states of spirituality, it must not be considered a unique way, or a 'correct way'."[2] On another occasion she said, "I'm a free-thinking Christian who believes in my way, but I don't believe it's the only way, with 6 billion people on the planet."[3]

You might not care what Oprah Winfrey thinks about faith, but many people find her spirituality—rooted in an acceptance of the validity of religious pluralism—highly compelling. A poll conducted at beliefnet.com found that 33 percent of 6600 respondents said Winfrey has had "a more profound impact" on their spiritual lives than their own clergypersons.[4] There's no doubt the idea of religious pluralism is compelling to many people (not just Oprah Winfrey fans!), but it has a glaring problem, as we're about to see.

Can All These Religions Really Point to the Same Truth?

Although the idea that all paths lead to the same truth sounds nice, the core beliefs of major religions contradict each other in logically irreconcilable ways. Consider the following sample of differences between Christianity and five other religions:

- Judaism denies that Jesus was the promised Messiah. Christianity affirms that Jesus was the promised Messiah.

- Islam affirms that Muhammad was the greatest prophet and that he fulfilled the ministry of Jesus. Christianity denies that Muhammad was a prophet at all.

- Christian Science denies the reality of sin. Christianity affirms the reality of sin and teaches that it's an eternally significant problem that separates humans from God.

- Mormonism affirms that there are three separate divine beings: the Father, the Son, and the Holy Ghost. Christianity denies the existence of multiple divine beings and emphasizes there is one God existing in three persons (known as the *Trinity*).

- Hinduism affirms a cycle of rebirths (*reincarnation*) that leads to a person's consciousness being absorbed into God or ultimate reality. Christianity denies reincarnation and teaches that a person has a single life, after which he or she will be judged.

These are not small differences. Religions differ in their claims of where we came from, why we are here, the problem of evil, the nature of ultimate reality, and where we're eventually headed. There is simply no logical way that all of these contradictory claims can point to the same truth. In fact, if religious pluralism is true, Christianity must be false because Jesus said He is the only way to God (John 14:6; see also Acts 4:12). This irony is lost on many.

Multiple Religions Can Have *Some* True Beliefs

There's a fine distinction we need to make when talking about religious pluralism. When we acknowledge the reality that all religions cannot logically point to the same truth, we're *not* saying that every belief of religions other than Christianity is entirely false. Multiple religions can contain *some* true beliefs. For example, Judaism, Islam, and

Christianity all affirm there is one God. From the Christian perspective, they all hold to that same true belief. It's when we compare the *totality* of their beliefs that we encounter the problem of irreconcilable claims that cannot point to the same total truth.

Because this is a fine distinction, it's often a source of confusion. Here's an example of that confusion from a website devoted to Jainism (an Indian religion). The author published the aforementioned story of the blind men and elephant, then concluded:

> The moral of the story is that there may be some truth to what someone says. Sometimes we can see that truth and sometimes not because they may have [a] different perspective which we may not agree too [sic]...In Jainism, it is explained that truth can be stated in seven different ways. So, you can see how broad our religion is.[5]

This writer is correct that there can be truth in what multiple people or religions say. But it doesn't follow that entire religions—large bundles of claims—are all just different perspectives on the same truth. Believing a "broad" religion is necessary or helpful is actually just one more truth claim that is irreconcilable with the truth claims of other religions.

The Lure of Religious Pluralism

It doesn't take long to show why the idea behind religious pluralism logically fails. However, it's an idea that your kids may find quite compelling for several reasons.

First, it seems to make sense on the surface. As Oprah Winfrey pointed out, there are billions of people on the planet. With that many people, doesn't it make sense we would have many equally valid perspectives on how to come to God? What makes sense on the surface, however, can be very misleading. We need to help our kids learn to critically evaluate these types of simplistic appeals to common sense (see chapter 13).

Second, it keeps religious conversations politically correct. Our culture values an ill-defined version of tolerance above all else (see chapter 9).

It's tempting for young people to wave off huge differences in belief in order to meet their peers' expectation of being "tolerant." Our kids need to understand that, as Christians, our calling is to tell the truth, not to tell what's politically correct. And we can tell that truth graciously and lovingly.

Third, it reduces religion to moral teachings. One online commenter responded to the question "Can all religions be true?" by saying, "They're all true. The 3 main religions Islam, Judaism and Christianity all go back to Abraham. They all also have one god. All religions teach fairness and equality and they all have the same golden rule [to] love each other."[6]

Good moral teachings are truths that many religions *do* have in common. People, like this commenter, frequently point to those commonalities as evidence that all religions point to the same truth overall. It's especially tempting to make that conclusion because it eases the tension of believing there are eternal consequences for other religious beliefs. But truth is truth. If the truth is that there *are* eternal consequences for your beliefs, as Christianity claims, then moral commonalities between religions don't point to the same truth any more than tires all point to the same vehicle. Our kids need to understand that religions can't be reduced to moral teachings, as uncomfortable as that reality may be.

Religions Offer Very Different Views on Truth

If the elephant in the Indian fable represents ultimate truth, our kids should understand that the elephant—God—has spoken. We don't have to be blind men feeling our way through darkness. If the elephant speaks to clear the confusion, the whole illustration falls apart. We can confidently teach our kids that God has spoken through the Bible to answer our big questions about reality, and those answers, when closely evaluated, are very different than the answers of other religions. Of course that prompts the important question of why we should believe the Bible really is God's Word—be sure to continue this conversation with the topics in part 4!

11. How can Christians claim they know what is objectively true?

For our fifteenth wedding anniversary, my husband and I had the opportunity to go on a local culinary-tasting tour. When planning the trip, I pictured tasting foods in a romantic outdoor setting perfect for celebrating an anniversary—perhaps involving a checkered tablecloth and butterflies, with the occasional bunny running by. The reality was more like an indoor cattle call where herds of people elbowed their way to tables for a taste of their next sample and engaged in small talk with strangers (for the record, I'm an introvert and what I just described was *not* a good thing).

I could tell the man standing alone next to us really wanted to talk, so I fought my introvert tendencies and offered a simple "Hi." That small greeting eventually led to a long conversation about what's most important in raising kids. Bill, as I'll call him, told me, "The most important thing is giving your kids good old Christian values. Your kids may make a different decision about religion when they grow up, but they'll always have those values." I asked him, "Why do you believe it's the values and not the Christian faith that's important for them to have?" He looked at me incredulously, then replied, "Well, no one knows *for sure* what happens after we die. But good values will be a foundation for the rest of their life."

Bill isn't alone in having the general attitude that "no one knows for sure about God, therefore we can't take our choice of religion too seriously." But is that really as far as we can take our knowledge of truth? So far we've established that objective truth exists (chapter 9), and that all religions can't logically point to the same truth (chapter 10). But if our kids can't get to the next step of claiming to know it's *Christianity* that's true (versus any other worldview), they're not much better off than where we started—chalking religious belief up to guesses about things that no one can know "for sure."

So how *can* Christians claim to know what's true? Let's start by considering what it means to know *anything* is true in our daily lives.

What Does It Mean to *Know* Something?

We use the word *know* in several ways. Sometimes we use it to say we have knowledge of someone by acquaintance ("I know my daughter"). Other times we use it to describe knowledge as competency, as in, "I know how to play the piano." Still other times we use it to make a claim about something that is true or false, as in, "I know the Civil War ended in 1865" (this is called *propositional knowledge*). This is the kind of knowledge we're dealing with when we talk about religious claims.

Traditionally, philosophers have defined propositional knowledge as "justified true belief." This definition, while admittedly not exciting at first glance, is very useful for considering what it means to know something. Let's walk through it.

As a first step to knowing something, you have to have a *belief* of some kind; you have to hold something to be true. It's possible to believe anything, of course. Simply having a belief doesn't mean it is right. I can believe that aliens exist, but that doesn't mean they do. Unfortunately, simple belief is the category to which many people assign religion. Like Bill on the culinary tour, they think no one can know what's true about God *for sure*, so all religious ideas are just simple beliefs. But this is an inadequate understanding of what it means to know something. Let's press on to understand why.

Because a belief can be wrong, we should have good *reasons* for thinking it's true before we claim to *know* it. This is called having *justification* for your beliefs (recall our definition of knowledge: *justified true belief*). Contrary to popular claims, the Bible never tells us to "just believe" in the sense that we should blindly accept Jesus without reason. First Peter 3:15 says, "In your hearts honor Christ the Lord as holy, always being prepared to make a defense to anyone who asks you for a reason for the hope that is in you." As Christians, we should be ready to explain the (good) reasons for our beliefs.

Here's the tricky part: Having justification for why you believe something doesn't guarantee the belief is true. For example, I may believe that the Earth stands still all the time, as justified by the fact I don't feel the ground moving. That would be a justified belief. But, as we know, that justified belief is not correct.

That leads us to one last and very important component of the definition of knowledge: The justified belief must be *true*.

How do we get from thinking our beliefs are justified to knowing they are true? Our beliefs are justified when there is evidence for them, but are counted as true when there is *overwhelming* evidence for them. If that sounds like a vague deciding line, you're right (philosophers have written a lot on this topic). But, at the same time, we apply this principle every day without thinking about it. Let's say you find cookie crumbs all over the floor, which is the same thing that happened the last time your cookie-loving toddler broke into the pantry. Based on that past experience, you would be justified in believing your toddler was the culprit this time too. However, you wouldn't say you *know* she did it if there are three other cookie-loving kids in the house. But if you find her favorite drinking bottle next to the crumbs and moments later she walks in with the same crumbs all over her mouth, the overwhelming evidence would lead you to conclude you *know* it was her—even if you couldn't say that with absolute certainty.

As this example demonstrates, we claim to *know* something in everyday life when we have overwhelming evidence for it. Now let's look at how that applies to Christianity.

Building a Case for Christianity

As we saw in chapter 8, atheists regularly state that religious beliefs are based on a total lack of evidence. That claim is practically a battle cry today, and one that is jarring for a young person to hear. The propaganda is far from the truth, however. *Christianity is a worldview based on many compelling lines of evidence, and those lines of evidence are the basis for reasonably claiming we know Christianity is true.*

Our kids need to know this evidence for Christianity *exists*, they need to *understand* it, and they need to be able to *articulate* it. Let's look at one big-picture example of how we can help them understand the case for Christianity based on evidence and reasoning.

1. *There is significant evidence that God exists.* In chapter 1, we looked at three of the most compelling arguments for God's existence: the cosmological argument, the design

argument, and the moral argument. If God exists, atheism and pantheistic religions like Hinduism and Buddhism cannot be true (*pantheism* is the belief that the universe is God and is eternal). Of major world religions, that leaves Judaism, Islam, and Christianity.

2. *If God exists, miracles are possible.* This is an important step between the existence of God and the evidence for Jesus' resurrection (see chapter 24).

3. *The New Testament is historically reliable and says Jesus claimed to be God.* This is where Judaism, Islam, and Christianity diverge. Judaism and Islam both say that the New Testament is false in what it claims about Jesus being God incarnate; Christianity says the New Testament is true. In part 4 we'll look at the evidence for the reliability of the New Testament. In chapter 18, we'll look at the evidence for Jesus claiming to be God.

4. *Jesus' claim to be God was miraculously confirmed by the resurrection.* There is compelling historical evidence to support a supernatural resurrection, as discussed in chapter 23.

5. *Therefore, Jesus is God and what Jesus taught was true.* We know what Jesus taught based on the (historically reliable) New Testament.

This brief summary provides one possible framework for thinking about the material in this book as a case for Christianity. Each point requires several levels of understanding, but a big-picture structure like this is very useful for helping kids understand the relevance of individual questions about faith.

Four Key Takeaways

I know there's a lot of information packed into this chapter. You may even want to go back and study the details again later. In the meantime, however, I want to be sure the following four big takeaways don't get lost in the mix.

1. *Our ultimate goal should* not *be for our kids to merely believe true things.* From our discussion of knowledge, we can see a true belief is necessary, but not sufficient. We want our kids to have solid justification for those true beliefs so they can have confidence that their knowledge about God is more than a lucky guess. When our kids encounter the atheist claim that there is a "total lack of evidence" for God's existence, they should be able to smell the propaganda a mile away.

2. *We need to make sure our kids have* good *reasons for their beliefs.* Not all reasons for belief are necessarily good. If our kids believe in Jesus for *bad* reasons, their faith may be easily crushed. For example, many kids say they are Christians simply because their parents are, and not because they've really thought about their beliefs (I was one of those kids). That kind of "borrowed" faith gets trampled easily.

3. *We need to make sure our kids can* articulate *the good reasons for their beliefs.* An atheist who frequents my blog once observed, "Most Christians can't even begin to explain why they believe what they do." In my experience, that's true. Teaching our kids the case for Christianity is a hugely important first step, but we need to make sure they can articulate that case to others. Giving them a framework like the one in this chapter can help significantly.

4. *We need to teach our kids how to evaluate reasons for* other *beliefs.* People with other worldviews can have convincing reasons for their beliefs as well. Passionate atheists are often especially well-prepared to discuss the reasons for their claims. Our kids need exposure to other people's reasons for belief and experience evaluating those reasons versus their own.

Claiming Knowledge Isn't Claiming Absolute Certainty

When people like Bill from the culinary tour assert that we can't know anything *for sure*—implying no one should claim they *know* their religion is true—they're appealing to a level of certainty beyond what we expect in everyday life. We regularly claim to know things when we have convincing evidence, and without absolute certainty. In the same way, Christians can claim to know what is objectively true based on multiple compelling lines of evidence.

12. How can personal experience help determine what is true?

In the previous chapter, we looked at the importance of helping our kids know good reasons for their faith. But what about the role of *personal experience* in determining what's true? Do the experiences we have with God (or lack thereof) constitute good reasons for our spiritual beliefs? These are the questions we'll address in this chapter.

People often trust their personal experiences over every other kind of evidence for their beliefs. The most common response I hear when I first explain what the word *apologetics* means is some version of, "I'm a Christian because I know in my heart Christianity is true." One mom told me, "I can only teach my kids what I know I've experienced, and they'll have to develop their beliefs based on their own experiences." If you've gotten this far in the book, you've hopefully seen that we have much more to offer our kids as reasons for belief than a description of how we've personally experienced God. But that's not to say personal experience isn't an important part of determining what is true. We just need to be careful about how we balance experience with other reasons for faith. What should that relationship look like? Let's begin to answer that question by looking at what the Bible says.

The Experience of the Holy Spirit

My great-grandmother had triplets who died after birth. She said that when she entered their room after they died, she saw an angel by the crib. My great-grandmother shared that experience with others as part of her Christian testimony for the rest of her life. I've wished many times that the privilege of supernatural encounters was hereditary!

While some people, like my great-grandmother, have unique religious experiences, there is one experience common to all believers that we should understand and acknowledge: the work of the Holy Spirit. The Bible tells us that the Holy Spirit transforms us, acts as a witness to the truth about God, and gives us conviction regarding our beliefs:

- "Hope does not put us to shame, because God's love has

been poured into our hearts through the Holy Spirit who has been given to us" (Romans 5:5).

- "Because you are sons, God has sent the Spirit of his Son into our hearts, crying, 'Abba! Father!'" (Galatians 4:6).

- "Our gospel came to you not only in word, but also in power and in the Holy Spirit and with full conviction" (1 Thessalonians 1:5).

We should be confident that this type of personal experience—the work of the Holy Spirit—is an important foundation for our knowledge of truth.

Two Major Challenges to the Validity of Personal Religious Experience

While the Bible affirms that the Holy Spirit is at work in the lives of Christians, there are two significant challenges to the validity of personal experience as evidence for the truthfulness of religious claims.

1. People have contradictory religious experiences.

Mormons often say they know the Book of Mormon is true and that Joseph Smith is a prophet from God because they have experienced a "burning in the bosom"—something they consider to be a confirmatory personal experience. As a non-Mormon, you probably dismiss that "evidence" because you don't believe Mormonism is true. But how is a Mormon saying, "My personal experience tells me *Mormonism* is true" any different than a Christian saying, "My personal experience tells me *Christianity* is true"? From the skeptic's perspective, the fact that people have contradictory religious experiences is one of the most significant challenges to their validity.

There are three possible conclusions a person could draw from the variety of religious experiences that people have: (1) All of them must be false because they contradict each other; (2) all of them point to a common core of truth; or (3) some may be true and some may be false. The conclusion that the vast majority of skeptics jump to is number 1, but that conclusion doesn't logically follow. Five people could witness a car accident and give contradictory reports of what happened. That doesn't necessarily mean no one gave the *correct* report. Similarly, the fact that there are contradictory religious experiences doesn't automatically mean they're all invalid or false. As for conclusion 2, it's possible that people of any religion may experience God, in terms of having a sense of the divine. That doesn't mean, however, that *all* experiential claims can be true; many are flatly contradictory. As you can see, the most logical conclusion is number 3: Some personal experiences may be true, and some may be false. This challenge to the validity of religious experience does nothing to debunk the logical possibility of the Holy Spirit's authentic work in the Christian's life.

2. Religious experience can be attributed to biological activity in the brain.

Skeptics commonly offer *neurological* explanations of religious experience in order to show that *supernatural* explanations are unnecessary. For example, events that occur in the brain during some types of religious experiences are very similar to events that occur during seizures, with some mental disorders, and with some kinds of drugs.[1] A skeptic who would hear about my great-grandmother's experience of seeing an angel would likely chalk it up to a hallucination triggered by deep grief.

It's beyond the scope of this chapter to evaluate whether neurological phenomena can actually be a sufficient explanation for describing the wide range of religious experiences that people have. But, for the sake of argument, let's assume they are. Would that automatically mean a given religious experience could not truly have been an encounter with the supernatural? Not at all. *Every* experience we have is accompanied by a neurological state. We shouldn't be surprised to find corresponding brain activity for religious experience if we are made with the God-given capacity to experience Him in that way. If humans can physically respond to God's presence through some kind of powerful experience, it follows that we might see that register in the brain. Seeing the associated brain activity in no way suggests that God doesn't exist or that religious experiences can't truly be encounters with the supernatural.

As we've seen, these two objections to the validity of personal religious experience have reasonable answers from a Christian perspective. That said, some cautions are in order when we consider the role of experience in faith.

Three Cautions on the Role of Religious Experience in Faith

1. The validity of personal religious experience does **not** negate the need to have other good reasons for faith.

Imagine for a moment that an atheist is challenging your child on his or her beliefs and all your child can say is, "My personal experience tells me Christianity is true." Just as you would give a person evidence to demonstrate that their experience confirming *Mormonism* is false, an atheist would give your child evidence to demonstrate that their experience confirming *Christianity* is false. If our kids have no reasons outside of themselves to help confirm that their personal experience is true, their faith can easily be crushed in light of such "evidence." This is why kids need good reasons for belief outside of personal experience (see chapter 11). Those external reasons help confirm the foundational work of the Holy Spirit.

2. Authentic religious experience should align with the Bible.

Dean Parave was an alcoholic before he converted to Christianity. After his fifth arrest for driving under the influence, he begged God for help. He received a lesser prison sentence than expected and took it as a sign. He felt convicted that he and his wife should begin sharing God's Word by swinging (swapping sex partners) with other couples. Parave says, "God has put me here to spread his word and our lifestyle community is a great place to do it."[2]

You've probably heard many other cringe-worthy stories about people who believe God told them to do outlandish things or live in unbiblical ways. It gives personal religious experience a bad name. But there's a simple test we can apply to our own experiences and those of others claiming to be Christians: *If Christianity is true, religious experiences should align with what the Bible says.* The fact that the Holy Spirit works through us in no way means that *every* feeling we have is from God. We must test our experiences using the Bible as our guide. In Parave's case, we know from Scripture that sex outside of marriage is wrong, so we have reason to question the validity of his claim.

3. A **lack** *of religious experience isn't evidence against God.*

I once attended a work-related convention and got into a conversation about religion with a fellow attendee after dinner. When I told him I was a Christian, he replied, "I'm agnostic. I actually would like to believe in God, but I've never had an experience that would show me He exists." He said this sadly, as if it was a total bummer that he had no other reason to believe.

It's not just Christians who are at risk for over-relying on experience as evidence for their beliefs. Many people decide that their *lack* of religious experience is evidence *against* God. If they haven't personally encountered an eight-foot-tall angel standing in their living room, they aren't going to believe. However, once again, we have to return to what the Bible says. If the Bible claimed that we would know Christianity is true because every individual would have a unique, undeniable encounter with God, then a lack of experience would indeed count as evidence against Christianity.

But the Bible says God chose to reveal Himself to everyone through Jesus (John 3:16). If we look in places other than where God promised we would find Him, we shouldn't deny His existence when we don't see Him there. It's like giving someone a map that shows where gold is buried, but they go looking for it somewhere else because that's where they think the gold *should* be. If they came back saying the gold doesn't exist, you would tell them they looked in the wrong place. Similarly, we have to look for God where He chose to reveal Himself.

Personal Religious Experiences Can *Help* Point to Truth

The Bible tells us that the experience of the Holy Spirit working through us is common to all believers. There's no reason to deny the validity of that or other religious experiences simply because people make contradictory claims or because some types of experiences happen to have corresponding brain activity. However, we should strongly value additional reasons for belief outside of ourselves in order to confirm that inner witness and be able to offer a case for Christianity to others—starting with our kids.

13. How can common sense help determine what is true?

> The light of common sense, thrown on the stories of making snakes out of rods, of the Red Sea dividing itself, of Christ's making wine from water, curing blind men by rubbing spit in their eyes, walking on water, the story of the flood, God's making the world in six days, of making a woman from Adam's rib and all the mythical, miraculous stories of the Bible would cause any sensible man to question the veracity of the whole book, including all the stories of the gods, spirits, angels, devils, and the things that common sense tells us are not true.[1]

This quote, from a website devoted to atheism, is an example of a frequent claim against Christianity: *Christianity defies common sense.* While there certainly are many Christians and skeptics engaging in deeper, more scientific or philosophical battles online, simplistic appeals to common sense are the down-and-dirty weapons often hurled through social media. You don't need to know one thing about logic, theology, history, biblical scholarship, philosophy, or science to cobble together an emotionally impactful statement that can make someone feel utterly stupid for what they believe. That's why appeals to common sense can be so powerful: They're easy and effective. Consider the general message of the quote at the beginning of this chapter: *What Christians believe is so ridiculous that anyone with just a little common sense can see it isn't true.* Common sense is presented as a one-size-fits-all bulldozer against faith.

If you're like me, your immediate reaction when reading a quote like this is a series of "But...but...but..." objections explaining why each thing really *does* make sense. As tempting as that is, it's not the best response. In reality, common sense isn't the intellectual tool we should be applying to the evaluation of religious truth claims. This chapter will explain why.

The Limits of Common Sense

Common sense is defined as "sound judgment based on a simple perception of the situation or facts."[2] It's an important part of our daily lives. For example, common sense tells us not to walk into the street when we see a car coming. We run into problems, however, when we attempt to make common sense-type judgments about matters that require more understanding than a "simple perception of facts." Here are two key reasons why.

1. Common sense is based on a person's individual experience.

Because our experiences are limited, they usually don't give us enough information from which to draw reliable conclusions on complex subjects. For example, no one would try to conduct surgery on another person without medical training. We accept that the ability to do surgery requires a deeper understanding of medical facts and not just simple evaluations when we cut someone open. You would find it quite bizarre if someone handed you a knife and said, "Don't worry— once you cut him open, just use your common sense!" Similarly, common sense isn't an appropriate tool for evaluating the truth of complex worldviews.

2. Many things are weird but true, defying common sense.

The definition of *weird* is "different from anything ordinary."[3] When we encounter the abnormal, we tend to question its reality because it's outside of our everyday experience. But many things are true despite their weirdness. It's weird but true, for example, that we live on a big rock that jets around the sun at an average speed of 66,600 mph and we don't feel a thing. If our test for truth is what we instinctively think is common sense, we'll indiscriminately reject almost any idea that strikes us as weird. Since religious claims usually involve unique revelations and events outside our experience, they're a natural target for rejection based on supposed common sense.

Bill Nye, the well-known host of the mid-1990s children's science show *Bill Nye the Science Guy*, recently wrote a book promoting evolution titled *Undeniable: Evolution and the Science of Creation*. An interviewer asked him, "Do you imagine a child in a creationist-friendly household managing to get his hands on the book and stealing away with it?" Nye replied, "It would be great if the book is that influential. My biggest concern about creationist kids is that they're compelled to suppress their common sense, to suppress their critical thinking skills at a time in human history when we need them more than ever."[4] Nye's assertion that creationism defies common sense is characteristic of atheist thought today: *Anything not explainable by science is outside of our experience and should be rejected based on our common sense.* Nye, like many others, has incorrectly applied the tool of common sense to questions beyond its scope.

Christianity Isn't Common Sense…But It Does Make Sense

As we've seen, religion isn't a subject that common sense alone can evaluate. However, that doesn't mean a religion can't *make sense*. People often confuse these two terms. When we say something *makes sense*, we're referring to whether it's "reasonable or comprehensible."[5] This is an entirely different question, though people sometimes use the terms interchangeably. Of course, this too is an objection to Christianity: *Christianity just doesn't make sense!* For example, here's an excerpt from an atheist's blog post that makes several observations about the Bible and repeatedly asks, "Does this make sense to you?"

> God who is so powerful he not only spoke the universe into existence but can control the most absolute smallest particle and yet his solution for [man's] plight is to be born of a virgin so he can grow up and be killed by his own creation. Does this make sense to you? It makes sense to Christians![6]

In this case, the writer is presumably talking about reasonable or rational sense, not common sense. The question of rational sense goes right back to the discussion in chapter 11: How can Christians claim they know what is objectively true? If our kids aren't equipped with good reasons for their faith—compelling reasons that demonstrate the fundamental rationality of what they believe—this kind of rhetoric can be devastating. That's why it's so important that we proactively work through the rational case for Christianity with our kids. Christianity makes sense, but not *necessarily* by default. As you can see from this blog excerpt, there are a lot of ways to look at Christian claims. Taken out of context, they can seem nonsensical.

Making Sense of Common Sense

It's easy and emotionally impactful for people to claim that Christianity defies common sense. However, common sense isn't even an appropriate tool for evaluating the truth of complex subjects like the nature of reality. That doesn't mean Christianity *doesn't* make sense. There are many compelling reasons for believing that God exists, that miracles are therefore possible, and that Jesus was miraculously resurrected (see chapter 11 on building a case for Christianity). Christianity may not be a matter of *common* sense, but it certainly makes *rational* sense when you consider the many compelling reasons for belief.

14. If Christianity is true, why are there so many denominations?

Let's assume for a moment that objective truth exists (see chapter 9), that religions don't all point to the same truth (see chapter 10), and that it's reasonable for Christians to claim they know what's true (see chapter 11). Even if we line up all those pieces, it doesn't necessarily follow that Christianity *is* true. It only means Christianity is *possibly* true. In this book, we discuss many objections to that possibility based on challenges to specific Christian beliefs.

Some objections to Christianity, however, aren't even about *what*

Christians believe; they're about the *results* of what Christians believe and the intellectual competence of believers. In this and the next two chapters, we'll address those challenges: If Christianity is true, why are there so many denominations? (chapter 14); is Christianity responsible for millions of deaths in history? (chapter 15); and, are Christians less intelligent than atheists? (chapter 16).

These three challenges are rarely issued as *primary* reasons for rejecting Christianity. More often, they're used as "nail in the coffin" arguments— objections that effectively say, "As if all the problems with Christian beliefs aren't enough, look at these obvious signs Christianity can't be true." Case in point for this chapter, here's how an atheist commenter on my blog once described his problem with multiple denominations existing within Christianity:

> The elephant in the Christian church is its thousands of sects, many of whom hold long-standing, diametrically opposed beliefs which all cannot be true. Such a situation seems inexplicable for an allegedly reasonable religion like Christianity. After all, other, far younger enterprises that are based on reason and evidence—science is a good example— for the most part lack this splintering...Let the first test of Christianity's reasonableness be whether it can convince its own adherents to shed incorrect gospels and unite behind a single doctrine. This achievement seems trivial for a religion that's truly reasonable, one headed by a deity who is supposedly no author of confusion.

By some estimates, there are more than 40,000 Christian denominations in the world.[1] Atheists such as this commenter look at that fact and ask, "How can Christianity be true if there is such disagreement over that supposed truth?" It's an important question that requires a thoughtful answer. If our kids come to believe that all churches labeled "Christian" are effectively the same, they may not be able to discern false teachings and eventually may be led astray. On the other hand, if they come to believe the mere existence of so many denominations proves that Christianity is unreasonable, they may walk away from faith completely. In this chapter, we'll look at how to navigate between those two extremes.

What Is a Christian?

Before we can look at what Christians disagree about and why, we need to first answer the more basic question: What *is* a Christian? The answer is the source of a lot of misunderstanding. For example, consider how the website religioustolerance.org "tolerantly" defines the word *Christian*:

> We accept as Christian any individual or group who devoutly, thoughtfully, seriously, and prayerfully regards themselves to be Christian. That is, they honestly believe themselves to be attempting to follow the teachings of Yeshua of Nazareth (a.k.a. Jesus Christ) as they interpret those teachings to be.[2]

In other words, this website says that any group who self-identifies as Christian is Christian. Major groups who would be Christian according to this commonly used definition include Protestants (with thousands of denominations), Roman Catholics, Eastern Orthodox, Mormons, Jehovah's Witnesses, Christian Scientists, New Thought, and the Unification Church. But within this one large and supposedly Christian group, some believe Jesus was God and some believe He was only a man; some believe there is one God and some believe there are many gods; some believe man needs redemption and some believe redemption is unnecessary. The list of contradictory beliefs could go on for pages.

If we define Christians as any group that follows Jesus' teachings in some way, *of course* it will seem like Christians disagree on a lot—using that definition, there are no beliefs necessary to agree on! Imagine if some parents pulled their daughters out of a Girl Scout troop to start a new group focused on theater instead of service, earning acting roles instead of badges, and selling performance tickets instead of cookies—all while claiming to still be Girl Scouts, based on their own interpretation of what troops should do. The new troop would function so differently that no one would still consider them Girl Scouts, regardless of how they wanted to identify themselves. Allowing people to self-identify may be politically correct, but it doesn't allow us to use words very meaningfully. To define groups of people in a meaningful way, we need to identify standards of "membership." For Christians, those standards come from the Bible.

Five Biblically Based Essential Christian Doctrines

It would be great if the Bible explicitly stated, "Here's how to define a Christian from now on," but it never comes straight out and says that. In fact, the word *Christian* is used only three times in the whole New Testament (Acts 11:26; 26:28; 1 Peter 4:16). Jesus' followers were called Christians because their behavior, activities, and speech were like his. Though we might not have an official membership guide for the early Christian community, it's not hard to create one. The Bible makes it clear that the first Christians held at least five essential beliefs, or doctrines:[3]

1. *One God:* "To you it was shown, that you might know that the LORD is God; there is no other besides him" (Deuteronomy 4:35; see also 6:4; Exodus 20:3; Isaiah 43:10; 44:6).

2. *The Deity of Jesus:* "Jesus said to them, 'Truly, truly, I say to you, before Abraham was, I am'" (John 8:58; note that this references Exodus 3:14, where God refers to Himself as "I am"; see also John 10:30; 20:28; Philippians 2:5-8; Colossians 2:9).

3. *The Resurrection:* "If Christ has not been raised, then our preaching is in vain and your faith is in vain" (1 Corinthians 15:14; see also 15:17; John 2:19-21).

4. *Salvation by Grace:* "By grace you have been saved through faith. And this is not your own doing; it is the gift of God, not a result of works, so that no one may boast" (Ephesians 2:8-9; see also Romans 3:20; Galatians 2:21; 5:4).

5. *The Gospel:* "I delivered to you as of first importance what
   I also received: that Christ died for our sins in accordance
   with the Scriptures, that he was buried, that he was
   raised on the third day in accordance with the Scriptures"
   (1 Corinthians 15:3-4; see also Galatians 1:8-9).

With these essential doctrines in hand, we can now see that several groups who call themselves Christian don't adhere to the basic beliefs that define Christianity. For example, Jehovah's Witnesses deny the deity of Jesus, His physical resurrection, and salvation by grace. Mormons deny there is only one God, that there is salvation by grace, and that Jesus is (uncreated) deity. Both groups hold beliefs contrary to the gospel given by Scripture. When we use essential doctrines to meaningfully define Christianity, it quickly becomes clear that major disagreements within "Christianity" are really major disagreements between Christianity and other *religions.* That fact must be the starting point for this discussion. With that established, we can now appropriately look at disagreements *within* Christianity.

Christian Denominations: Unity, Not Uniformity

As a kid, I remember being fascinated by the number of churches we passed between school and home each day. There was a Nazarene church, a Church of Christ, a Lutheran church, three Baptist churches, an Assembly of God church, and a Free Methodist church on a single stretch of road. I had absolutely no idea what the differences were between them, but I distinctly remember thinking that the Free Methodist church must have started because they didn't believe in taking an offering (a pretty enticing thought for an eight-year-old with a small piggy bank!).

These churches are examples of some Christian *denominations.* They generally agree on the essential doctrines we just looked at, but have emerged as unique denominations within Christianity because they disagree on what are often considered *nonessentials.* Unlike the religions described previously that differ on major doctrines like the number of gods and the deity of Jesus, Christian denominations differ on things like baptism methods, who should take communion, church governance, and worship styles. It's true that these disagreements have been significant enough to lead to the formation of new denominations, but it would be disingenuous to say that they represent thousands of individual "sects," as the commenter on my blog claimed. These denominations *do* "unite behind a single doctrine"—and much more than a single doctrine. They agree that there is one God, that Jesus was fully human and fully God, that Jesus died for our sins in accordance with the Scriptures, that He was physically resurrected, and that we have been saved by grace through faith in Jesus as our Savior. In other words, denominations agree on far more than they disagree on. There is clear *unity* amongst Christians (when appropriately defined), even if there is not *uniformity*.

Two final points should be made.

First, the vast majority of Christians belong to just a handful of denominations. While it's popularly said that there are 40,000+ denominations, that number includes every minor church separation ever documented around the world—most of which shouldn't even qualify as a denomination. There certainly aren't 40,000+ substantially different versions of Christianity.

Second, disagreement is not specific to Christianity. In nearly every field of study, multiple experts can look at the same set of facts and end up disagreeing over their interpretation. All major branches of science are rife with disagreement (unlike my blog commenter claimed). Just as in science, the very existence of disagreement in religion doesn't falsify the entire enterprise. Even if there actually *were* 40,000+ substantially different denominations, it wouldn't negate the possibility that somewhere among them, truth could be found.

Theology Matters

In an effort to make theology understandable for kids, we sometimes oversimplify Christianity to "Jesus died for our sins." While that's important for kids to know, they need a more complete understanding of the essential doctrines that define Christianity. With that understanding, they'll be able to appropriately discern between non-Christian religions and Christian denominations despite living in a world that frequently blurs those lines. They'll also be able to more clearly see the fundamental unity that exists within Christianity, regardless of denominational disagreements on nonessentials.

15. Is Christianity responsible for millions of deaths in history?

The very first purchase my son ever made with his allowance was a set of Legos. We were so proud of him that day, thinking of how our little boy was getting old enough to make "big boy" decisions. But when we got home from the store, his actions quickly dismissed any idea we had that he crossed some magical line of maturity that day. Before he even opened the box, he got into an argument with his little sister and promptly used his new purchase to hit her over the head. Our daughter cried, "Mommy! You have to take those Legos back to the store—they hurt me!"

Perhaps you've had times when one of your children is bawling but you have to laugh given the circumstances (which, of course, leads to a downward spiral of *more* bawling). This was one of those times. I sat my daughter down and explained that even though her brother *used* the Legos to hit her, there was nothing wrong with the Legos; it was her brother's bad choice that hurt her. I explained that if the Legos had come with instructions to hit someone, *then* we could say there was a problem with the Legos. She looked at me skeptically and replied, "Then we better look at the Lego instructions to make sure they're safe!"

Just as my daughter was determined to place the blame on the Legos for her brother's behavior, many people today are determined to place the blame on religion for the history of human violence. For example, atheist author Sam Harris, in *The End of Faith: Religion, Terror, and the Future of Reason*, claims religion is "the most prolific source of violence in our history." Many Internet authors focus on Christianity specifically and have attempted to publish every atrocity ever committed in the name of Christ.[1] The motivation for all these claims, of course, is to show that Christianity can't be true if it's responsible for so much evil in the world.

To address this issue, we have to distinguish between human behavior and the "instructions" that supposedly directed that behavior. For Christians, those instructions are found in the Bible. *We should only fault Christianity for the alleged millions of deaths if support for the actions leading to those deaths is found in Scripture.* Otherwise, we should conclude that it was actually sinful human behavior that is to blame, even if those people erroneously thought they were acting in the name of Christ. We don't want to be like my daughter and blame the Legos when the instructions never said to use them that way in the first place.

In this chapter, we'll look at historical deaths supposedly attributable to Christianity to (1) understand what happened, and (2) evaluate whether Christianity is rightfully to blame based on the teachings of the Bible. Although there are many historical atrocities for which people blame Christianity, there are three events that get the most attention: the Crusades, the Inquisition, and witch hunts. Those are the representative events we'll focus on in this chapter (see chapter 3 for questions about the "atrocity" of the Canaanite genocide).[2]

Evaluating the Crusades, Inquisition, and Witch Hunts

People who attempt to catalog all of the deaths caused by Christianity arrive at wildly varying death tolls. This is for two reasons: (1) different authors include different historical events in their lists, and (2) published death estimates for any given historical event vary significantly themselves. That said, all the death toll estimates have one thing in common: They're in the millions—some in the hundreds of millions. This isn't a small concern that's easily waved off, so we need to get into the details...

The Crusades
What happened?

When Islam's prophet Muhammad was born in AD 570, Christendom stretched from the Middle East, all along North Africa, and throughout much of Europe. But in the 80 years after Muhammad's death in 632, a new Muslim empire quickly displaced Christianity from most of the Middle East (including the Holy Land), all of North Africa, and most of Spain.[3] Fighting between Muslims and Christians over these and other lands continued for hundreds of years.

In 1095, the Byzantine Empire (the *eastern* half of Christendom) was losing significant territory to the invading Seljuk Turks, who had recently converted to Islam. The Turks had invaded the Middle East, captured Jerusalem, and driven to within a hundred miles of Constantinople, which was the capital of the Byzantine Empire. Byzantine emperor Alexius Comnenus sent a letter to Pope Urban II (head of the *western* half of Christendom) pleading for help to save the Holy Land and make it safe once more for Christians.[4] Pope Urban II responded by calling a meeting in Clermont, France, urging Western Christians to help Eastern Christians recapture the Holy Land from Muslim hands. Over the next 200 years, a series of 9 military campaigns were undertaken in the Middle East. The crusaders were ultimately expelled from the area, failing to regain the Holy Land from Muslim control. An exact count of the death toll doesn't exist. However, the commonly cited total is 1-3 million deaths, including Muslims, Jews, and the crusaders themselves.[5]

Is Christianity to blame?

Although many terrible things happened during the Crusades, support for those actions cannot be found in the Bible. There are no instructions for us to fight other religious groups for land, to massacre innocent people, to force conversions to Christianity, to rape, or to plunder (see chapters 3 and 31 for discussion of some Old Testament events that people may incorrectly classify as "instructions" to carry out these activities). The Crusaders, unfortunately, were misled in their zeal. In addition, many were Christian in name only and acted in ways clearly inconsistent with the faith. The Bible makes clear that Jesus came to "guide our feet into the way of peace" (Luke 1:79), that we are to love and pray for our enemies (Matthew 5:44), that peacemakers will be called the sons of God (Matthew 5:9), and that we should "seek peace and pursue it" (Psalm 34:14).

Some skeptics specifically point to Matthew 10:34, 38-39 as biblical support for the Crusades. In those verses, Jesus said, "Do not think that I have come to bring peace to the earth. I have not come to bring peace, but a sword...Whoever does not take his cross and follow me is not worthy of me. Whoever finds his life will lose it, and whoever loses his life for my sake will find it." However, the sword and cross in these verses are metaphors. The sword is a metaphor for the separation between those who believe in Jesus and those who do not (even within a family, as is made clear in verse 35). The cross is a metaphor for discipleship, in that a disciple must be willing to "die" to their self-will. When appropriately considered in context, these verses in no way support the actions of the crusaders.

The Inquisition

What happened?

The Inquisition was a group of judicial institutions within the Roman Catholic Church that aimed to combat heresy (nonorthodox religious beliefs) amongst professing Christians in the Middle Ages. In the Roman law of the time, anyone who opposed the beliefs of the emperor was an enemy of the state; religious heretics were considered a threat to society itself. At a time when certain heretical groups were gaining in popularity, the church decided to institute a formal inquisition process to locate and try suspected offenders (local civil authorities carried out the sentencing).

There were three major Inquisitions—the first beginning in 1184, and the last beginning in 1542. The most famous was the Spanish Inquisition, authorized by Pope Sixtus IV in 1478. The goal was to investigate charges against Jewish and Muslim converts to Christianity who were suspected of secretly practicing their former religions. The Spanish Inquisition is well-known because of the cruelty used by local authorities to elicit confessions and punish offenders. It's estimated that about 6000 people were killed throughout the Inquisition period, though undocumented Internet sources frequently (and inaccurately) place this number in the millions.[6]

Is Christianity to blame?

There's no doubt the cruelty used to root out heretics during the Inquisition was awful, as were the thousands of deaths.[7] But, as with the Crusades, even if the Inquisition was carried out in the name of Christ, we have to look to the Bible to see if it supports what was done.

You might be surprised to learn that there *are* Bible verses that tell God's people to "inquire" about heretics in the community and kill them. For example, skeptics will gladly point you to Deuteronomy 17:2-5 to demonstrate that the Bible supports the Inquisition:

> If there is found among you, within any of your towns that the LORD your God is giving you, a man or woman who does what is evil in the sight of the LORD your God, in transgressing his covenant, and has gone and served other gods and worshiped them, or the sun or the moon or any of the host of heaven, which I have forbidden, and it is told you and you hear of it, then you shall inquire diligently, and if it is true and certain that such an abomination has been done in Israel, then you shall bring out to your gates that man or woman who has done this evil thing, and you shall stone that man or woman to death with stones.

There's no denying that sounds pretty severe. However, context is everything: *These laws were given to the nation of Israel when it was a theocracy—the one and only time when a country legally and politically came under the direct authority of God.* The strict laws of this period were designed to keep the community as theologically pure as possible in order to fulfill its unique role of pointing other nations to the one true God. These laws are in no way instructions for individual Christians or Christian communities outside of that context.

Witch Hunts
What happened?

During the Middle Ages, Satan began to take on a more prominent and visually menacing image in many Christian parts of Europe. Christians started to believe that the world would soon end and that

Satan's activities on Earth would become more frequent. This led to paranoia, as people began to think society's troubles were all a result of their neighbors performing witchcraft and consorting with the devil. People were accused of being witches for anything from causing a village death to causing crop failure.

In the 16th and 17th centuries, a frenzy of witch hunts took place in which communities sought out their local "witches" and promptly executed them. In mainland Europe and Scotland, suspected witches were burned at the stake. In England and the American colonies, witches were hanged. An estimated 60,000 people were put to death during this time.[8]

Is Christianity to blame?

Skeptics commonly point to two verses as evidence that the witch hunts were a result of Christians obeying the Bible. First, Exodus 22:18 says, "You shall not permit a sorceress to live." Second, Leviticus 20:27 says, "A man or a woman who is a medium or a necromancer shall surely be put to death. They shall be stoned with stones; their blood shall be upon them" (a necromancer is someone who practices witchcraft).

While those verses sound harsh, once again we have to look at the context. And again, they are part of the laws God gave to the nation of Israel when it was a theocracy. Those verses are in no way applicable to individuals or communities outside of that context.

What About Millions of Deaths *Not* Attributable to Christianity?

It's not just skeptics who point the finger for big death tolls in history. Christians engaging in these discussions often point the finger back to show that the *most* killings have come from modern atheist regimes. Consider the following:

- The rule of Mao Zedong, founder of the People's Republic of China, resulted in the deaths of 40-70 million people from starvation, forced labor, and executions.[9]

- The regime of Joseph Stalin, communist dictator of the Union of Soviet Socialist Republics (USSR) from 1929 to 1953, led to 20-60 million deaths from artificial famine, executions, and forced labor.[10]

- Adolph Hitler and his Nazi party were responsible for the genocide of about 6 million Jews (and other victims deemed racially inferior) during World War II.[11]

- Pol Pot and his communist Khmer Rouge movement in Cambodia killed at least 1.5 million people—out of a population of 7-8 million—by starvation, execution, disease, or forced labor.[12]

I'm including these details to give you a broader perspective on the nature of this debate and the extent of human depravity—mass killings have certainly never been limited to people who act in the name of religion. However, Christians really have nothing to gain by somehow proving that an atheist or irreligious worldview has led to more deaths than Christianity. Millions of deaths resulting from other worldviews don't absolve Christians from addressing the historical evils committed in the name of Christ. Our primary concern in these conversations needs to remain on demonstrating that the Bible (when properly interpreted) in no way permitted those evils, not on how many deaths other worldviews are responsible for.

It's Not the Legos, It's the Person

There is no doubt that the Crusades, Inquisition, and witch hunts would not have happened if Christianity didn't exist. In that sense, a person could claim that Christianity is to "blame" for those events. But acknowledging that the mere *existence* of Christianity enabled people to use it for harm hardly proves the point skeptics usually want to make—that Christianity *itself* is responsible for evil. As we've seen, Christians who have committed evils were not acting based on the teachings of the Bible. This doesn't necessarily mean they weren't Christians (though many surely were not), but rather, that even Christians do wrong. We have to carefully distinguish between what people do, what they claim to be doing, and what their "instructions" actually say.

16. Are Christians less intelligent than atheists?

In July 2014, Ohio State University made the news when a quiz question from one of the school's psychology classes implied Christians aren't as smart as atheists. The question asked students to pick which scenario they found most likely given that a person named Theo has an IQ of 100 and a person named Aine has an IQ of 125 (IQ is a measure of intelligence). The correct answer? "Aine is an atheist, while Theo is a Christian."[1] The story went viral and launched an online flurry of atheist commentary about the intellectual inferiority of Christians.

You may assume the Ohio State story is an example of baseless atheist bias against religion. That's actually not the case. The question-and-answer choices were poorly worded, but it's true that a number of studies have found a negative relationship between intelligence and religiousness—in other words, they suggest that the more intelligent a person is, the less likely they are to be religious. Many passionate atheists are well aware of these studies and use them as ammunition for their arguments that religion is for the poor, ignorant, and unintelligent.

Is this a valid claim? Can people legitimately say, based on these studies, that Christians are less intelligent overall than atheists? Absolutely not. I have an MBA in marketing and statistics and have taught university-level market research, so I'm a numbers geek...one who's a little too excited to set the record straight in this chapter.

Before we move on, however, I have to point out what is hopefully obvious: *Even if we could reliably measure which group is smarter, the answer wouldn't tell us anything about the truth of Christianity; intelligence doesn't equate to always having the right answer.*

Theoretically, we could end all conversations on this topic by pointing that out. But if your child asks you one day why Christians aren't as smart as atheists, do you really want to reply, "Well, that doesn't mean Christianity isn't true"? We owe it to our kids to be able to address the claim itself. This chapter will help you do that.

What Exactly Do These Studies Say?

There are two major studies people typically reference when this subject comes up—one at the country level, and one at the individual (person) level.

Country-Level Study Findings

In 2009, researchers compared the average national IQ with the national percent of atheists for 137 countries around the world.[2] This analysis showed a significant positive relationship between those two measures: the higher the average national intelligence, the higher the percent of atheists in a given country.[3] There are two key things you should know about this frequently quoted study.

First, the validity of national measures of intelligence and atheism is questionable. Measuring national intelligence is a controversial area of study due to the complex interaction of cultural factors such as environment, education, literacy, nutrition, and health care.[4] This means that IQ numbers will vary across nations due to a variety of factors, making cross-country comparisons of intelligence extremely difficult, if not impossible.

Calculating a reliable estimate of the percent of atheists in a country is equally difficult. The researchers themselves acknowledged four problems with the data set used to estimate atheist percentages: low response rates, weaknesses in random sample selection, regime or peer pressure influencing responses, and problems of terminological variation between cultures over words such as *religious* or *secular*.[5] No data is perfect, but the data used in this study is especially subject to concern.

Second, a more detailed analysis shows that the relationship between atheism and intelligence is limited to countries within a specific national IQ range. For a moment, let's ignore my last point and assume the IQ and atheism measures for the 137 countries are reliable. Is the reportedly strong relationship between intelligence and atheism accurate based on the data points used? Yes and no. I obtained the raw country-level data from the published research study to dissect the reported results. While it's true that the data as a whole shows a relationship between national intelligence and atheism, a closer analysis shows that this effect *is mostly limited to countries with a national IQ between 85 and 95.* In the 63 countries with an IQ less than 85 (almost half of the total), there is a statistically *zero* relationship between IQ and atheism.[6] In the 36 countries with an IQ of 96 or greater, there is also a statistically *zero* relationship between these measures. Only in the 38 countries with an IQ between 85 and 95 is there a statistical relationship between IQ and atheism. These are predominantly Central Asian, Southeast Asian, and South American countries.

So what's the bottom line? Taking the questionable data as it is, the only thing we can conclude is that in a specific range of national IQ levels there may be a weak relationship between IQ and atheism—and the countries falling in that range are almost all in three specific regions of the world (which suggests underlying region-specific factors). This is hardly conclusive.

Individual-Level Study Findings

In 2013, researchers from the University of Rochester and Northeastern University pulled together all past studies conducted on the relationship between religiousness and intelligence at the individual (person) level.[7] Of the 63 studies identified:

- 35 showed a significant *negative* relationship between intelligence and religiousness (the more intelligent a person was, the less likely they were to be religious).

- 2 showed a significant *positive* relationship between intelligence and religiousness (the more intelligent a person was, the more likely they were to be religious).

- 26 showed *no* significant relationship between intelligence and religiousness.

In other words, only about half of the 63 studies suggest that the more intelligent a person is, the less likely they are to be religious. The other half of the studies don't show that at all. The researchers *themselves* acknowledged, "The relation between intelligence and religiosity has been examined repeatedly, but so far there is no clear consensus on the direction and/or the magnitude of this association."[8]

First major takeaway: The common claim that studies have shown repeatedly that religious people are less intelligent is highly misleading. It ignores the results of almost half of the studies conducted. Overall, the results are inconclusive.

The goal of the researchers in 2013 was to look at these studies *as a group* for the first time in order to better quantify the nature and magnitude of the relationship between intelligence and religiousness. Before we look at the results, it's important to note that combining 63 individual studies is problematic. The studies varied extensively on: [9]

- *Who was studied:* Some studied precollege teens, some studied college students, and some studied noncollege adults (people recruited outside an academic context).

- *How many people were studied:* Sample sizes ranged from 20 to more than 14,000.

- *When the studies were conducted:* The studies were done over an 84-year span of time (the earliest study was conducted in 1928 and the most recent in 2012).

- *What the studies measured:* Some studies measured religious behavior (for example, church attendance and/or participation in religious organizations) and some measured religious beliefs (for example, belief in God and the Bible).

- *How the studies measured:* 23 different types of tests were used to measure intelligence (for example, university entrance exams, vocabulary tests, scientific literacy tests, etc.). Details weren't provided on how exactly each study measured religious behavior and beliefs, but that surely varied extensively as well.

Cornell statistics professor William M. Briggs summarized the problem with this variety, saying, "Data of every flavor was observed, data that should not be mixed without an idea of how to combine the uncertainty inherent in each study and in how, say, kinds of IQ measurements map to other kinds of IQ measurements. In other words, they mixed data which should not be mixed, because nobody has any idea how to make these corrections."[10]

Methodological concerns aside, let's assume for a moment that it's valid to combine the results of these 63 studies. Ultimately, there were 2 factors researchers found to be significant in the relationship between intelligence and religiousness. The first was the *life stage* of who they studied (precollege, college, or noncollege). The second was the *measure of religiousness* (behavior or belief). The results suggested:

- Religious *behavior*, such as church membership, has almost no relationship with intelligence at any life stage.[11]

- Religious *belief* has almost no relationship with intelligence in the *precollege* years (presumably because beliefs are more influenced by parents).

- Religious *belief* has a *weak* negative relationship with intelligence for *college and noncollege adults* (the higher the intelligence, the less likely a person is to have religious beliefs).[12]

Second major takeaway: The results suggest a negative relationship between intelligence and religious belief for adults, but the mathematical magnitude of that relationship is *very small.* The vast majority of variation in religious belief amongst individuals is explained by (unidentified) factors other than intelligence.

If you're not a numbers person, your head might be spinning a bit right now. That's okay—consider this a reference chapter to revisit when the subject comes up. You'll be happy to know we're all done with the data now. But before we call it a day, it's important to consider what the Bible says on this subject too. Referencing what Scriptures say about intelligence and faith won't get you far in a conversation with an atheist (which is why you need to understand the data), but as a *Christian*, it's important to know what God has told us.

What Does the Bible Say About Intelligence and Faith?

The Bible is clear: *Belief is not a function of intelligence.* Scripture says:

- We are born with a spiritually dead mind (Ephesians 2:1).

- People without the Holy Spirit's leading do not accept the things that come from God and consider them foolishness (1 Corinthians 2:14).

- People think in futile ways and can be darkened in their understanding due to a hardness of heart (Ephesians 4:17-18).

- The mind governed by the flesh is hostile to God (Romans 8:7).

- Because of these realities, people are unable to come to God without His prompting (John 6:44; Romans 3:11).

The Bible also makes it clear, however, that we shouldn't check our minds at the door. Thinking, *in its appropriate place*, is a core part of faith. Jesus told us to "love the Lord your God with all your heart and with all your soul and *with all your mind*" (Matthew 22:37). The apostle Paul told the Corinthians, "Do not be children in your thinking. Be infants in evil, but in your thinking be mature" (1 Corinthians 14:20). The kind of thinking that the Bible repeatedly cautions against is a purely *self-reliant* thinking. Make no mistake: Christians are called to a *Spirit-enabled* use of our minds.

No Need for Shame

As a Christian, you may wonder why anyone ever gets caught up in discussions about who's more intelligent. After all, as I pointed out earlier, the most intelligent people (whoever they might be) don't necessarily have all the right answers. But atheists often bring this up to show that religion is for ignorant people who don't know better. It's an emotionally impactful claim that can shame your kids for being Christians and make them question their own judgment—an outcome truly unnecessary given the actual data. Make sure your kids have the full picture: Only about half the studies ever conducted on the topic have suggested that more intelligent people are less likely to be religious, and, even in those studies, the relationship between intelligence and religiousness is *very* weak.

PART 3:

Conversations About
JESUS

17. How do we know Jesus existed?

If you grew up in church, you may never have considered the following question: How do we know Jesus existed? In fact, it may seem like a rather strange thing to ask. I admittedly had never considered it before an atheist wrote this comment on my blog one day: "There's actually not a shred of evidence that Jesus ever existed. Check it out for yourself."

When I first read that, it seemed like an outlandish claim. How could someone think Jesus never even existed as a person in history? But as crazy as that sounded, I had no idea how to respond. Clearly, just citing the Bible wasn't going to convince someone who didn't believe in its authority. Off I went to do some research.

To my surprise, I learned there are many people who make an extensive case for Jesus being purely mythical. They're called *mythicists* and they write prolifically online. To give you a feel for the types of claims your kids are likely to see, here's a representative Internet quote from a mythicist:

> All reliable evidence points to Jesus Christ being just a myth. There is no reliable evidence that Jesus even existed, and significant evidence that he didn't. The evidence is in the Bible, the other religions of the time, the lack of writings about Jesus by any historians of the 1st century, and the lack of writings about Jesus by anyone until a decade or more after his supposed life.[1]

Interestingly, mythicists such as this person are generally only found at the popular (nonscholar) level. Dr. Bart Ehrman, agnostic author of *Did Jesus Exist?*, commented in an interview:

> [Mythicists] are not influential among scholars of antiquity, historians of the ancient world, classicists, and biblical scholars. There, they've made virtually no impact. Where they have made an impact is in popular circles, especially with the advent of the Internet. There is an increasing following of these people on the Internet, and a number of them have written books that have sold a lot of copies.[2]

Unfortunately, it's this popular-level impact we most need to be concerned about as parents. Our kids aren't usually seeking out what the scholars say. They're stumbling upon entire websites dedicated to making sweeping, unscrutinized claims that Jesus is just an elaborate myth. That's why it's important to know how to respond.

Evidence for Jesus' existence comes from both Christian and non-Christian sources. The evidence from non-Christian sources is especially important for engaging with nonbelievers, since they usually dismiss the Bible as a source of historical information. With that in mind, let's first consider the evidence from non-Christian sources.

Evidence from Non-Christian Sources

While there are several ancient references typically discussed in this conversation (less than ten), there are four that are considered to be the most important. You don't need to get consumed by the details if you're not wild about history. What's important is understanding the nature of these mentions and how they support the historicity of Jesus. Here they are, listed in their order of importance:

1. *Flavius Josephus* (AD 37–c. 100) is perhaps the most famous ancient Jewish historian. During the Jewish-Roman wars, he defected and became a Roman citizen. He personally did not believe Jesus was the Son of God. This is important because it means he wasn't incentivized to promote Christian beliefs. Josephus mentioned Jesus in two separate passages of his writings.

The first passage is controversial because it doesn't sound like the original writing of a Jew who didn't believe that Jesus was the Messiah. For that reason, most scholars assume Christians edited it when copies were made in later years. Many scholars believe, however, that there is still an authentic core that references the historical Jesus:

> Now there was about this time, Jesus, a wise man, if it be lawful to call him a man, for he was a doer of wonderful works, a teacher of such men as received the truth with pleasure. He drew over to him both many of the Jews, and many of the Gentiles. He was the Christ, and when Pilate, at the suggestion of the principle men among us,

had condemned him to the cross, those that loved him at the first did not forsake him; for he appeared to them alive again the third day; as the divine prophets had foretold these and ten thousand other wonderful things concerning him. And the tribe of Christians so named from him are not extinct at this day.

The second passage of interest is less controversial because it was written in a more disinterested way. It describes how the high priest Ananus was preparing to kill the apostle James, brother of Jesus:

So he assembled the Sanhedrin of judges and brought before them the brother of Jesus, who was called Christ, whose name was James.

This is significant because James was important to the historical narrative solely through his affiliation with Jesus. If Jesus hadn't lived, there would be no need to mention Him, and no need to mention James.

2. *Cornelius Tacitus* (AD 56–c. 117) was a first-century Roman senator who wrote a history of the Roman Empire from AD 14–68. He provided a valuable mention of Jesus when he described how Emperor Nero tried to blame Christians for Rome's fire in AD 64:

Hence to suppress the rumor, he falsely charged with the guilt, and punished Christians, who were hated for their enormities. Christus, the founder of the name, was put to death by Pontius Pilate, procurator of Judea in the reign of Tiberius: but the pernicious superstition, repressed for a time broke out again, not only through Judea, where the mischief originated, but through the city of Rome also, where all things hideous and shameful from every part of the world find their center and become popular.

Skeptics argue that this cannot be considered independent evidence for Jesus because we don't know what Tacitus's source was. They claim it could have been hearsay. However, Tacitus's position gave him access to many official documents, and it is likely he had a reliable source for the information.

3. *Pliny the Younger* (AD 61–c. 112) was a Roman official who is known for his hundreds of surviving letters to notable people in the Roman Empire. In his correspondence with the emperor Trajan, he reported on the worship activities of early Christians and asked for instruction on how to deal with them. These early Christians would have had firsthand knowledge that Jesus actually existed, and developed their worship accordingly.

4. *Thallus* was one of the first Gentile writers to mention Jesus. In AD 52 he wrote a natural explanation for the darkness that covered the land at the time of Jesus' crucifixion (Matthew 27:45).[3] His original writings no longer exist, but we know of them from the citations of other writers. For example, Julius Africanus, a Christian writer, wrote the following around AD 221:

> Thallus, in the third book of his histories, explains away this darkness as an eclipse of the sun—unreasonably, as it seems to me (unreasonably, of course, because a solar eclipse could not take place at the time of the full moon, and it was at the season of the Paschal full moon that Christ died).

While these four references from non-Christian sources may not seem like much historical evidence, it's important to keep in mind that there are very few documents of any kind that survive from Jesus' day. Jesus ministered for only three years and lived in a remote corner of the Roman Empire. What's surprising is that we have *any* ancient extrabiblical references to Him!

That said, we have significant additional evidence when we include Christian sources. Let's turn now to the Bible and the early church fathers.

Evidence from Christian Sources
The New Testament
The New Testament is comprised of 27 individual historical documents (books) that provide evidence of Jesus' existence. You don't have to accept any theological claims of the New Testament to acknowledge

that these books support the existence of a historical Jesus. Regardless of whether historians believe Jesus' claims to be God, most agree that these sources alone are sufficient to testify to Jesus' *existence*.

Writings of the Early Church Fathers

The earliest church fathers (church leaders who lived within the first half of the second century) left writings that provide important additional historical evidence for Jesus. These writers presumably had firsthand knowledge independent of the New Testament sources. Especially important are Clement of Rome, Ignatius of Antioch, and Polycarp of Smyrna.

Clement of Rome wrote the earliest Christian letter outside of the New Testament around AD 96. In his letter, called 1 Clement, he addressed a dispute over leadership of the church in Corinth and urged readers to remember the words of Jesus.

Ignatius of Antioch was a student of the apostle John and wrote a series of letters en route to his martyrdom (about AD 110). The following quote from Ignatius describes his all-consuming passion for Jesus:

> It is not that I want merely to be called a Christian, but to actually be one. Yes, if I prove to be one, then I can have the name...Come fire, cross, battling with wild beasts, wrenching of bones, mangling of limbs, crushing of my whole body, cruel tortures of the devil—only let me get to Jesus Christ!

Polycarp of Smyrna was a Christian bishop who was probably the last surviving person to have known an apostle. He was martyred around AD 160 at about 86 years old. Just before he was killed, he prayed:

> Father, I bless you that you have deemed me worthy of this day and hour, that I might take a portion of the martyrs in the cup of Christ...Among these may I today be welcome before thy face as a rich and acceptable sacrifice.

These church fathers clearly wrote with passion and were willing to die for a Jesus they knew existed. Their writings offer compelling historical evidence.

Virtually All Historians Acknowledge Jesus Existed

The combined evidence of non-Christian and Christian sources provides a powerful testimony that Jesus existed, despite the passionate and insistent claims of mythicists. It is this very evidence that explains why serious scholars and historians generally do not argue against Jesus' historical existence.

The question of whether or not Jesus existed is a good example of a challenge to faith that many of us might never have considered ourselves. The questions we encounter and those that our kids will encounter can be very different. That's why it's so important to learn what specific claims are challenging the younger generation today. In this case, the statement that there's "not a shred of evidence that Jesus ever existed" is simply an unsubstantiated claim touted by a vocal minority.

18. Did Jesus really claim to be God?

In the book *Soul Searching: The Religious and Spiritual Lives of American Teenagers*, sociologists Christian Smith and Melinda Lundquist Denton describe in detail the results of a study on the spiritual lives of 3000 American teenagers.[1] The authors found that many young people hold a combination of beliefs not exclusive to any world religion— a worldview the authors labeled *Moralistic Therapeutic Deism*. The key beliefs that describe this view are:

- A god exists who created and ordered the world and watches over human life on Earth.

- God wants people to be good, nice, and fair to each other, as taught in the Bible and by most world religions.

- The central goal of life is to be happy and to feel good about oneself.

- God does not need to be particularly involved in one's life except when He is needed to resolve a problem.

- Good people go to heaven when they die.[2]

It's called *moralistic* because these young people believe you should be "good." It's called *therapeutic* because they believe the goal is to feel good about oneself (it's all about what God can do for *you*, not what you should do for God). And it's called *deism* because they believe that God at least exists and created the world.

The problem is that a lot of young people equate Moralistic Therapeutic Deism with Christianity. They see no effective difference. And that's a dangerous trap our kids can fall into. It's a belief system that at first *sounds* like Christianity, but it couldn't be more different. It doesn't involve *Jesus*.

Let's get brutally honest for a minute. Jesus was either God or He wasn't. If He was, then *everything* He said and did is of critical importance for our lives. If He wasn't, He was just a human like the rest of us and there's no reason to believe His words have any authority. There's a lot of gray in the world, but that is black and white.

Why do so many kids with a Christian upbringing end up believing some version of Moralistic Therapeutic Deism? *They clearly lack the conviction that Jesus was actually God.* If they believed He truly was God, their faith couldn't possibly exclude Him. But it's not necessarily easy for kids (or adults) to believe this fundamental building block of Christianity. Realize what we're suggesting: Someone who lived 2000 years ago claimed to be God, was believed by His followers to be God, performed miracles, and came back to life from the dead. In today's world, our kids will have many opportunities to (rightly) question why they should believe something so extraordinary. In this and the next six chapters, we'll look at the basics they need to know about Jesus in light of the challenges they're likely to face.

So first things first: Did Jesus even *claim* to be God?

Did Jesus Claim to be God?

If you've never had the occasion to study this particular topic, you might be surprised to hear that there's no place in the Bible where Jesus actually says the words, "I am God." That seems a bit strange at first, right? If God were going to take on human form, wouldn't He immediately want to make His identity known? That logic isn't lost on skeptics, who frequently point it out as a problem. For example, ex-Christian New Testament scholar Bart Ehrman claims Jesus only understood Himself to be a prophet who was predicting the end of the current evil age and the future king of Israel in the age to come. Ehrman concludes in his book *How Jesus Became God*, "What we can know with relative certainty about Jesus is that his public ministry and proclamation were not focused on his divinity; in fact, they were not about his divinity at all."[3]

Oftentimes, as Christians, we take for granted what we believe the Bible says and aren't aware of nuances that can drive a major divide between believers and nonbelievers. In this case, it's the question of whether or not Jesus actually claimed to be God. If He *didn't* claim to be God, there would be little reason to conclude he actually *was* God, regardless of what others thought.

The key to answering this question is understanding that we don't need the exact words "I am God" from Jesus to know that's who He claimed to be. Dr. Norman Geisler, in *When Skeptics Ask: A Handbook on Christian Evidences*, identifies six ways in which Jesus *effectively* (if not directly) claimed to be God.[4]

1. Jesus claimed to be Yahweh.

Yahweh is the unique name given by God for Himself in the Old Testament. Other titles used for God in the Old Testament were also used for humans or false gods, but Yahweh was *uniquely* God's name. Therefore, if anyone were to claim to be Yahweh, there would be no question they were claiming to be God Himself. And that's exactly what Jesus did.

In Exodus chapter 3, God appeared to Moses from a burning bush. Moses asked God His name, and God replied, "I AM WHO I AM" (Exodus 3:14). God then revealed His name as Yahweh. Fast-forward to John 8:58. Jesus said, "Truly, truly, I say to you, before Abraham was, I am." At first glance, that sentence looks grammatically incorrect. You would think it should say "I was" at the end. But it says "I *am*" because

Jesus was intentionally referencing Exodus 3:14. In doing so, He not only claimed that He existed before Abraham, but also claimed equality with Yahweh—God. The Jews clearly understood the reference and picked up stones to kill Him for blasphemy (John 8:59). Jesus identified Himself with similar statements in Mark 14:62 and John 18:5-6.[5]

2. Jesus claimed to have the same unique rights as God.

The New Testament also records several examples of Jesus claiming to have certain *rights* that only God was believed to have. He claimed:

- *The right to forgive sins:* In Mark 2:5, Jesus told a paralytic, "Son, your sins are forgiven." The scribes questioned, "Why does this man speak like that? He is blaspheming! Who can forgive sins but God alone?" (Mark 2:7) Jesus then healed the man to prove that He could both heal *and* forgive sins—just like God.

- *The right to raise and judge the dead:* In John 5:25-27, Jesus said, "Truly, truly, I say to you, an hour is coming, and is now here, when the dead will hear the voice of the Son of God, and those who hear will live. For as the Father has life in himself, so he has granted the Son also to have life in himself. And he has given him authority to execute judgment, because he is the Son of Man." The Old Testament teaches that only God can raise and judge the dead, so Jesus (referring to Himself as the "Son of Man" here) is clearly claiming God's authority (see also Deuteronomy 32:35; 1 Samuel 2:6; Psalm 49:15; Joel 3:12).

- *The right to be honored like God:* In John 5:23, Jesus said, "All may honor the Son, just as they honor the Father. Whoever does not honor the Son does not honor the Father who sent him." By claiming that the Son (Jesus) has the right to be honored like the Father (God), Jesus was essentially declaring His divinity.

3. Jesus claimed to be the Messiah (God).

The Hebrew word *Messiah* means "anointed one" or "chosen one." The Greek equivalent is the word *Christos*, which is where we get the English word *Christ* from (Jesus Christ literally means Jesus the Messiah). In the Old Testament, people were anointed as prophet, priest, or king. But the Old Testament also predicted a *unique* "anointed one" who would be chosen by God to redeem Israel.[6] There are several indications in the Old Testament that this Messiah would be God. For example, Isaiah 9:6 calls the Messiah "Mighty God, Everlasting Father." Isaiah 7:14 prophesied the birth of the Messiah, calling Him "Immanuel"—a name meaning "God with us." Therefore, if a person claimed to be this unique Messiah, they were also claiming to be God. Once again, we'll see that's what Jesus did.

Jesus frequently referred to Himself as the *Son of Man*, which is precisely the term used for the unique Messiah in Daniel 7. At Jesus' trial, the high priest asked, "Are you the Christ, the Son of the Blessed?" (Mark 14:61). Jesus answered:

> "I am, and you will see the Son of Man seated at the right hand of Power, and coming with the clouds of heaven." And the high priest tore his garments and said, "What further witnesses do we need? You have heard his blasphemy. What is your decision?" And they all condemned him as deserving death (verses 62-64).

Clearly, the Jews understood Jesus was claiming to be the Messiah—God—based on His "Son of Man" reference to Daniel 7. He was quickly condemned to die for it.

4. Jesus claimed His words had as much authority as God's words.

There are several times when Jesus put His words on par with God's words:

- The phrase, "You have heard that it was said…But I say to you…" is repeated several times in Scripture (for example, see Matthew 5:21-22). In these instances, Jesus was challenging the prevailing views of Moses' law and was implicitly claiming the authority to declare its full meaning.

- In Matthew 5:18, Jesus made clear that He was not changing the laws God gave to Moses; it was the people's *understanding* of those laws that needed correction. He said, "Truly, I say to you, until heaven and earth pass away, not an iota, not a dot, will pass from the Law until all is accomplished." Later, He made the same claim about the everlasting nature of His words: "Heaven and earth will pass away, but my words will not pass away" (Matthew 24:35).

- In Matthew 28:18-19, Jesus asserted He has all authority: "All authority in heaven and on earth has been given to me. Go therefore and make disciples of all nations."

5. Jesus accepted worship.

The Old Testament forbade people to worship anyone but God (Exodus 20:1-5; Deuteronomy 5:6-9). On multiple occasions, however, people worshiped Jesus and He never rebuked them, implying He saw their actions as appropriate:

- A leper (Matthew 8:2), a ruler (Matthew 9:18), a Canaanite woman (Matthew 15:25), and the mother of the disciples James and John (Matthew 20:20) all knelt before Jesus with their requests (a posture of worship).

- In Matthew 14:33, after Jesus calmed the storm, we read that "those in the boat worshiped him, saying, 'Truly you are the Son of God.'"

- A blind man said, "Lord, I believe," then "worshiped" Jesus (John 9:38).

- When some of the women were on their way to tell the disciples about the resurrection, Jesus appeared to them. Matthew 28:9 says, "They came up and took hold of his feet and worshiped him."

6. Jesus accepted prayer in His name.

Jesus asked people to pray in His name, claiming that He would answer prayers and be a unique conduit to God:

- "Whatever you ask in my name, this I will do, that the Father may be glorified in the Son. If you ask me anything in my name, I will do it" (John 14:13-14).

- "If you abide in me, and my words abide in you, ask whatever you wish, and it will be done for you" (John 15:7).

- "I am the way, and the truth, and the life. No one comes to the Father except through me" (John 14:6).

Jesus Did Far More Than Say "I Am God"

No, Jesus never said the exact words "I am God." But He claimed to be God in other substantial ways: He claimed to be Yahweh, He claimed to have the same unique rights as God, He claimed to be the (divine) Messiah, He claimed His words had as much authority as God's words, He accepted worship, and He accepted prayer in His name. People have identified several additional claims to deity within the Gospels as well.[7]

Now that we've established Jesus *claimed* to be God, we need to ask this: Did His *followers* believe that about Him? That's the subject of the next chapter.

19. Did Jesus' followers really believe He was God?

One night during Bible time with our kids, I posed the following question: "Why do you think the disciples believed Jesus was God?"

My daughter offered, "Because He told them so!"

To my kids' amusement, I got up and confidently walked around the living room claiming, "I'm God! I'm the Creator of the universe. Believe everything I say!"

When they started laughing, I looked at them crestfallen. "Why don't you believe I'm God?"

My son replied, "Because God would never yell at us!"

Not exactly the answer I was shooting for.

The point was not completely lost, however. I explained that Jesus did live a perfectly moral life (unlike me, as my son was overly quick to point out), but that even more importantly, He performed miracles to provide his followers with *evidence* of His claims to divinity (see the previous chapter).

That said, imagine for a moment that you witnessed Jesus' miracles. Even then you wouldn't necessarily assume that Jesus was God. Perhaps you'd think there was some natural explanation. Or maybe you'd think Jesus only had God's *power* to perform miracles (like Moses, for example). Or perhaps you just wouldn't know *what* to make of it! Even if we assume the reality of biblical miracles, it doesn't necessarily mean the disciples believed Jesus was God.

Knowing what Jesus' followers believed, of course, is quite important: If *they* didn't believe Jesus was God, there's little reason for *us* to. And skeptics claim there's plenty of room to doubt they actually did—they make the case that it wasn't until long after Jesus' death that people elevated Him to the status of God.[1]

To answer this chapter's question, we need to look at what the Bible tells us about the disciples' beliefs in two distinct time periods: (1) during Jesus' life, and (2) after Jesus' resurrection.

During Jesus' Life

The disciples witnessed amazing events during the three years of Jesus' ministry. In that time, Jesus healed people of all kinds of sicknesses, demonstrated His power over nature, raised people from the dead, and resisted every temptation.

When we read about these things, we have the privileged position of seeing the full picture of Jesus' life, death, and resurrection. The disciples did not—they experienced it all in real time. They had to learn about Jesus little by little, working to make sense of all that He said and did. For that reason, we shouldn't be too surprised to see that during Jesus' life, the disciples weren't always certain of His identity and mission.

Let's look at some examples.

In Matthew 8:23-27, Jesus and the disciples were on a boat when a great storm arose. The disciples were terrified and begged Jesus to save them from dying. Jesus "rebuked the winds and the sea, and there was a great calm." The disciples marveled, saying, "What sort of man is this, that even winds and sea obey him?" They were amazed by the miracle, but we aren't told if, at that point, they believed Jesus was God.

In Mark 8:29, Jesus directly asked the disciples who they thought He was. Peter answered, "You are the Christ." Recall from chapter 18 that *Christ* is the word for the Messiah foreshadowed in the Old Testament. As we saw, Jesus claimed that identity for Himself, and there were several clues in the Old Testament that the Messiah would be God. That said, the Jews in Jesus' time imagined the Messiah as an *earthly* political deliverer who might free them from their subjugation to Rome. Given that context, we can better understand why Peter rebuked Jesus for telling the disciples He would be rejected and killed (Mark 8:32)—that wasn't what Peter had in mind for the Christ at all! So even in Peter's confession of Jesus' identity we can see he didn't unequivocally understand Him to be God.

In John 14:8, the disciple Philip said to Jesus, "Lord, show us the Father, and it is enough for us." It appears as if, at that point, Philip didn't believe that Jesus was God. Jesus replied, "Have I been with you so long, and you still do not know me, Philip? Whoever has seen me has seen the Father. How can you say, 'Show us the Father'?" (John 14:9).

In John 2, Jesus cleared out the temple with a whip of cords because of the disgraceful commercial activity taking place there. In verse 18, the Jews asked Jesus, "What sign do you show us for doing these things?" Jesus answered them, "Destroy this temple, and in three days I will raise it up" (verse 19—He was referring to His body as the temple and to His resurrection as "raising it up"). The Jews didn't understand what He was saying, and verse 22 suggests the disciples didn't either at the time: "When therefore he was raised from the dead, his disciples remembered that he had said this, and they believed the Scripture and the word that Jesus had spoken." John made similar statements about the disciples not understanding Jesus' words during His life—but remembering and believing after the resurrection—in John 12:16 and John 20:9.

As you can see, the disciples' words and actions while Jesus was alive suggest that they didn't necessarily understand Him to be God.

But the resurrection changed everything.

After Jesus' Resurrection

When the disciples encountered the risen Jesus, their view of His identity changed drastically. For several reasons, we can see they finally understood Jesus' claims to deity.

First, we can see that they believed Jesus was God because they identified Him as the Creator of the universe. God is explicitly revealed as the Creator of the universe in Genesis, so to ascribe that role to Jesus is to equate Him with God.

In John 1:1-3, the disciple John wrote, "In the beginning was the Word, and the Word was with God, and the Word was God. He was in the beginning with God. All things were made through him, and without him was not any thing made that was made." In these verses, John established that the "Word" existed before creation, the "Word" is the Creator, and the "Word" is God. So what exactly is the "Word"? A few verses later, that clarification is made: "The Word became flesh and dwelt among us, and we have seen his glory, glory as of the only Son from the Father, full of grace and truth" (John 1:14). Clearly, John was referring to Jesus.

The apostle Paul, to whom Jesus also revealed Himself after the resurrection, referenced Jesus as the Creator as well:

> By him all things were created, in heaven and on earth, visible and invisible, whether thrones or dominions or rulers or authorities—all things were created through him and for him. And he is before all things, and in him all things hold together (Colossians 1:15-17).

Second, the disciple Thomas verbally proclaimed that Jesus was God. Thomas, who had doubted the resurrection even after hearing eyewitness testimony, saw the risen Jesus and immediately proclaimed, "My Lord and my God!" (John 20:28).

Third, the disciples and Paul saw Jesus as the forgiver of sins. Acts 5:31 says, "God exalted him at his right hand as Leader and Savior, to give repentance to Israel and forgiveness of sins." Similarly, Colossians 3:13 says, "As the Lord has forgiven you, so you also must forgive." Since only God was believed to have the right to forgive sins, this equated Jesus with God.

Fourth, Paul wrote that Jesus would judge sin. In 2 Timothy 4:1, he said, "I charge you in the presence of God and of Christ Jesus, who is to judge the living and the dead." Again, this was a right only God was believed to have (see chapter 18 for more on this).

Fifth, the disciples were willing to die to proclaim the truth of the gospel—that Jesus died for the forgiveness of sins, was buried, and was resurrected. As we'll see in chapter 23, the fact that they were willing to *die* to proclaim this provides significant historical evidence for the truth of the resurrection; no one dies for what they *know* to be a lie. And if the disciples truly believed they had seen the risen Jesus, it implies they then understood and believed all of His prior claims to deity (see chapter 18).

The Resurrection Made Jesus' Deity Clear

The New Testament provides several clues that the disciples were unsure what to make of Jesus' identity and mission during His life—even given His amazing miracles. However, we see a drastic and immediate change in their understanding after Jesus' death and resurrection. All of His claims to deity could at that point be seen in full perspective. Jesus was then described as Creator, Forgiver, and Judge—God.

20. Why did Jesus need to die on the cross for our sins?

Something my husband and I like to do each week is have a "questions night" for our kids. We simply ask them what questions they have about God or the Bible and do our best to answer them. For example, this week my six-year-olds asked: "Why did God create the Garden of Eden if He knew Adam and Eve would disobey?" "Why did God tell Noah his whole family could go on the ark when he was the only one found to be righteous?" "Why isn't heaven a physical place like a house?" "Why did Jesus pray to God if He *was* God?" "Why was Jesus baptized if He was without sin?"

In the last year that we've done this, we've never had a shortage of good questions like these. Recently, however, I realized that conspicuously missing from the topics they've raised is any question to the effect of "Why did Jesus need to die for our sins?" It's not that they aren't aware of the concept. They hear it regularly at both church and home. In fact, my son recently pointed to a cross off the freeway and said, "There's a cross, like where Jesus died for our sins!" So why wouldn't they ask questions about such a frequently discussed topic that's admittedly difficult to understand?

To answer that, I can look at my own childhood. I grew up in a Christian family and went to church every week, but I don't think I ever questioned what it meant for Jesus to "die for my sins." That phrase was repeated so much in my spiritual development that it became like a slogan—something you accept as a given and don't think more deeply about. At age 18, if you had asked me why Jesus needed to die for our sins, I would have said something like "because we need to be forgiven." If you had asked, "Why?" I wouldn't have had an answer. And if you had asked questions just deeper than the surface, like "Why couldn't God just forgive us when we do bad things?" or "Why did Jesus have to die a bloody, gruesome death—couldn't He have forgiven us some other way?" or "Why did God want a human sacrifice?"...I would have been utterly speechless. Yet Jesus' death is central to the entire Christian faith!

It's easy to get so comfortable in our own beliefs that we take for granted what our kids understand about fundamental concepts. Perhaps nowhere does this happen more often than on the question of why Jesus died for our sins (clearly I've been guilty of this myself). But when our kids don't have a clear understanding of the nature of Jesus' sacrifice, skeptics can easily get a foot in the door of their hearts by characterizing the Christian God as a horrible, bloodthirsty being who demands human sacrifice. As one example, consider this YouTube video in which a skeptic posed a "One Question Challenge" to Christians: "Why does blood sacrifice make anything better?" He says,

> We would agree that a tribe that took a virgin and tossed her into a volcano to appease the wrath of the volcano gods, that that's absolutely ridiculous. It's absurd. It's cruel. It's barbaric…And yet, you would celebrate taking a pure-hearted virgin, beating the crap out of him and then nailing him to a cross…Could you please explain to me exactly why it is that this particular blood sacrifice made anything better?[1]

This popular perspective on Jesus' death betrays a fundamental misunderstanding of the Christian worldview. In this chapter, we'll look at three core points our kids need to know in order to answer such questions: (1) Sin is real and is a major problem; (2) God is just; and (3) God has chosen to *justly* forgive.

Sin Is Real and Is a Major Problem

By definition, sin is "an immoral act considered to be a transgression against divine law."[2] Divine law, of course, must come from a divine law*giver*—God.

If God doesn't exist, the concept of sin is meaningless.

This ultimately is the gulf that sits between the atheist and Christian views of Jesus' death on the cross, so we need to dig deeper here. From the Christian perspective, a perfectly good God exists, and His goodness is the *objective standard* for our morality (see Deuteronomy 32:3-4; Psalm 5:45; 1 John 1:5). An objective standard is a standard that supersedes our personal opinion; it's what gives meaning to the words *right* and *wrong*. If there's no divine lawgiver, right and wrong are simply a matter of personal opinion, and no opinion can be objectively better than another. In an atheistic worldview, it follows that sin is a meaningless concept because there's no way for a person to actually do something *wrong*. As we'll see, if sin isn't a real concept, it's not possible to make sense of Jesus' death.

Now we need to go one step further. Not only does sin *exist* in the Christian worldview, it's a major *problem* that needs a solution. Because we rebel against God when we sin, our sin separates us from the Creator and Sustainer of life. That's why the Bible says that the wages of sin is death (Romans 6:23). This doesn't mean that we physically die as soon as we sin, of course. It means that we are *spiritually* dead because sin separates us from the Source of "the truth, and the life" (John 14:6). If you believe that a wonderful, all-loving, all-knowing, and all-powerful God exists, there's no question that spiritual separation from Him is a major problem that desperately begs for a solution. Ultimately, Jesus' death on the cross was that solution, but before we can understand why, we must first establish a fundamentally important aspect of God's character: God is *just*.

God Is Just

In *The God Delusion*, atheist Richard Dawkins asks, "If God wanted to forgive our sins, why not just forgive them, without having himself tortured and executed in payment?"[3] It's a good question. But the answer quickly becomes clear when you understand what it means for God to be just.

Imagine for a moment that a judge in your city regularly let murderers and rapists go free without penalty because he wanted to be as "loving" as possible. Do you think the citizens of your community would consider that loving? Of course not. There would be a public outcry from Christians, atheists, and everyone else at the *injustice*. Love without justice is not love at all.

The Bible makes it clear that God is a God of both love *and* justice. Because we discussed what the Bible says about God's justness in chapter 4, I'm not going to repeat that here. For our current purposes, suffice it to say that God's justness and love go hand-in-hand: Overlooking sin would actually make a perfectly holy God *unjust*, like letting murderers and rapists go unpunished would make our imaginary judge *unjust*.

God, as our ultimate judge, also sets the penalty for our sin: death (Romans 6:23). We may not agree with or completely understand that verdict, but that doesn't make it any less true. God made the law, we broke the law, and God says the penalty is death.

So where does that leave us? We're sinners who must pay the price for our sin because God is just. That's why God can't simply let us off the hook, as Dawkins proposed. But what about the rest of his point—why is the payment Jesus' own death on the cross?

God Has Chosen to *Justly* Forgive

There's an important difference between our imaginary judge and God. In the case of God, He's both the judge *and* the offended party. That means He's in the unique position to both set the penalty *and* absolve humans of their guilt as He sees fit within His just character. How did He "see fit"? God Himself paid the debt we owed by sending Jesus to die in our place. In this way, He *justly* forgave us. He didn't simply ignore the debt incurred by our sin against His laws. Payment was made as required by His justness. As an act of love, however, He made that payment *Himself*.

For Christians, this was an amazing act of love by a God who wanted to reconcile mankind to Himself, enabling our rescue from spiritual death. But many skeptics characterize Jesus' death as a form of divine child abuse. That notion greatly misunderstands the nature of the Trinity. Christians believe that God is three persons in one, including the Father, the Son, and the Holy Spirit. That means God didn't sacrifice some poor third-party human as the method of payment for our sins. Because He and Jesus are one, God paid the penalty *Himself*.

The Bible makes it clear in several places that the Father and Son were working together to accomplish salvation on the cross. Jesus was not an unwilling victim. He clearly understood His mission on Earth, and part of that mission involved giving His life as a sacrifice:

- Mark 8:31 says, "[Jesus] began to teach them that the Son of Man must suffer many things and be rejected by the elders and the chief priests and the scribes and be killed, and after three days rise again" ("Son of Man" is how Jesus often referred to Himself; see chapter 18).

- Mark 10:45 says, "Even the Son of Man came not to be served but to serve, and to give his life as a ransom for many."

- In John 10:18, Jesus says about His life, "No one takes it from me, but I lay it down of my own accord. I have authority to lay it down, and I have authority to take it up again. This charge I have received from my Father."

- When approaching the time of His death, Jesus said, "Now is my soul troubled. And what shall I say? 'Father, save me from this hour'? But for this purpose I have come to this hour" (John 12:27).

All of us have sinned and fall short of God's standards (Romans 3:23); we're all in the same boat. The difference between Christians and nonbelievers is that Christians acknowledge their guilty position and accept God's gift of forgiveness, paid for by Jesus on the cross. The Bible says that those who do so are reconciled to God and will stand blameless before Him (John 3:16; Romans 5:10; 1 Corinthians 1:30; 2 Corinthians 5:21). That *imputed righteousness*—righteousness we have been credited with despite not achieving it on our own—is what allows us to spend eternity with God.

Why Blood Sacrifice "Makes Things Better"

Now we can come back to the YouTube video question of why "blood sacrifice makes anything better." In the Christian worldview, sin is real and it's a serious problem that needs a solution. This is the critically important backdrop against which Jesus' death on the cross—the ultimate solution—makes sense. Without a real problem of sin to solve (as in the atheist's worldview), all you have is ancient people believing in the need for a human sacrifice to ambiguously appease an angry

God. But when we acknowledge the reality of sin, our resulting separation from the Source of life, God's stated penalty for sin, and God's just character, we can begin to understand our deep need for reconciliation. Jesus' death was the ultimate solution for mankind's ultimate problem. *That's* how blood sacrifice "makes things better."

21. What are the historical facts of the resurrection that nearly every scholar agrees on?

When my husband and I were first married, we both worked long hours. By the time the weekend rolled around, we just didn't have much desire to go to church. Neither of us was a passionate believer at the time, so the thought of joyfully launching ourselves out of bed on a Sunday morning when it was "unnecessary" seemed outlandish. Because we were both raised in Christian homes, however, we felt a sense of duty to get to church at least once in a while.

As part of this "duty," we haphazardly selected a nearby mainline denominational church to attend. We went there for about three years. My general spiritual apathy continued until an Easter sermon caught my attention in the third year. While preaching about the resurrection, the pastor stated, "Whether or not Jesus physically came back to life isn't important. What *matters* is that He lives on in our hearts and we can make the world a better place."

What?!

I wasn't about to bother dragging myself to church, occasionally praying, and calling myself a Christian in any sense if there wasn't reason to believe Jesus came back to life as the Bible said. Warm, fuzzy feelings as I commemorate Jesus' life by making the world a better place wasn't going to cut it.

It took a couple more years and a new church before I made a full commitment to Jesus, but that day was the turning point when I realized the importance of believing in the resurrection. Perhaps because of that experience, my favorite verse in the Bible is the apostle Paul's pointed words to the Corinthians: "If Christ has not been raised, then our preaching is in vain and your faith is in vain" (1 Corinthians 15:14).

If the resurrection isn't true, Christianity is meaningless.

If Jesus didn't rise from the dead as He predicted, He was a false prophet and there's no reason to follow any of His teachings—regardless of who He *or* His followers thought He was (see chapters 18 and 19). But if He *did* rise from the dead, that event would have confirmed His radical claims to divinity and *everything* He said is of utmost importance.

So why should we believe the resurrection is true? While the truth of the resurrection is undoubtedly a matter of personal conviction, there's actually significant *historical evidence* to support its veracity. To be sure, most people don't come to Jesus because they first learned about this evidence. But learning about it can give your kids a much deeper level of confidence that the convictions they already have are true. The kind of confidence that isn't shaken when their atheist friend asks, "You seriously believe a dead person came back to life?" The kind of confidence that allows them to reply, "Absolutely. There's good reason to believe God raised Jesus from the dead when you look at the historical data. Let me explain why."

This and the next two chapters will focus on the historical evidence for the resurrection. In this chapter, we'll look at the basic historical facts surrounding the resurrection that even nonbelieving scholars agree on.

The Minimal Facts Approach to the Resurrection

When historians want to investigate something that happened 2000 years ago, obviously they're going to have limited information to work with. But that doesn't mean they throw their hands in the air and conclude they can't know *anything*. It's their job to uncover whatever historical facts are available, form hypotheses that might explain those facts, and make conclusions about what happened based on the strongest hypothesis. We can follow this same process when looking at the historical events surrounding the resurrection.

In the book *The Case for the Resurrection of Jesus*, Drs. Gary Habermas and Michael Licona detail what they call the "Minimal Facts" approach to the resurrection. Their basic objective is to strip away any religious assumptions about what happened and consider "only those data that are so strongly attested historically that they are granted by nearly every scholar who studies the subject, even the rather skeptical ones." Habermas and Licona explain why this "Minimal Facts" approach is so important:

> One of the strengths of this approach is that it avoids debate over the inspiration of the Bible. Too often the objection raised frequently against the Resurrection is, "Well, the Bible has errors, so we can't believe Jesus rose." We can quickly push this point to the side: "I am not arguing at this time for the inspiration of the Bible or even its general trustworthiness. Believer and skeptic alike accept the facts I'm using because they are so strongly supported. These facts must be addressed."[1]

In a culture where the reliability of the Bible is frequently questioned, you can see why this approach can be so powerful in discussions with nonbelievers. The following four historical facts are the ones that Habermas and Licona say are generally accepted, even by skeptics (we'll consider possible explanations for them in the next chapter).

Fact 1: Jesus died by crucifixion.

We know from many historical sources that crucifixion was a common form of execution used by the Romans. It isn't suspicious at all that the Gospels say Jesus died on a cross. His crucifixion is also referenced by several non-Christian historical sources, including Josephus, Tacitus, Lucian of Samosata, and the Jewish Talmud.[2]

It might not seem like this fact about Jesus' death gets you very far toward evidence for a *resurrection*, but in the next chapter you'll see that some people believe Jesus only *appeared* to die. They believe He lost consciousness and later revived, enabling Him to fake a resurrection.

However, we'll see in that chapter that the fact He was *crucified* means His survival was virtually impossible, so this fact is actually an important starting point.

Fact 2: Jesus' disciples believed that He rose and appeared to them.

This is arguably the most important fact of all. Habermas explains:

> There is a virtual consensus among scholars who study Jesus'
> resurrection that, subsequent to Jesus' death by crucifix-
> ion, his disciples really believed that he appeared to them
> risen from the dead. This conclusion has been reached by
> data that suggest that (1) the disciples themselves claimed
> that the risen Jesus had appeared to them, and (2) subse-
> quent to Jesus' death by crucifixion his disciples were rad-
> ically transformed from fearful, cowering individuals who
> denied and abandoned him at his arrest and execution into
> bold proclaimers of the gospel of the risen Lord.[3]

A skeptic may claim that there are natural (as opposed to supernatural) explanations for what happened to the disciples, but very few deny
that the disciples actually experienced *something*. That *something* must
have been significant in order to have triggered their transformation
into "bold proclaimers of the gospel"—a role that required the disciples to willingly face severe persecution and death. This is a powerful
fact, and we'll look at the implications in more detail when we consider
possible explanations in the next two chapters.

Fact 3: The church persecutor Paul was suddenly changed.

Paul wrote several books of the New Testament and was undeniably one of the most influential Christians who ever lived. But he wasn't
always a devoted follower of Jesus. Initially, he was a passionate enemy
of the early church.

Paul (whose Hebrew name was Saul) is first mentioned in Acts 7:58,
where it's noted that he observed the stoning of the first Christian mar-
tyr, Stephen (Acts 8:1 explicitly states Paul approved of the execution).

Acts 8:3 goes on to say, "Saul was ravaging the church, and entering house after house, he dragged off men and women and committed them to prison." In his letters to the Corinthians, Galatians, and Philippians, Paul later described these persecutions himself (1 Corinthians 15:9; Galatians 1:13; Philippians 3:6).

But something changed everything for Paul. Acts 9:3 tells us that he was on a journey to Damascus when "suddenly a light from heaven shone around him." Acts 9:4-6 says:

> Falling to the ground he heard a voice saying to him, "Saul, Saul, why are you persecuting me?" And he said, "Who are you, Lord?" And he said, "I am Jesus, whom you are persecuting. But rise and enter the city, and you will be told what you are to do."

After this experience, Paul converted to the Christian faith and tirelessly preached that Jesus died for the sins of the world, was buried, and was resurrected. Paul was willing to endure great suffering to spread this message and was eventually martyred for his claims.

Paul's conversion is a particularly compelling historical fact because he was an enemy of the church at the time he claimed to have seen the risen Jesus. It takes something significant for a zealous enemy to switch sides. You might think, *What's the big deal? Lots of people convert to other beliefs.* But there's an important difference here. People usually convert to other religions because they believe a message they heard from a secondary source—*not* because they claim to have heard a message from the source of the religion Himself.

Fact 4: The skeptic James, brother of Jesus, was suddenly changed.

Although we don't have as much information on Jesus' brother James as we do on Paul, we know enough to conclude that James converted to Christianity because he believed the resurrected Jesus appeared to him. We can conclude this based on the following points:

- Jesus' brothers (including James) were not believers during Jesus' ministry (Mark 3:21,31; 6:3-4; John 7:5).

- First Corinthians 15:7 says Jesus appeared to James.
- After Jesus' alleged resurrection, James is described as a leader of the church (Acts 15:12-21; Galatians 1:19).
- James was martyred for his beliefs, as recorded by both Christian and non-Christian historical writings (Hegesippus, Clement of Alexandria, and Josephus).[4]

As with Paul, the question is, *What happened to cause such a drastic change in belief?*

So What Should You Conclude from the Facts?

To recap, here are our minimal facts: Jesus died by crucifixion, the disciples believed He rose and appeared to them, and the church persecutor Paul and Jesus' skeptic brother James were suddenly changed after the alleged event. That might not sound like a lot of historical data to work with, but, as you'll see in the next chapter, it's not very easy to find natural explanations that fit those few facts. We'll now look at seven major theories that attempt to do so.

22. What are the major theories people use to explain those facts?

When I first started studying the resurrection, I was surprised that there were multiple theories about what happened. I assumed that people who didn't believe in the resurrection just...didn't believe it. But once you establish that there are several historical facts involved (see chapter 21), you realize those facts require an *explanation*. In other words, we can ask someone: Given that almost everyone agrees that Jesus died by crucifixion, that the disciples truly believed a resurrected Jesus appeared to them, and that the church persecutor Paul and Jesus' skeptic brother James were suddenly changed after Jesus died, what do *you* think happened?

In this chapter, we'll look at the most frequently cited theories used to challenge a supernatural resurrection and ask of each, *Does this theory account for the basic historical facts?*

Theory 1: "Jesus only appeared to die."

Some skeptics say that even if Jesus was crucified, He may not actually have *died*. He may have lost consciousness and only *appeared* to die. After His body was placed in the tomb, He could have revived and showed Himself to people, faking a resurrection.

I know that sounds crazy to us as Christians. But to nonbelievers, this is no crazier than claiming a dead person came back to life. So let's take it for what it is and look at two reasons this theory is no more plausible than the supernatural explanation it attempts to defeat.

First, assume for a moment that Jesus really did survive the cross and emerge from the tomb after a failed crucifixion. Would the disciples have concluded that He had been *resurrected*? With horrible wounds, they would have concluded he was a *dying* man who needed help—not a Savior and conqueror of death. It's extremely unlikely that such a sight would have led the early Christians to believe all that they did about Jesus.

Second, given what we know today medically and historically about the crucifixion process, it's virtually impossible that Jesus survived. John 19:34 tells us that after Jesus died, a soldier pierced His side with a spear and "at once there came out blood and water." We now know that this description is consistent with a piercing of the heart—a certain death. In 1986, an article in the *Journal of the American Medical Association* stated, "Interpretations based on the assumption that Jesus did not die on the cross appear to be at odds with modern medical knowledge."[1]

This theory fails to explain the basic fact of what the early Christians believed, *and* it's medically implausible.

Theory 2: "The disciples lied or stole Jesus' body."

Some people propose that the resurrection was nothing more than a deception by Jesus' followers—that they either lied or stole Jesus' body for any number of self-serving reasons.

This is extremely unlikely in light of the minimal facts we established in the previous chapter. Recall that it's generally accepted the disciples at least *believed* that Jesus rose from the dead and appeared to them. Their lives were radically transformed by what they claimed to have witnessed, to the point they were willing to endure severe persecution and die for it. Why would anyone be willing to risk their life for something they *knew* to be a lie?

At first you might think, *Well, many people are willing to die for their religion today, and those religions aren't all true.* This is quite different, however. The disciples would have *known* if they were risking their lives for something untrue. People who die for their religion today, like the 9/11 terrorists, are dying for what they *believe* to be true, not for what they personally witnessed and *know* to be true. It would be strange indeed if the disciples all lied, never admitted it, and were willing to suffer and die for what was only a tall tale.

There's another problem with this theory if you consider the conversions of the nonbelievers Paul and James. Paul and James almost certainly wouldn't have converted if the disciples were simply being deceptive. James was a skeptic during Jesus' life, so something significant must have happened to him after Jesus' death to explain his conversion. Paul said he believed because Jesus *appeared* to him (Acts 9). Neither of these conversions would likely be explained by a simple deception on the part of the disciples. This theory fails on multiple levels.

Theory 3: "Someone (other than the disciples) stole Jesus' body."

Given that the evidence points to the disciples truly believing that they had seen the risen Jesus, other people suggest that someone else may have stolen the body and tricked the disciples into believing Jesus rose from the dead.

In this theory, all we have is a possible explanation for an empty tomb. But no one claimed to believe in the resurrection of Jesus just because His body was missing. This does nothing to explain why the disciples, Paul, and James all believed they *saw* Jesus. This theory simply can't account for the basic facts.

Theory 4: "Witnesses went to the wrong tomb."

What if no one was being deceitful, but the women and disciples simply went to the wrong tomb, saw it was empty, and reasoned that Jesus had risen from the dead?

This theory suffers from the same problem as the last one: It does nothing to explain why the disciples, Paul, and James all believed they *saw* Jesus. That said, even if an empty tomb somehow spurred a belief in Jesus' resurrection, the Roman and Jewish authorities would have immediately wanted to destroy that belief by going to the *right* tomb and digging out the body. Once again, this theory fails.

Theory 5: "The people who saw Jesus were hallucinating."

It's common for grieving people to have hallucinations following the death of a loved one (a *hallucination* is a false perception of something that isn't there).[2] If the disciples deeply loved Jesus and were grieving after His death, isn't it possible they were just hallucinating, as people are known to do in such circumstances?

This theory doesn't work for two major reasons. First, hallucinations are in the mind of *one* person; they're not group experiences. While all of Jesus' followers may have experienced the same *grief*, they would not all have experienced the same *hallucination* of Jesus being raised from the dead. Not only is it highly improbable that multiple individuals had the same hallucination, it's highly improbable that *groups* of individuals had a *simultaneous* hallucination. In 1 Corinthians 15:5, Paul said that Jesus appeared to "the twelve," in verse 6 he said that Jesus appeared to "more than five hundred brothers at one time," and in verse 7 he said that Jesus appeared to "all the apostles." Paul even noted in verse 6 that many of the five hundred were still alive, suggesting they were available to confirm his account. To propose that all these individuals and groups had the same hallucination defies what we know about psychology.[3]

Second, hallucinations aren't likely to account for the conversion of Paul. Paul was *not* a follower of Jesus during His lifetime and wouldn't have been grieving when He died. There is no reason, therefore, to think Paul would have experienced a grief-based hallucination. This theory fails to reasonably explain the basic historical facts.

Theory 6: "People invented Christianity based on pagan myths."

Of all the theories here, this is the one your kids are most likely to encounter in popular culture. Countless images have floated through social media with comparison charts between Jesus and pagan deities, suggesting that the resurrection was just something ancient people invented based on other myths of the time. For example, one popular image says that the god Mithra was born of a virgin on December 25, had 12 disciples, performed miracles, was buried in a tomb, rose after 3 days, had followers who celebrated his resurrection annually, and was considered the "way, the truth, and the light."[4] The bottom of the image asks, "Why can't Christians at least be original?" Other deities with various alleged parallels include Horus, Krishna, Attis, Dionysus, Adonis, Osiris, and Perseus.

There are two key questions we need to consider with this theory: (1) Are there *truly* close parallels between Christianity and the pagan myths of Jesus' time? (You have to admit that if the Mithra story really included all of the above elements, it would give anyone pause to consider its relationship to Christianity.) And (2) if there are parallels, does it really matter?

Let's start with the first question. Contrary to popular Internet claims, the vast majority of alleged parallels aren't even true. For example, there is no reference in historical writings to most of the quoted facts about Mithra, like that he came back to life after three days (see the endnotes of this chapter for an article with a detailed evaluation of each supposed fact).[5] These are just unfounded claims that have been copied repeatedly online. In other cases, the "parallel" is hardly parallel when you look at the details of the myth. For example, the Egyptian god Osiris was murdered and his body parts were scattered. His wife put him back together, enabling him to journey to the underworld and become the lord of the dead. He never returned to the world of the living. Can this really be considered parallel to the accounts of Jesus' resurrection?

In yet other cases, the alleged parallel is so broad that it would be true in any religion. For example, many gods supposedly performed miracles. That's not exactly a suspicious parallel, given that any god should be able, by definition, to act supernaturally. Perhaps most incredibly, some alleged parallels were written many years *after* Christianity arose![6] For information on individual myths (and why they fail to be close parallels), please see the website in the endnotes to this chapter.[7]

All that said, let's still consider the second question and pretend for a moment that we could find legitimate, close parallels between ancient myths and Christianity. Would it matter? No. The claims of resurrections in other religions can't explain the evidence that exists for *Jesus'* resurrection. The minimal historical facts remain. Any supposed "resurrection" must be judged on its own merits. This theory is popular, but completely falls apart under scrutiny.

Theory 7: "As Jesus' teachings spread, they were embellished with supernatural details."

This theory assumes Jesus was a historical person, but states that all the supernatural details of His life and resurrection crept into the accounts years later as legend.

To understand the context for this theory, it's important to know that the New Testament authors didn't record their writings immediately after Jesus died. There's at least a 20-year period separating Jesus' death and the earliest Christian writings. What if those writings reflect rumors that snowballed during that 20-year period? If that *were* the case, how could we ever know?

You might be surprised to learn that we actually *can* know some truly important things about that period based on evidence from

Paul's writings—in particular, 1 Corinthians. Within 1 Corinthians is a creed that most scholars agree dates to just four to six years after Jesus' death (a *creed* is a formal statement of Christian belief). In other words, although the passage doesn't say as much, scholars can tell the words aren't Paul's and that he's referencing a formal statement of faith that already existed.[8] The verses of note are 1 Corinthians 15:3-7:

> I delivered to you as of first importance what I also received: that Christ died for our sins in accordance with the Scriptures, that he was buried, that he was raised on the third day in accordance with the Scriptures, and that he appeared to Cephas, then to the twelve. Then he appeared to more than five hundred brothers at one time, most of whom are still alive, though some have fallen asleep. Then he appeared to James, then to all the apostles.

At the beginning of this passage, Paul said he "received" this information. The most likely time for him to have received it would have been in the early AD 30s when, according to Galatians 1:18, he "went up to Jerusalem to visit Cephas [Peter] and remained with him fifteen days." *That means this creed was already formulated and being transmitted within four to six years of Jesus' death.*[9] This shows that Jesus' resurrection was far from a legend that arose decades or more after His death. Christians were asserting He came back to life since right after He died.[10]

Where's the Explanation That Fits All the Facts?

When we consider all of these theories in light of the minimal facts from chapter 21, we can see that they fail to make sense of the basic historical data on one or more levels. There are several other theories not discussed here, but all have similar weaknesses.[11] Christians, of course, have another explanation: that Jesus really did rise from the dead. In the next chapter, we'll look at how a supernatural resurrection best explains the historical facts.

Keeping Your Kids on God's Side

23. Why do Christians believe a supernatural resurrection best explains the facts?

Pretend for a moment that you just sent three kids out to play in the backyard. Knowing they'll clearly occupy themselves for a reasonable amount of time without getting hurt, becoming bored, destroying the yard, or fighting with each other, you realize you can relax on the couch with a good book for the next hour. (What? That's not a realistic scenario in your home? Don't worry, it's not in mine either.)

Much to your shock, your relaxation is interrupted a few minutes later by all three kids screaming. They run into the house shaking and scared. One explains, "We just saw three pigs fly by!" You smile in relief that it wasn't a *real* problem and calmly explain that pigs can't fly, so they must have seen something else. But the kids are emphatic and all agree. They go on to give you all kinds of reasons for believing their claim.

Let me ask you something: Is there any amount of evidence that would convince you they actually saw three flying pigs, short of witnessing it yourself? Probably not. Why? Because you know, based on how our world works, that *pigs can never fly*. No matter what evidence there is, you're simply never going to believe the kids actually saw flying pigs.

That is very much the problem most nonbelievers have with the resurrection. We can lay out "minimal historical facts" that nearly everyone agrees on (see chapter 21) and establish that competing theories about what happened fail to explain those facts (see chapter 22), but many people will never seriously consider the idea that Jesus came back to life because *we know dead people don't come back to life*. It's as simple as that for them—just as it's as simple as that for you to know pigs don't fly and conclude that any claims to the contrary are undoubtedly wrong.

Therein lies the sticking point. We *do* all know that dead people don't come back to life...*naturally*. Christians and nonbelievers agree on that! But if God exists, He could *supernaturally* cause events to happen that we know could never happen *naturally*. If God does *not* exist, such events are impossible.

In this chapter, we'll look at how the "theory" of a supernatural resurrection performs as an explanation of the historical facts. But it's important to read this with the understanding that most nonbelievers reject any supernatural theory from consideration in the first place. That has nothing to do with the generally accepted historical data or the ability of a supernatural resurrection to fit the historical facts. It has everything to do with whether or not a person accepts the possibility of *miracles*. Given the importance of this connection between a person's worldview and how he or she evaluates the evidence for the resurrection, we'll take a deeper look at the specific topic of miracles in the next chapter. For this chapter's purpose, we'll treat the hypothesis of a supernatural resurrection just like we would any other historical hypothesis. After all, there's no point in arguing for the possibility of miracles if the resurrection doesn't even fit with what we know historically.

Evaluating the Resurrection as a Historical Hypothesis

When historians study the past, there's a lot of information they don't have access to. They must form conclusions about what happened based on the limited facts they have to work with. Oftentimes there are multiple possible explanations for the data. To choose between them, historians weigh hypotheses based on certain criteria (a *hypothesis* is just one proposed explanation for something). The hypothesis that best meets those criteria is usually the preferred explanation of what actually happened.

Michael Licona, in *The Resurrection of Jesus: A New Historiographical Approach*, outlines four key criteria used by historians to weigh hypotheses: explanatory scope, explanatory power, plausibility, and less ad hoc.[1] In the last chapter, we evaluated various competing theories of the resurrection somewhat informally by looking at how they did or didn't account for our four basic historical facts. Here, we'll do a more formal evaluation of the resurrection hypothesis using these criteria (space didn't permit me to evaluate the other theories at this level of detail).

Explanatory Scope

This criterion considers the number of facts accounted for by a hypothesis; the hypothesis that accounts for the most facts has the greatest *explanatory scope*.

As we saw in chapter 22, many of the theories on the resurrection fail to explain the basic historical facts. Recall, for example, that the theory of the disciples lying failed to explain why they would be willing to die for their beliefs, and why the apostle Paul would have believed Jesus appeared to him. From the historian's perspective, the more facts a theory accounts for, the stronger the theory is. A supernatural resurrection easily accounts for *all* of the facts:

- *Jesus died by crucifixion:* You can't have a resurrection (in the sense described by the disciples and Paul) without Jesus having died.

- *Jesus' disciples believed He rose and appeared to them:* If Jesus was truly resurrected, it would explain why the disciples claimed He appeared to them.

- *Paul and James (former nonbelievers) were suddenly changed:* A true resurrection would also easily explain why these nonbelievers suddenly became believers.

Unlike the theories we considered in the last chapter, a supernatural resurrection can easily account for all the basic historical facts.

Explanatory Power

This criterion considers how *well* each hypothesis explains the facts. This is important because there might be multiple hypotheses that *can* explain a set of facts (satisfying the *explanatory scope*), but that doesn't mean each explanation is equal in *quality*. For example, if Jesus didn't actually die after being crucified, and was somehow able to show Himself to the disciples, it would explain the fact that they believed He appeared to them. But it wouldn't explain that fact very *well*. As we saw in the last chapter, the disciples would have been more likely to conclude Jesus was a dying man who needed help—not a conqueror of death.

The hypothesis that Jesus was supernaturally resurrected has extremely strong explanatory power. If the disciples truly witnessed a supernatural resurrection, you would expect the event to completely transform their lives—and dramatic life transformation is exactly what we see. Disciples who were cowering in fear for their lives at Jesus' arrest (Matthew 26:56; Mark 14:50) were later willing to endure great suffering and persecution in order to spread the news of what they saw. If the Gospels simply claimed that Jesus came back to life from the dead, but the disciples never *did* anything with that information, the claim would be highly suspect. A lot of hypotheses might account for something like that. But in this case, they didn't just make a claim; they *demonstrated* they truly believed it by being willing to suffer and die for it.

At the same time, a true resurrection very effectively explains why Paul—someone who was seeking to *destroy* the Christian church (Galatians 1:13)—was suddenly transformed by what he claimed to have witnessed. Similarly, a true resurrection also explains why James, who didn't believe in Jesus' divinity during His life, suddenly changed his mind after Jesus' death.

A true resurrection not only explains all the facts, it explains them in a powerful way.

Plausibility

This criterion considers how well hypotheses account for a wide variety of accepted truths or background knowledge.

Plausibility is the most difficult criterion to evaluate for the resurrection hypothesis because there are no generally agreed-upon facts about God's existence. As we discussed at the beginning of the chapter, if God exists, the resurrection could happen; it's a *plausible* hypothesis. If God *doesn't* exist, it couldn't; it's an *implausible* hypothesis.

That said, it's important to note that even if we believe God exists, it doesn't mean we should accept every miracle claim as true. Some miracle claims are more *plausible* than others when you consider their religious context. In our flying pigs example, there is absolutely no religiously significant context involved. Even if we believe in God and the possibility of miracles, we have no reason to believe He would make that particular event happen. Given the lack of *context*, a flying pigs miracle is quite implausible.

But consider the context of the resurrection. Jesus performed miracles during His life as signs to demonstrate that God's kingdom was breaking into human history; He claimed to be equal to God (see chapter 18); and He predicted that He would die and come back to life (Matthew 17:22-23; Mark 8:31; Luke 9:22). When you consider the historical data from chapter 21 in light of this context, a supernatural resurrection becomes a *very* plausible hypothesis. It's only implausible if you rule out God's existence before consideration.

Less Ad Hoc

Historians say an explanation is *ad hoc* when it incorporates assumptions that go beyond what the evidence suggests. Hypotheses are *less ad hoc* when they rely on fewer presuppositions.

The resurrection hypothesis requires only one additional assumption beyond the evidence from the four minimal historical facts: that God exists. Of course, if you already believe in God, that's not an additional assumption at all. However, this is once again where a person's worldview becomes a deciding factor in how one evaluates the historical data.

A Supernatural Resurrection Best Fits the Facts

Using established criteria for evaluating historical hypotheses, a supernatural resurrection undoubtedly best fits the facts. But because a supernatural event is impossible if God is assumed to not exist, many people reject the resurrection without consideration. It's important to understand that this rejection isn't based on historical evidence, but rather on a philosophical commitment to an atheistic worldview. Wolfhart Pannenberg, one of the world's best-known theologians, eloquently summarized this tension:

> The historical solidity of the Christian witness [to the resurrection] poses a considerable challenge to the conception of

reality that is taken for granted by modern secular history. There are good and even superior reasons to claiming that the resurrection of Jesus was a historical event, and consequently the risen Lord himself is a living reality. And yet there is the innumerably repeated experience that in the world the dead do not rise again. As long as this is the case, the Christian affirmation of Jesus' resurrection will remain a debated issue, in spite of all sound historical argument to its historicity.[2]

Given the importance of the subject of miracles, the next and final chapter in this section will look at this question in more detail.

24. How can Christians believe miracles are even possible?

I recently had the opportunity to watch apologist Sean McDowell speak to my church's high school youth group. McDowell did a presentation he calls the Atheist Encounter, in which he role-plays an atheist and raises tough questions for his Christian audience. It was a fantastic chance for teens to get exposed to atheist thinking, and McDowell held nothing back—calmly and confidently challenging them on everything from why they believed in the Bible to why they thought morality was anything more than a product of evolution.

The group seemed to thoroughly enjoy the opportunity to "stump the atheist." But, toward the end of the session, a 14-year-old girl in the back stood up with tears streaming down her face. She confidently cried out to McDowell, "I can prove there's a God! I was born six weeks early and my mom didn't know if I would live. She prayed that I would be okay, and here I am today. I believe in God because I'm the result of a miracle! What do you have to say to *that*?"

You could hear a pin drop as the room waited to see how McDowell would respond. By that point in the session, most of the older kids realized the "atheist" on stage wouldn't be convinced by such an argument at all. Clearly, there could be a perfectly natural explanation for the girl's survival. One of every nine infants in the United States is born premature, and most survive.[1] We typically don't consider every premature birth survivor a miracle. McDowell graciously ended his role-playing at that point and gently explained how atheists believe there are natural explanations for *any* proposed miracle—from personal experiences to Jesus' resurrection.

My heart went out to this young girl, who had obviously been taught that her survival was a miracle that proved God's existence. Perhaps her survival *was* a miracle. I have no idea. But basing your faith on whether or not you've experienced a modern-day miracle misses the boat completely. For Christians, it misses the boat because our faith should be grounded first and foremost in the truth of *one* particular miracle: the resurrection of Jesus (see chapters 21-23). For atheists, it misses the boat because a lack of *personally-experienced* miracles says nothing about the truth of a possible *resurrection* miracle.

The common question "How can Christians believe miracles are even possible?" therefore needs some clarification before we answer. When our kids are challenged in this area, it's important that they immediately understand there's just *one* miracle that determines the truth of Christianity. The specific question they need to be able to answer is "How can Christians believe the miracle of Jesus' resurrection is possible?" Giving them this clarity can help them quickly wade through the many tangential conversations that take place around this topic.

In this chapter, we'll look at three key questions that will help our kids navigate the issue: What is a miracle? Are miracles possible? And why believe in biblical miracles?

What Is a Miracle?

One dictionary definition of a miracle is "an extraordinary event manifesting divine intervention in human affairs."[2] A second definition is "an extremely outstanding or unusual event, thing, or accomplishment." People often use these definitions interchangeably, but they have very different meanings.

Biblical miracles follow the first definition. The Bible explicitly attributes its extraordinary events to God's intervention in human history. These events are not simply unusual occurrences with an ambiguous cause. When we defend the truth of biblical miracles, therefore, we're specifically defending why we believe God exists (see chapter 1) and why we believe there is evidence that He intervened in human history (see chapters 21-23).

Are Miracles Possible?

In the last chapter, we saw that the answer to this question is quite straightforward: If God exists, miracles are possible. If God doesn't exist, miracles are impossible. That's the very short answer to this chapter's broad question.

But let's go one step further to address a common related question. Even if we grant the possibility of God's existence, doesn't science preclude a miracle from actually *happening*? That's what many people claim. Oxford mathematician and Christian apologist John Lennox explained this perspective in a talk he gave to Harvard University students:

> Let's remind ourselves, then, of the contemporary scientific perspective. Since scientific laws embody cause and effect relationships, scientists nowadays do not regard them as merely capable of describing what has happened in the past...such laws can successfully predict what'll happen in the future with such accuracy that even Newton's laws will land somebody on the moon. It is very natural, therefore, that such scientists resent the idea that some God could "arbitrarily intervene and alter, suspend, reverse or otherwise violate these laws of nature"...To them, that would seem to contradict the immutability of the laws and thus overturn the very basis of the scientific understanding of the universe.[3]

Lennox went on to explain, however, why our knowledge of science doesn't logically preclude the idea that God could choose to intervene in the world.

As a scientist, I believe in the laws of nature. Indeed, God, who is responsible for them, created an orderly universe; otherwise, as I said before, we'd never recognize an exception. But God is not a prisoner of the laws of nature…God, who set the regularities there, can Himself feed a new event into the system from the outside. Science cannot stop Him doing that…Unless you have evidence that the system is totally closed, you cannot argue against the possibility of miracles."[4]

In short, the fact that humans are able to explain the world through science doesn't rule out the possibility of divine intervention. Natural laws by definition don't automatically add some kind of divine barrier—in fact, as Lennox points out, those laws suggest God's very existence! If God exists, He can intervene.

Now, the *possibility* of miracles doesn't mean we should believe every miracle claim. Saying, "I believe miracles are possible because I believe God exists and can choose to act in the natural world" is not the same as saying, "I believe that every surprising event in life is an act of divine intervention." Christians need to critically examine miracle claims like we would anything else. If we don't, we're as gullible and superstitious as skeptics often make us out to be.

We've established so far that miracles are possible if God exists, but that we need good reason to believe a miracle has actually occurred. So what constitutes good reason to believe in the all-important *biblical* miracles? Context is key. Let's look at that now.

Why Believe in Biblical Miracles?

A lot of skeptics have the idea that the Bible reads like a fairy tale—page after page of events that defy common experience. Given the lack of a continual stream of similar events today, they say the Bible lacks credibility. Why believe God used to endlessly play in the world during biblical times but not today? Don't we know these things don't happen?

If you read the Bible carefully, however, you'll notice that throughout thousands of years of history, there were actually just three relatively brief but prominent periods of miracles, separated by centuries of no recorded miracles. Most importantly, those periods served a very specific purpose leading up to and through Jesus' life.

- *The time of Moses and the Exodus:* God used many miracles to deliver the Israelites from Egypt and bring them to the Promised Land, such as the plagues, the parting of the Red Sea, the provision of manna in the wilderness, bitter water made sweet, and the collapse of Jericho's walls.

- *The time of the prophets Elijah and Elisha:* After Israel split into two kingdoms, the northern kingdom quickly strayed from God. As a warning, God raised up the prophet Elijah, who performed many miracles to demonstrate God's power and presence. Similar miracles accompanied Elijah's successor, Elisha.

- *The time of Jesus and the early church:* Miraculous activity greatly intensified when Jesus was on Earth. Jesus' miracles demonstrated control over nature, the ability to heal, and the ability to raise the dead.

Here's the key point: *Biblical miracles primarily occurred when God would have needed to authenticate His messengers and their message at key times in history.* There were plenty of teachers among God's people whose words were not authenticated by such signs. But the individuals above claimed to speak words directly from God, not simply teach what had already been revealed. Powerful signs would have been necessary to prove their unique status. When considered in this context, there's good reason for believing that if God exists, and He wanted to reveal Himself to mankind, He would have used miracles in exactly the way we see.

In Jesus' case, He was claiming that God's kingdom was breaking into human history, that He was the anticipated Messiah, and that He was equal to God Himself (see chapter 18). Why should anyone believe such audacious claims? Jesus needed to perform miracles to *demonstrate* that what He said was true. He needed to give people *evidence.*

The biggest of these miracles was Jesus' resurrection. Jesus predicted that He would die and come back to life (Matthew 17:22-23; Mark 8:31; Luke 9:22). Only if He truly was God could He deliver on such a prediction. In addition, all of Old Testament history pointed toward Jesus as Savior: the sacrificial system under Moses, the Messianic prophecies, and many foreshadowings. It's in this extensive context that we can look at the historical evidence for the resurrection (see chapter 23) and conclude that it's reasonable to believe a miracle took place.

Why Christians Can Believe in Biblical Miracles

Only if you assume God doesn't exist or the Bible is unreliable for providing the theological and historical context we just discussed can the miracle of Jesus' resurrection be quickly relegated to the realm of superstition. That's why it's so important that our kids understand the evidence for God (see chapter 1) and the evidence for a reliable Bible (see part 4). The possibility of miracles boils right down to those two considerations. If God does exist, and He wanted to reveal Himself to mankind, there's good reason to believe He would have used miracles in exactly the way the Bible says.

PART 4:

Conversations About
THE BIBLE

25. How were the books in the Bible selected?

In the last section, we looked at why we as Christians can confidently believe what we do about Jesus—most importantly, that He was divine, that He died on the cross for our sins, and that He was resurrected. This understanding, of course, comes primarily from an examination of what the Bible says. *But how do we know we should trust the Bible in the first place?* That's the vital subject for this next part of the book.

We'll get right to it with a basic first question: How were the books in the Bible selected? Or, more formally stated, how did we get our *canon*? The word *canon* simply means a standard. In the context of the Bible, the canon refers to the writings we consider to be the *standard* for our faith. The Protestant canon has 39 Old Testament and 27 New Testament books.[1]

The Old and New Testaments have very different canonization histories. Space prohibits me from going into detail on both, so in this chapter we'll look at the development of the New Testament canon in particular, given its special importance to Christianity. If you're interested in learning more about the Old Testament canon, I've listed resources in the endnotes.[2]

A Picture of Winners and Losers?

The development of the canon is admittedly not the most exciting topic for most Christians, despite its obvious importance. Ironically, however, the canon is a favorite topic of skeptics. The popular skeptical view of the canon goes something like this:

- In the first centuries after Jesus, there were many rival versions of Christianity, but the representative writings were suppressed by those in power.

- Our New Testament books represent the version of Christianity that happened to "win" over time.

- The winning books weren't picked until some 300 years after Jesus' death, and they won because they found political favor at the time.

The implication here, of course, is that we have no reason to believe our canon gives us the right understanding of Jesus. New Testament scholar Bart Ehrman promotes this kind of view in *Lost Scriptures: Books That Did Not Make It into the New Testament*:

> The victors in the struggles to establish Christian orthodoxy not only won their theological battles, they also rewrote the history of the conflict; later readers, then, naturally assume that the victorious views had been embraced by the vast majority of Christians from the very beginning, all the way back to Jesus and his closest followers, the apostles. [3]

If this view is correct, we have a lot to be concerned about. What if we're getting Jesus all wrong because we've been handed erroneous books as an unfortunate consequence of political history? After all, it's true that there were many books written about Christianity in the first centuries after Jesus. We know of at least 280! [4] It's also true that our 27 New Testament books weren't *officially* recognized as the canon until AD 393. But the heart of the matter, regardless of the number of books written and when the canon was officially recognized, is this: *Which of all these writings tell us the truth about the faith that was taught by the apostles—the people who actually knew Jesus?*

To answer this, we can look at the early historical consensus of the church fathers. Generally speaking, we can see there were four categories of books: (1) books accepted by all, (2) books accepted by most, (3) books accepted by a few, and (4) books rejected by all. *Our New Testament books—and those books only—fall into the first two categories.* We'll look at the historical acceptance of those books now, and the historical rejection of books in the last two categories in the next chapter.

Early Acceptance During the Lives of the Apostles

The process of Scripture recognition started very early in the life of the church. For example, in 1 Timothy 5:18, the apostle Paul quoted from Luke's writings, calling them part of "the Scripture." Similarly, the book of 2 Peter referenced Paul's letters as Scripture (3:15-16). Other verses show that the New Testament writings were already being collected and circulated amongst churches during the lives of the apostles (Colossians 4:16; Revelation 1:3).

Early Acceptance by the Apostolic Church Fathers

The apostolic church fathers (those who wrote in the first half of the second century) quoted extensively from and alluded to almost all of our New Testament books in their writings. This is effectively a stamp of approval from those who personally had contact with the apostles or lived just after them and had received their teaching. New Testament scholar Dr. Craig Blomberg explains, "The nature and context of these quotations and allusions suggest that these early patristic authors viewed such writings as uniquely authoritative and occasionally declared them explicitly to be Scripture, in the sense of being on a par with the Old Testament."[5]

While the apostolic church fathers didn't compile any formal lists of books similar to a canon, their quotes and allusions provide strong evidence of early support for our New Testament books. Key apostolic church fathers include Clement of Rome, Ignatius of Antioch, and Polycarp of Smyrna.

The Emergence of Heresies

The early church fathers likely didn't compile formal lists of accepted books because *there wasn't yet a need*. But by the middle of the second century, two major heresies (teachings opposed to accepted doctrine from the apostles) emerged, prompting the next generations of church fathers to define which writings were authoritative for Christians—and which were not.

First, there was a man named Marcion who rejected the Old Testament, denied that Jesus came in the flesh, and attempted to establish an early canon in line with his personal doctrine. This included some of Paul's letters and an edited version of Luke. Marcion is the first person we know of who published a fixed collection of New Testament books.

Second, there was a movement called *Gnosticism*. Gnostics believed that only spirit and soul are good, that Jesus only appeared to be human, and that special knowledge available to only a few was the means to salvation. Valentinus was the most well-known Gnostic leader.

New Testament scholar Dr. F.F. Bruce explains the significance of these developments:

> The distinctive features of Marcionitism and Valentinianism had this at least in common—they were recognized as innovations. This, the leaders of the catholic church knew, was not what they had heard from the beginning. But their followers had to be shown where those new movements were wrong: if the teachings of Marcion and Valentinus were unsound, what was the sound teaching, and how could it be defended?[6]

In other words, it was in response to these *deviations from what had been taught since the beginning* that the canon started taking shape.

Shaping the Canon

Over the next 200 years, Christian literature exploded, and we have many more opportunities to read about the debate over which books were considered authoritative. Below are a few historical highlights (approximate dates of writings are in parentheses):

- *Muratorian Fragment (c. AD 180):* This anonymous document contains a list of books recognized as authoritative in the late second century. It lists 22 of the books we have today. It does *not* list Hebrews, James, 1 and 2 Peter, or 3 John. Aside from Marcion's abridged canon, this is the earliest list of books we have.

- *Irenaeus (c. AD 180):* Irenaeus was a bishop and the student of Polycarp, who knew the apostle John. He never made a list of accepted books, but appealed to the same writings as listed in the Muratorian fragment (with the exception that he included 1 Peter).

- *Tertullian (c. AD 207):* Tertullian was an early Christian apologist (defender of the faith). He acknowledged the four Gospels we have today and noted they were written by apostles or associates of the apostles. He cited all the writings of our New Testament except 2 Peter, James, and 2 and 3 John. Tertullian was the first person we know of to actually use the term *New Testament*.

- *Origen (early third century):* Origen was a scholar and theologian. He distinguished three categories of books in his writings: those widely acknowledged, those disputed by some, and those rejected as false doctrine. Widely acknowledged books included the four Gospels, Acts, all of Paul's letters, 1 Peter, 1 John, and Revelation. Disputed books that are now in the New Testament included Hebrews, James, 2 Peter, 2 and 3 John, and Jude (Origen was the earliest Christian writer to mention 2 Peter).[7]

- *Athanasius (AD 367):* Athanasius was the bishop of Alexandria and the most prominent theologian of the fourth century. In an Easter letter to his churches, he named the 27 books that were considered authoritative—the same 27 we recognize today.

- *Council of Hippo (AD 393):* This council formally ratified the recognition of the 27 books in our New Testament canon. At that time, it was said that "nothing should be read in church under the name of the divine scriptures except the canonical writings."[8]

As you can see from these historical highlights, we can trace the development of our canon to *centuries* before the Council of Hippo ruled on it. Twenty of our 27 New Testament books were accepted from the very beginning and were never in dispute.[9] The only books that some questioned were Hebrews, James, 2 Peter, 2 John, 3 John, Jude, and Revelation. To conclude this chapter, we'll look briefly at the key reasons they were questioned:[10]

- *Hebrews:* The author of Hebrews didn't identify himself, leading to concerns over the book's authority. Most, however, believed the author was Paul or one of his disciples, giving the book the apostolic authority necessary for acceptance.

- *James:* The book of James raised questions because its emphasis on good works at first appeared to conflict with Paul's emphasis on salvation by grace *apart* from works. After closer inspection, it was determined to be compatible with Paul's teachings.

- *2 Peter:* There's a marked style difference between 1 and 2 Peter, leading some to question the authenticity of 2 Peter. It's now believed that the difference in style can be accounted for by Peter's use of a scribe and the difference in time, topic, and recipients.

- *2 and 3 John:* These short books were questioned because of their anonymity and limited circulation. They were later accepted as likely works of the apostle John.

- *Jude:* Jude was questioned by some because it quoted from a nonbiblical source (the Book of Enoch in Jude 14). Nevertheless, it was recognized by the early church fathers and was eventually canonized.

- *Revelation:* Concerns about Revelation weren't raised until the fourth century, when a heretical group called the Montanists tied their doctrines to it. However, key church leaders came to its defense and its place in the canon was confirmed.

Sometimes Winners Deserve to Win

There were many early writings about Christianity, but the only ones that were either accepted by all or accepted by most are the ones we have in our New Testament today. These were the books the early church fathers *knew were consistent with the apostles' teaching*, and were accepted long before they were formally canonized in AD 393. F.F. Bruce summarized this history well in *The New Testament Documents: Are They Reliable?*:

> One thing must be emphatically stated. The New Testament books did not become authoritative for the Church because they were formally included in a canonical list; on the contrary, the Church included them in her canon because she already regarded them as divinely inspired, recognizing their innate worth and generally apostolic authority, direct or indirect.[11]

So let's now turn to the books that *didn't* make the cut. Why were they rejected?

26. Why were books left out of the Bible?

As we saw in the previous chapter, our New Testament books have a well-documented line of connection to the earliest days and figures of the Christian faith. They were eventually included in the canon because they were known to be directly connected with the apostles' teachings.

But what if a case can also be made for the connection of *other* books to the apostles or other early followers of Jesus? Just because the New Testament books have these connections doesn't necessarily mean other books *don't*. We have to consider those other books on their own historical merits.

That said, there are far too many writings to discuss each individually here. Instead, we'll look at the two broad *categories* of writings that will complete our survey from chapter 25: books *accepted by a few*, and books *rejected by all* (recall that chapter 25 addressed books *accepted by all*, and books *accepted by most*).

Though we're continuing to focus on the New Testament, it should be noted that no references to competing, unorthodox Hebrew writings from Old Testament times exist anywhere. As far as we know, no writings rivaled the Old Testament books we have in the Bible today.[1]

Books Accepted by a Few

There are several writings not in the canon that were widely circulated amongst Christians and were occasionally accepted as authoritative by early church fathers. It's difficult to give a precise number of books that fall into this category because there isn't a definitive criterion that determines what exactly it means to have been "accepted by a few." For example, what church fathers or lists should be included in the "vote"? If they merely quoted from a work, does that mean they *accepted* it? If they believed it should be read in churches, does that mean they accepted it as *authoritative*? As you can see, there are reasons it's hard to cite an exact count, but most lists of books "accepted by a few" include around ten.

Most of the books in this category are the writings of the apostolic church fathers. Recall from the prior chapter that these men had personal contact with the apostles or lived just after them. We have several of their writings, including: *1–2 Clement*, seven letters of Ignatius, one letter of Polycarp, the *Martyrdom of Polycarp*, *Didache*, *Pseudo Barnabas*, *Shepherd of Hermas*, *Epistle of Diogenes*, and the *Fragments of Papias*.[2]

These writings were greatly valued by early Christians. Some were especially esteemed, even being called "Scripture" (not all of the writings listed above were respected to that degree). For example, the *Shepherd of Hermas* was the most popular noncanonical book in the early church. It was quoted as inspired by the church fathers Irenaeus and Origen. The church historian Eusebius reported that it was used for instruction in the faith. Despite its popularity, however, it never gained widespread acceptance as divinely inspired. The Muratorian fragment (see chapter 25) noted the broader consensus: "It ought to be read; but it cannot be publicly read in the church to the people, either among the Prophets, since their number is complete, or among the Apostles, to the end of time."[3]

There were some other books that were accepted by a few, but were not part of the writings by the apostolic church fathers. The most significant ones were the *Apocalypse of Peter*, *Gospel According to the Hebrews*, and *Acts of Paul and Thecla*. These books were much less accepted than the writings of the church fathers. However, I've included them here for the sake of thoroughness, given that they were positively acknowledged by at least one later church father or list.

In summary, the writings accepted by a few were esteemed for their historical, moral, or literary value. They were accepted by a limited group of Christians for a limited time, but for various book-specific reasons, never gained widespread recognition as having the same authority as the writings that now comprise the New Testament.

Books Rejected by All

As we just saw, the number of books accepted by a few but ultimately rejected from the canon was small. The number of books *rejected by all* is much greater. This includes books that were obvious forgeries, books that were knowingly written too late to be associated with the apostles, and books that clearly did not conform to the teachings of the books *already known* to be authentic. *We shouldn't be concerned that our Bible is "missing" these books because we have no reason to believe they were connected with the apostles.* Even so, there are certain books in this category you should know more about because they get a lot of "air time" from skeptics today: the so-called Gnostic writings.

Recall from chapter 25 that the most widespread alternative form of Christianity (with explicit written evidence) was called Gnosticism. Gnosticism wasn't a single movement, but rather a worldview that "produced a myriad of viewpoints on the themes tied to its definition."[4] As we saw, this typically involved the ideas that only spirit and soul are good, that Jesus only appeared to be human, and that special knowledge available to only a few was the means to salvation.

Once again, it's hard to say how many writings are in this category. For example, if a work contains one Gnostic-type statement but is largely about something else, should it be classified as Gnostic? Lists of Gnostic works differ given this definitional challenge. Generally speaking, though, at least 30 writings are recognized as Gnostic, and sometimes more than 50. Some of the most well-known are *Gospel of Thomas*, *Gospel of Philip*, *Gospel of Truth*, *Gospel of Mary*, and *Gospel of the Egyptians*.

Because there was never a single Gnostic church, individual expressions of Gnosticism took ideas from a variety of sources. This makes the historian's task of untangling Gnostic roots difficult, and has led to many different opinions on the timing and nature of Gnostic origins. The key issue of interest for our current purpose, however, is this: *What evidence, if any, is there for connecting the teachings of these Gnostic writings to Jesus and the apostles?* If no connection can be found, there's no need to be concerned that Gnostic writings have any authority with respect to what Jesus taught.

There are two key criteria we can look at to answer that question: antiquity and theology.

Antiquity

Most scholars agree that all 27 books of the New Testament were written by the end of the first century—within 70 years of Jesus' death.[5] There are *no* Gnostic works that scholars date to the first century with the *possible* exception of the *Gospel of Thomas* (making this particular work of special interest to historians).[6] The Gnostic books we have were all written in the second century or later. You might think this one fact swiftly answers the question of whether this material can be traced back to Jesus and the apostles. But we shouldn't be so hasty.

There are actually three scenarios that could account for this first-century silence: (1) Gnostic teachings can be traced back to Jesus, but the first-century Gnostic writings were lost over time; (2) Gnostic teachings can be traced back to Jesus, but the first-century Gnostic writings were actively suppressed; or (3) Gnostic teachings *cannot* be traced back to Jesus, and first-century Gnostic writings are missing because they didn't exist.

Let's consider the first two scenarios. Is it *possible* that there were first-century Gnostic writings connected to the apostles, but they were lost over time or suppressed? Yes. *Anything* is possible. And it's that possibility that has spurred much scholarly discussion. But we have to consider what is *probable* based on the evidence we have. As it stands now, these scenarios are mostly arguments from silence—hypothesizing what *could* have happened.

The third scenario, however, is well-supported by the evidence. Apostolic associations are *nonexistent* for the Gnostic writings we have. They don't even *claim* the authority of having had their teachings passed down in oral or written form. Instead, they appeal to *new* revelation and special spiritual knowledge. This is in great contrast to the emphasis of the church fathers on being faithful to the original teachings of the apostles who knew Jesus. In addition, the ideas reflected in existing Gnostic writings produced a negative reaction as soon as they appeared.[7] If these Gnostic writings were truly preceded by other Gnostic writings leading back to the apostles, we would expect them to appeal to that authority or to see reactions from earlier church fathers.

Theology

The criterion of antiquity is easier for us to apply in retrospect than it was for Christians who lived in the second to fourth centuries, when many of these works appeared. New Testament scholar F.F. Bruce explains, "Most of the churchmen who concerned themselves with this problem lacked the information or the expertise to appeal confidently to the evidence for dating such documents: they preferred to judge them by their theology."[8]

In other words, the writings *already known* by early church fathers to be authentically connected with the apostles served as a theological benchmark. As we saw from our brief look at Gnosticism, Gnostic beliefs varied significantly from the theology taught by the writings known to be connected with the apostles (those of our New Testament). There was good reason for the early church fathers to not just reject these works, but to actively write against them.

New Testament scholar Dr. Darrell Bock sums up the skeptics' current interest in Gnostic writings nicely:

> The rehabilitation of the Gnostics does not mean the re-imaging of Christianity. A comprehensive look at the missing gospels and Gnostic teaching does not make them a light

for the twenty-first century, despite [scholars'] recent claims. To regard them as such is an anachronism of the worst kind, doing immense damage to the Christian faith and to our culture's roots. Such reimaging is a distortion of Gnosticism, the Christian faith, and early Christian history.[9]

Noncanonical Books Were Rejected for Good Reason

Several popular books today have piqued the public's interest in possible "missing gospels," as if Christians have gotten Jesus totally wrong. Many skeptics are quick to tout these noncanonical books as evidence against traditional Christianity—simply because they *existed*. But the mere existence of dozens of "Christian" writings that never made it into the Bible says absolutely nothing. What matters is whether any of those writings can legitimately claim spiritual authority by way of connection to Jesus and His apostles. None of the books that were ultimately rejected from the canon have an authoritative connection on par with the writings of the New Testament.

27. How do we know we can trust the Bible's authors?

One day on my blog, an atheist commented that there's "absolutely no evidence" for Jesus' resurrection. I took the bait and replied by outlining the significant historical evidence that does exist for Jesus' resurrection (see chapters 21–23). A few minutes later, the commenter wrote back and dismissively replied, "There's no evidence I would accept for Jesus being God because you'll never be able to put him in a test tube and scientifically see who he actually was."

Jesus in a test tube? Yes, this person had taken the current secular emphasis on science to the extreme. Can you imagine how limited our knowledge would be if we truly couldn't accept anything that isn't "test tube-verifiable"? That would rule out most knowledge of history!

Much of what we know about history comes from recorded eyewitness accounts—accounts like the Gospels purport to be (the Gospels are the books of Matthew, Mark, Luke, and John). Given that we can't reasonably expect to put Jesus in a test tube, we have to rely on the word of those who witnessed His life and resurrection. But how do we know we can trust them?

Assessing the reliability of eyewitnesses isn't a challenge unique to the Bible. Historians and detectives have to do it all the time. In fact, cold-case homicide detective (and former atheist) J. Warner Wallace wrote a fascinating book in which he investigates the Gospels' claims from a detective's perspective. In *Cold-Case Christianity: A Homicide Detective Investigates the Claims of the Gospels*, Det. Wallace assesses the reliability of the Gospels' authors by asking the four key questions detectives use to evaluate *any* eyewitness:[1] (1) Were they present? (2) Were they corroborated? (3) Were they accurate? and (4) Were they biased?

In this chapter, we'll look at each of these questions. I highly recommend Det. Wallace's book for further reading on the topic.

1. Were They Present?

The first criterion of eyewitness reliability is whether the alleged eyewitnesses were actually present. For our purposes, we need to know if the Gospels are based on the testimony of people who actually saw Jesus' life and resurrection.

To evaluate that, it helps to know who the Gospel authors were. That's not as simple as you might think. All four Gospels are technically anonymous, just like many other ancient works. The names we have (Matthew, Mark, Luke, and John) didn't become associated with the Gospels until the second century. That said, *no one* in antiquity attributed the Gospels to anyone other than the four authors we recognize today. There was no debate.

According to the early witness of church fathers, the disciples Matthew and John were the authors of their own eyewitness accounts, Mark was the author of the disciple Peter's eyewitness account, and Luke was a physician and historian who wrote an account based on the eyewitness testimony of the disciples and the apostle Paul (Paul was an eyewitness to the resurrection, but not to Jesus' life).[2]

As supporting evidence for this authorship, there's good reason to believe that the Gospels were written in the mid- to late-first century. (If the Gospels were written in the second century, as some have proposed, they couldn't have been written by these four authors.) Some key points made in support of an especially early dating for Matthew, Mark, and Luke are as follows (most scholars believe John wrote his Gospel in the 90s):

- The book of Acts, written by Luke, is a history of the Christian church after Jesus' ascension. There are several relevant and important historical events, however, that Acts doesn't mention: the destruction of the Jewish temple in AD 70 and the deaths of the apostles Peter (AD 65), Paul (AD 64), and James (AD 62). This strongly suggests Acts was written *before* these events happened (that is, by AD 62).

- Luke wrote his Gospel before he wrote Acts, so the book of Luke can be dated even earlier (in Acts 1:1-2, Luke referenced his "first account").

- The early church unanimously said that Matthew was the first Gospel written. Many scholars today believe Mark was the first. In either case, that means at least one of these books was written even earlier than Luke (before AD 62).

Based on (1) the identities of the authors provided by the early church fathers, and (2) the supporting evidence of first-century authorship, we have good reason to believe the Gospels are based on the accounts of people who were actually present in Jesus' life and at His resurrection.

2. Were They Corroborated?

Even if an eyewitness was present, it's important to look for *independent evidence* which supports their claims. That's called *corroboration*. With respect to the Gospels, there are two kinds of corroboration we can evaluate. *Internal corroboration* is evidence from within the

Gospels themselves—we can see if the eyewitness accounts support each other. *External corroboration* is evidence independent of the Gospels that may verify what they say.

First, let's consider internal corroboration: Do the Gospel accounts support each other? Skeptics often say no. Much has been made of the differences between the Gospels (see chapter 29), but corroboration *doesn't* mean eyewitnesses must provide identical details. To the contrary, Det. Wallace explains, "True, reliable eyewitness accounts are never completely parallel and identical. Instead, they are different pieces of the same puzzle, unintentionally supporting and complementing each other to provide all the details related to what really happened."[3]

This "unintentional support" is exactly what we see in the Gospels. On multiple occasions, two or more Gospel writers describe the same event and inadvertently support each other's accounts with clarifying detail. For example, Matthew 8:14-16 says Jesus went to the house of Peter's mother-in-law and healed her. Verse 16 says many other people were brought to Jesus for healing *that evening*. Why did they wait until evening? Mark 1:21 and Luke 4:31 happen to note the answer by including an extra detail: It was the Sabbath.

Another example comes from Luke 23:1-4, where Pilate asked Jesus if He was King of the Jews. Jesus said, "You have said so," and Pilate responded, "I find no guilt in this man." Why didn't Pilate charge Jesus even though He claimed to be a King? John 18:33-38 unintentionally provides that answer by including Jesus' longer response. Jesus specifically said His kingdom *was not of this world*—a claim Pilate wasn't concerned about.

In addition to many such examples of internal corroboration, several nonbiblical sources provide *external* corroboration of key details from Jesus' life. In chapter 17, we looked at the ancient non-Christian sources that provide those details, so I won't repeat the discussion here. Suffice it to say that those sources offer independent evidence of the Gospels' historical claims.

3. Were They Accurate?

The next test for eyewitness reliability is *accuracy*: What did they say, and how well has their testimony been preserved?

These questions are of particular importance for assessing the reliability of the Gospels, given that they were written almost 2000 years ago. Even if we're confident that the authors were *present* and that they were *corroborated*, how do we know their accounts have been *accurately preserved* over all that time?

This is such an important question that I've devoted the entire next chapter to it. For now, you can note that the accurate preservation of a few passages *is* in question, but those passages have no bearing on any essential Christian belief.

4. Were They Biased?

Many people claim we can't trust what the Gospels say because the writers were Christians who were trying to convince others of their religious perspective. Skeptics say this *bias*—a predisposition toward someone or something—makes the Gospels unreliable.

There's a critical difference between bias *prior to* an experience and conviction *after* an experience, however. As we saw in chapter 19, the disciples weren't necessarily sure what to make of Jesus during His life. The Jews at that time were expecting a Messiah who would save them from Roman oppression. They were hardly biased toward believing that Jesus would be killed like a criminal and raised back to life as a *spiritual* Savior. They became convicted of Jesus' deity only *after* they claimed to have experienced His resurrection.

There's no reason, therefore, to think that simple bias predisposed the disciples to believe or say what they did about Jesus. But what about the related and more self-serving issue of motive? Was there something they were explicitly hoping to gain from saying what they did?

Det. Wallace says that in his experience, there are really just three motives that drive dishonesty: financial greed, sexual or relational desire, or the pursuit of power.[4] Let's see if one of these motives can reasonably account for the disciples' beliefs and actions.

- *Financial greed?* In several places, the New Testament
  speaks of the apostles' hard lifestyle. Paul told the Corinthians, "To the present hour we hunger and thirst, we are
  poorly dressed and buffeted and homeless" (1 Corinthians 4:11). In 2 Corinthians 6:10, Paul described himself as
  "having nothing." In Acts 3:6, Peter told a poor lame man,
  "I have no silver and gold, but what I do have I give to you.
  In the name of Jesus Christ of Nazareth, rise up and walk!"
  There's no hint that the apostles were driven by greed.

- *Sexual or relational desire?* The Bible doesn't say much
  about the families of the apostles. We do know, however, that Peter was married (Matthew 8:14), and Paul suggested in 1 Corinthians 9:5 that other apostles were as well.
  Clearly, the apostles weren't a bunch of single guys who
  were seeking relational gain from their message.

- *Power?* Some Christians did rise to significant power...cen-
  turies after Jesus lived. The earliest Christians, however,
  faced immediate hostility. The ancient extrabiblical sources
  consistently state that the apostles were persecuted and
  martyred for proclaiming their beliefs. There is no record
  of any apostle ever changing his testimony to avoid death.

We have no evidence that the apostles benefited in any way from
their preaching. We can confidently conclude that it was not bias or
motive that was responsible for their testimony.

We Can Take the Gospel Authors' Word for It

We all like to see things ourselves before we believe them, but in
the case of historical claims, that's not possible. We have to assess the
word of others and determine if there's enough evidence to conclude
their claims are reliable. In this chapter, we saw there's good reason to
believe the Gospels are based on reliable eyewitness testimony: the people were *present*, the accounts are *corroborated*, what they said has been
accurately preserved, and there's no reason to believe that *bias* or motive
was responsible for their claims.

28. How do we know the Bible we have today says what the authors originally wrote?

The answer to this chapter's question has the potential to discredit the entire foundation of Christian belief, so it's an important topic that skeptics are understandably very interested in discussing. Christians, on the other hand, typically take for granted that the Bible says what the authors wrote and often aren't aware the question even needs to be asked. But there's a big reason why we shouldn't take it for granted: *None of the original texts have survived.* As far as we know, they no longer exist.

The reason we have a Bible at all today is that the original texts were copied many times for use by different people in different places (just as a publisher today produces many copies of an author's work). Our Bible is based on those copies.

Sounds simple, right? Well, there's one detail that makes it more complicated: The people making copies hundreds of years ago had to make them *by hand.* They didn't yet have the technology to make perfect replicas of a text. As you might imagine, that process introduced copies with changes (both intentional and unintentional) versus the original texts. And, of course, copies weren't only made from the originals. Copies were made from copies. Copies were made from copies of copies. Copies were made from...you get the idea. The result?

We have 20,000-plus handwritten copies of the New Testament—with hundreds of thousands of differences between them.

The conclusion skeptics draw from that fact should be pretty obvious: We have no idea what the authors originally said. In a debate between New Testament scholars Bart Ehrman and Daniel Wallace, Ehrman (an agnostic) said:

> Is the text of the New Testament reliable? The reality is there is no way to know. If we had the originals, we could tell you. If we had the first copies, we could tell you. If we had copies of the copies, we could tell you. We don't have copies in many instances for hundreds of years after

the originals. There are places where scholars continue to debate what the original text said, and there are places where we will probably never know.[1]

Given these facts, recreating the original New Testament writings sounds like an impossibility—and skeptics like Ehrman often promote it as such. But the situation is not nearly as dire as it appears. In this chapter, we'll answer four key questions to understand why: (1) What is textual criticism? (2) How many textual variants are there in the New Testament? (3) What is the nature of the variants? and (4) What theological issues are at stake?

What Is Textual Criticism?

If someone shipped you or me 20,000-plus hand-copied documents and asked us to use them to figure out what the original text must have said, we'd probably give up before we tried. But there's a whole field of study dedicated to precisely that kind of task: the field of *textual criticism*.

Textual criticism is the study of the copies of any written document whose original is unavailable, for the purpose of determining what the original said. To broadly understand how textual criticism works, you can think of a set of copies as part of a "family tree" branching off from an original. For example, let's say an original document said, "I like cats and dogs." Imagine that ten people copied that document, but one accidentally copied it as, "I like bats and dogs." Now imagine that ten people copy each of those copies. Everyone copying from the "I like bats and dogs" copy will carry that error forward. With another round of copying, imagine that someone makes a further mistake, writing "I like bats and hogs." Without knowing beforehand how these changes came about, you could look at the final set of all the copies and reconstruct the likely copying sequence. For example, you would know that the document with the unique "I like bats and hogs" version was most likely copied from a document that already had the "bats" error—not from one that still said, "I like cats and dogs."

Of course, New Testament textual criticism is much more complicated than that, taking into consideration many complex factors, such as the dating and geographic origin of a given copy. As Erhman stated, even the experts can't always arrive at an agreement on some questions. But, as you'll see in the rest of this chapter, that doesn't mean the New Testament we have is unreliable.

How Many Textual Variants Are There in the New Testament?

A *textual variant* is any place amongst manuscripts where there is a variation in wording. In our prior example, if "I like cats and dogs" is the base text to which we're comparing, we saw one variant for cats (bats) and one variant for dogs (hogs).

The best estimate of textual variants in New Testament manuscripts is between 300,000 and 400,000.[2] There are 140,000 words in the New Testament, so that means there are, on average, 2 to 3 variants *for every word*.

The fact that there are hundreds of thousands of variants between manuscripts is widely quoted by skeptics because it sounds so grim. But it's important to understand that we have so many variants *because we have so many manuscripts*. For example, if we only had one New Testament manuscript, there would be *zero* variants because there would be no other manuscripts for it to vary with! But in reality, we have more than 5800 Greek manuscripts, more than 10,000 Latin manuscripts, and 5000-plus other ancient translations. With every additional copy found, there are automatically new opportunities for differences to arise. Wallace, in his debate with Erhman, emphasized, "To speak about the number of variants without also speaking about the number of manuscripts is simply an appeal to sensationalism."[3]

Understanding this relationship between the number of variants and the number of manuscripts is a key first step in putting the 400,000 number in context. But, even more importantly, we need to look at the *nature* of all those variants.

What Is the Nature of the Variants?

Generally speaking, New Testament variants fall into four categories:[4] (1) spelling differences; (2) minor differences that don't affect translation; (3) differences that affect the meaning of the text but aren't viable; and (4) differences that affect the meaning of the text and *are* viable. Let's take a closer look at each of these.

1. *Spelling differences:* The vast majority of all textual variants in the New Testament are simply spelling differences. A modern-day example would be spelling the word color *colour.* Such differences in no way affect the meaning of the text.

2. *Minor differences that don't affect translation:* These variants involve different words (not just different spellings of the same word), but they don't change the meaning of the text once translated. For example, the sentence "Jesus loves John" can be expressed at least 16 different ways in Greek, but would be translated the same in English. Again, no meaning is affected by this type of variant.

3. *Differences that affect the meaning of the text but aren't viable:* The first two categories of variants don't affect the meaning of the text at all. Variants in this category *do* affect the meaning of the text, but there's little reason to think they might actually represent what the original text said (they're not "viable" possibilities). For example, suppose that one manuscript from the ninth century has a variant that significantly alters the meaning of a verse. There's little chance that this one manuscript retained the wording of the original text while all the other manuscripts from preceding centuries got it wrong.

4. *Differences that affect the meaning of the text and* are *viable:* For all intents and purposes, this is the only category that Christians should be concerned about. These variants affect the meaning of the text *and* there's reason to consider them viable candidates for the original wording. *Less than one percent of all textual variants belong to this group.*[5] While that's a very small number relative to the total, it's important to still ask what theological issues may be at stake. A small number of variants *could* equal a big difference in theology.

Keeping Your Kids on God's Side

What Theological Issues Are at Stake?

As we saw in the last category of variants, there *are* some significant questions about passages in the New Testament. For example, John 7:53–8:11 tells the story of the woman caught in adultery. The scribes and Pharisees asked Jesus if she should be stoned. Jesus replied, "Let him who is without sin among you be the first to throw a stone at her" (8:7). They all turned away, and Jesus told the woman to go "sin no more" (verse 11). Most New Testament scholars (both Christians and nonbelievers) believe this story wasn't in the original text that John wrote because it's not in the earliest manuscripts. Knowing that may impact our understanding of this passage, but does it change any core theological doctrine? No.

Another major example is the ending to Mark's Gospel (Mark 16:9-20). Although the vast majority of later Greek manuscripts have these verses, two of the oldest and most respected manuscripts do not. These older manuscripts end at verse 8, with "[the women] went out and fled from the tomb, for trembling and astonishment had seized them, and they said nothing to anyone, for they were afraid." The vocabulary in verses 9-20 is also not consistent with the rest of Mark. Most scholars believe this longer ending was added many years after Mark was originally written (check your own Bible, and you'll likely see a note about the doubtful authenticity of these verses). Knowing this may impact our understanding of this passage, but does it change any core theological doctrine? Again, no.

We could continue looking at examples, but we'll get to the same bottom line: *No core doctrine is called into question by any New Testament variant.* Even Dr. Ehrman has acknowledged, "Essential Christian beliefs are not affected by textual variants in the manuscript tradition of the New Testament."[6]

No Essential Christian Beliefs in Question

This chapter's subject offers a great example for your kids of how facts often don't speak for themselves. Even once we verify that the facts we're working with are correct, we have to ask what those facts really *mean*. In this case, we have 20,000-plus New Testament copies and

400,000 variants, but 99 percent of those variants are *irrelevant*. Most importantly, the 1 percent of variants that genuinely impact our understanding of a passage have no bearing on essential Christian beliefs. We have every reason to believe that the New Testament we have today accurately represents what the authors originally wrote.

29. Does the Bible have errors and contradictions?

My kids have been going through a phase in which they seem to love bad logic. In order to minimize the opportunities for getting into trouble, they often try to give vague or cleverly-worded answers in response to certain questions. As an example, here's a conversation I had with my daughter one morning this week:

"Honey, did you brush your teeth yet?"

"No, of course not."

"Why 'of course not'? You know you have to do that every day."

"Well, mommy, I did. Why are you asking?"

"Because you just said you didn't. Now you're saying you did. Which is it?"

"Mommy, you're just not understanding what I'm saying."

I present this mind-numbing conversation to you as a calm dialogue, but in reality, my daughter's contradictions drive me crazy. She either brushed her teeth or she didn't, but both responses can't be true at the same time.

Skeptics charge that the Bible is filled with hundreds of such contradictions and factual errors (statements that are verifiably untrue). One website, called bibviz.com, lays out 472 alleged problems from the *Skeptics Annotated Bible* and "conveniently" offers a slick graphic interface to further explore them (the site gets 30,000-50,000 page views every month).[1]

If the Bible really has hundreds of errors and contradictions, we would be hard-pressed to confidently trust that it's God's Word. This is undoubtedly a very serious claim, but it can be difficult to address because there's no "blanket" answer that applies to every alleged problem. That said, there are some big-picture considerations that can help provide a framework for discussing this challenge with your kids. In this chapter we'll look at those considerations—first for alleged errors, then for alleged contradictions.

Two Types of Alleged Biblical "Errors"

There are two kinds of biblical "errors" necessary to understand: (1) alleged errors that aren't *truly* errors, and (2) true errors.

Alleged Errors That Aren't Truly Errors

Skeptics have a long list of supposed factual errors that they claim demonstrate the Bible is a purely man-made book. The vast majority of these, however, are not actual errors.

For example, in a parable about the kingdom of heaven, Jesus called the mustard seed the "smallest of all seeds" (Matthew 13:31-32). But the mustard seed is *not* the smallest of all seeds. Many have claimed that's a factual error. However, Jesus was referencing the mustard seed in a *proverbial* sense—using an example familiar to His audience of a seed known for its smallness (He used a mustard seed reference proverbially in Matthew 17:20 as well).

Another example of an alleged factual error comes from Leviticus 11:13-19. God prohibited the Israelites from eating several kinds of "birds," including *bats*. But bats are mammals, not birds. That sounds like a scientific error. However, the scientific classifications we have today didn't exist 3500 years ago. The Hebrew word that's translated "birds" literally means "flying creatures"—which is what a bat is.[2] We can't retroactively impose our modern classification system on this group of animals and call it an error.

There are many such examples of alleged errors that aren't *actual* errors when further historical, linguistic, or literary factors are taken into account. The overarching takeaway is that just because someone cries, "Error!" doesn't mean there's actually an error. Do your research on the individual issues, and teach your kids how to do theirs.

True Errors

Recall from chapter 28 that the Bible we have today is based on copies that were made from the original writings—originals we no longer have. Although most copyists took tremendous care when producing their work, the process did result in some known errors.

As one example, 2 Kings 8:26 says that Ahaziah was 22 years old when he began to reign. Second Chronicles 22:2, however, says he was 42 years old. Obviously, these ages cannot both be correct. Based on the historical information in other passages, most scholars believe that the text in 2 Chronicles is the one that's been transmitted in error.

Given the existence of copyist errors, it's important to note here that Christians only affirm that the Bible's *original manuscripts* are inerrant (which can be ascertained from the copies with great, if not perfect, accuracy; again, see chapter 28).[3]

Three Keys to Evaluating Alleged Contradictions

A contradiction exists when there is no logical way to reconcile two statements—like that my daughter both brushed her teeth and did not brush her teeth. When skeptics allege that the Bible is filled with such contradictions, they're not properly interpreting the passages in question. Here are three of the most important keys to evaluating their claims.

1. Always Consider Context

If you remember nothing else from this chapter, remember this: The most frequent reason for alleged contradictions is that skeptics fail to consider *context*—context of a passage within its chapter, within its book, within the Old or New Testament, or within the Bible overall. For example, Romans 15:33 calls God a "God of peace," but Exodus 15:3 says, "The Lord is a man of war." These sound contradictory, but in the greater context of the Bible, they're not—we know that God desires peace, but in His justness, He punishes evil. Skeptics are often guilty of plucking isolated verses like these out of the Bible and claiming they contradict one another. But context is almost always the key to seeing their error.

2. Interpret Difficult Passages in Light of Clearer Passages

There are quite a few passages in the Bible that contain cultural or historical references we don't fully understand. When paired with other verses, they sometimes seem contradictory. For example, 1 Corinthians 15:29 contains an obscure reference to baptism for the dead. We know from the clarity of other Scriptures, however, that a dead person cannot be saved by someone else (Ephesians 2:8; Romans 3:28; 6:3-4). There's no reason to conclude that this is a contradiction. Always let clear passages interpret more obscure ones.

3. Don't Confuse Descriptive and Prescriptive Passages

The Bible *describes* many historical events that it doesn't necessarily *prescribe* (approve of). Skeptics often make the mistake of citing God's prohibitive command in one place, then pointing to another place where that command was violated as evidence of a "contradiction." For example, God clearly condemned human sacrifice in Deuteronomy 18:10 (a *prescriptive* passage), but we read of King Ahaz sacrificing his son in 2 Kings 16:3 (a *descriptive* passage; see chapter 32). These passages aren't contradictory—they're completely different in nature.

Three Special Considerations When Evaluating Alleged Gospel Contradictions

Because the Gospels are based on eyewitness accounts of the same events (Jesus' life and resurrection; see chapter 27), there are some considerations that are unique to these four books.

1. Authors sometimes present events in thematic rather than chronological order.

The Gospels recount many of the same events, but often in a different order. For example, the temptations of Jesus are sequentially different in Matthew 4:1-11 and Luke 4:1-13. The two sequences technically contradict each other because they can't both be correct. However, authors often write thematically rather than chronologically for different narrative purposes. Most Bible scholars believe Matthew's account is sequential and Luke's is thematic.

2. Partial accounts are not (necessarily) contradictory accounts.

When eyewitnesses recount details of an event, they may each reference a different part of it. On the surface, those varied accounts can seem contradictory, but closer investigation shows they are simply different parts of the same story. For example, Matthew, Mark, and Luke record different responses from Peter when Jesus asked him who Peter thought He was:

- In Matthew, Peter said, "You are the Christ, the Son of the living God" (16:16).

- In Mark, Peter said, "You are the Christ" (8:29).

- In Luke, Peter said, "The Christ of God" (9:20).

These responses are not identical, but they're also not contradictory. Mark and Luke were likely recounting a partial version of the fuller response we see in Matthew.

3. Different perspectives are not (necessarily) contradictions.

In chapter 27, we looked at homicide detective J. Warner Wallace's approach to evaluating the reliability of eyewitness accounts in the Gospels. As we saw, it's expected that eyewitnesses *corroborate* each other, but not that they provide *identical details* (if witnesses describe an event in exactly the same way, investigators often question their honesty!). Similarly, we should expect the Gospels to differ to some degree as the result of varied perspectives.

One major example of this is in the resurrection accounts, which differ on several points. For example, they differ on the number of women at the tomb (Matthew says two, Mark says three, Luke says five, John says one), the messengers at the tomb (Matthew says one angel, Mark says men, Luke says men, John says two angels), and whom the woman/women told (Matthew says the disciples, Mark says no one, Luke says the disciples and others, John says only Mary Magdalene told the disciples). Several other differences have been noted as well.

Many possible harmonizations of the accounts have been proposed.[4] Though we can't say with certainty how *all* the details fit together, we do know that the differences between the accounts is consistent with the varied perspectives to be expected from eyewitnesses. The central truths that Jesus was resurrected from the dead and appeared to many are clear in each.

Big Claims with Little Investigation

Skeptics consider it a given that the Bible has loads of "errors and contradictions," but often haven't actually investigated them. When you do take the time to properly evaluate the passages in question, there are good reasons to believe they're complementary. It's important to work with your kids on how to *do* those evaluations, rather than simply telling them, "There are no errors and contradictions in the Bible!" Giving them a framework for understanding the nature of alleged discrepancies empowers them to confidently make the evaluations themselves.

30. Does the Bible support slavery?

Kids who are raised in a Christian home make contact with biblical teachings in a lot of different ways: through devotionals, children's Bibles, Sunday school classes, youth speakers, and sermons, to name a few. But if they don't actually read a complete Bible from start to finish (which most kids don't), there's a good chunk of stuff they'll likely never encounter.

Some of this missed "stuff" will have minimal consequences for a kid's eventual faith. For example, they may never run into the content of books like Ezra and Nehemiah, but that material is highly unlikely to later challenge them. Other frequently missed parts of the Bible, however—particularly in the first few books of the Old Testament—contain seemingly shocking verses that *can* greatly challenge a person's faith once discovered. Most significantly, these passages raise questions about God's stance on *slavery, rape,* and *human sacrifice.*

Skeptics are well aware of these frequently-missed-but-alarming passages. In fact, many joke, "The best way to turn a Christian into an atheist is to have them actually read the Bible." They know most Christians don't have a clue what to do with these tough passages, and they're eager to "educate" you and your kids about them (using their own interpretation, of course). For example, one popular atheist website, www.EvilBible.com, says it's devoted to helping people "learn about all the nasty things in the Bible that are usually not talked about by priests and preachers."[1] EvilBible.com has been visited 3.8 million times since 2003.[2]

So what should parents do? We need to proactively address these passages with our kids before they encounter the twisted, out-of-context interpretations skeptics enthusiastically promote. Many kids won't ask about these issues, given that such passages can easily remain off their radar throughout childhood, but it's in their best interest for *you* to bring them to light. This and the next two chapters will help prepare you for those discussions. We'll start with slavery.

Does the Bible Support Slavery?

Does the Bible support slavery? There's actually not an easy answer to that question. It completely depends on what a person means when they say "support." I'm not playing word games here. The answer to this question really does require extended discussion to have any meaningful value for Christians and skeptics alike. Before we get into the biblical details, however, three important observations must be made.

First, there's no passage in the Bible that explicitly condemns slaveholding. God undeniably allowed various forms of slavery to take place amongst the Israelites. So, if that's what someone means when they say "the Bible supports slavery," they're right. But to stop there is like saying you know everything you need to know about World War I because you know the United States "supported" it. There's a lot more to know about slavery in the Bible if you want to have any constructive understanding of the topic.

Second, the fundamental question about slavery and the Bible has nothing to do with whether or not people have *used* the Bible to justify slavery in later time periods (such as early America). People often get caught up in discussions about whether the Bible is to blame for various historical periods of slavery, but that's a tangential issue—one that may be of historical interest, but *not* one that gets to the heart of the theological issue (why a good God would allow a terrible thing like slavery). Not everything done in the name of Christianity is a legitimate expression of the faith, so we need to evaluate the Bible by looking at the Bible itself.

Third, it's not adequate to answer this chapter's question by saying, "The Bible's laws on slavery were a lot nicer than the laws of surrounding cultures!" If you've ever heard a Christian respond to the question of slavery, it's probably been something along those lines. While it may be true, the fact hardly addresses the skeptic's concern about biblical morality. As one skeptic explained, "Even granting this point for the sake of argument, this fails to answer the simple question: is owning another human ever moral, or not? The relative kindness of a slave owner does not enter into the basic moral question of owning other humans as property."[3] This is an important point and requires more than a cursory answer.

With these three points in mind, let's now look at Old Testament slavery laws.

Slaves in the Old Testament

The key to understanding the complexity of Old Testament slavery is recognizing that there were several different *categories* of slaves, each under a unique set of laws. We can't talk about biblical "slavery" without talking about the following specific categories of slaves.

Indentured Servants (Male or Female)

When most modern people think of slavery, they think of the devastating *chattel* slavery common in the 17th to 19th centuries. Chattel slaves were treated as property rather than humans. They had no rights and were bought and sold as commodities.

Most of the "slaves" in Israel were not slaves in this sense at all. They were *indentured servants*. Again, this isn't a word game. Indentured servitude was completely different in nature than chattel slavery. Generally speaking, indentured servitude was a safety net to prevent extreme economic hardship in a society where there weren't other options. A debtor could voluntarily sell himself to his lender, or he could sell himself to a person who would pay off the debts in return for work. Most Old Testament slavery laws pertain to indentured servitude.

While indentured servitude was in no way like chattel slavery, it certainly wasn't seen as an ideal in its own right. Several laws existed to prevent people from getting to the point of servanthood in the first place. For example, God instructed the Israelites to not reap their field right up to the edge nor to strip their vineyard bare. This command to leave a remnant made it possible for the poor to gather food for survival (Leviticus 19:9-10; 23:22; Deuteronomy 24:20-21). The Israelites were told to lend to their poor countrymen without charging interest (Exodus 22:25; Leviticus 25:36-37). The poor were allowed to sacrifice smaller, less expensive animals in their worship of God (Leviticus 5:7,11). In spite of these provisions, however, circumstances sometimes became dire enough that these laws weren't sufficient to allow for a person's survival. In such cases, indentured servanthood became a welcome option.

Here are the most important things you should know about this form of "slavery:"[4]

- It was entirely voluntary—no one was forced to become an indentured servant. If anyone was caught trying to force a fellow Israelite into servanthood by kidnapping, the penalty was death (Deuteronomy 24:7).

- Indentured servants were required to work for only six years. In the seventh year, they were to be set free (Exodus 21:2; Deuteronomy 15:12).

- Servants were to rest on the Sabbath along with everyone else (Exodus 20:9-10).

- Physical punishment was allowed, but any permanently injured slave had to be set free (Exodus 21:26-27).

- An indentured servant could *choose* to become a permanent servant (Exodus 21:5-6; Deuteronomy 15:16-17).

- Freed servants were to be generously supplied with grain, wine, and livestock (Deuteronomy 15:12-15).

In short, an indentured servant was more like a hired worker than anything resembling the common notion of slavery.

Servant Girls as Future Wives

One of the most often-discussed and misunderstood passages on slavery is Exodus 21:7-11. Skeptics often claim these verses speak of God's support for sex slavery:

> When a man sells his daughter as a slave, she shall not go out as the male slaves do. If she does not please her master, who has designated her for himself, then he shall let her be redeemed. He shall have no right to sell her to a foreign people, since he has broken faith with her. If he designates her for his son, he shall deal with her as with a daughter. If he takes another wife to himself, he shall not diminish her food, her clothing, or her marital rights. And if he does not do these three things for her, she shall go out for nothing, without payment of money.

To understand what's going on here, we need some context. Every girl in that culture faced an arranged marriage. Normally a man would demonstrate his intent to marry a woman by giving her father a substantial monetary gift (a "bride-price"). In some cases, however, a father, driven by poverty, might choose to "sell" his daughter before marriageable age to be a servant—with the understanding that her "master" would later marry her. This was a way for the poverty-stricken father to receive money for his daughter's marriage much earlier, and it allowed his daughter to marry into a higher socioeconomic class than she otherwise would have. These verses regulate this practice to *protect* the girls who were entering into such arrangements.

Three key points should be made on this passage. First, the reason it says the girl was not to go free like male slaves was because working toward freedom was *never the intent* of this particular arrangement. The intent of this arrangement was for eventual *marriage*, not temporary indentured servitude (unmarried female indentured servants were to go free just like the male indentured servants, as made clear in Deuteronomy 15:12).

Second, if the future husband (the "master") decided to not go through with the marriage, the girl was to be taken back ("redeemed") *by her family*. He had no right to treat her as a slave who could be sold to someone else (a "foreign people").

Third, once she was married to either the "master" or his son, she was to be treated as *family*—again, not as a slave ("he shall deal with her as with a daughter"). He was to always provide for her and, if he did not, she was to go free with no reimbursement of what he had paid.

To summarize, there is nothing in this passage about a daughter being sold into perpetual chattel-like slavery (for sex or any other purpose). This passage speaks to an arranged marriage contract and the legal protection of the girl's rights in such cases.

Foreigners

So far we've looked at two types of "slaves" covered by slavery laws, neither of which resembles our common notion of slavery. Christians often point skeptics to this fact and assert that there really wasn't "slavery" (as we think of the term) at all. But this ignores one glaring passage—the laws on foreign slaves, found in Leviticus 25:44-46:

> As for your male and female slaves whom you may have:
> you may buy male and female slaves from among the
> nations that are around you. You may also buy from among
> the strangers who sojourn with you and their clans that are
> with you, who have been born in your land, and they may
> be your property. You may bequeath them to your sons
> after you to inherit as a possession forever.

Frankly, addressing the question of slavery would be much easier if this particular passage didn't exist, but it would be disingenuous to ignore it. Foreign slaves *could* be held for life and passed down as a "possession." The law did state that they were not to be mistreated (Exodus 23:9; Leviticus 19:33-34) and, generally speaking, Israel's slave laws were much more moderate than those of surrounding nations. However, the fact remains that God allowed the Israelites to permanently hold foreign slaves.

Why Did God Allow Any of This?

You may have noticed that, until now, I've avoided any discussion of *why* God allowed any of this. That's because most people are unaware of what "this" actually was, and an important starting point for discussing the *why* is understanding the *what*.

As we saw, indentured servitude—the predominant form of "slavery"—was more of a crude safety net than anything. It existed to provide economic relief in a time when there were no other options for the financially desperate. This shouldn't be morally controversial.

As for girls being sold as future wives, we need to understand that arranged marriages were a deeply embedded part of society at the time. Most women were uneducated and completely dependent on their male family members (a father or husband) for security. Israel's laws regulated this institution and protected the rights of its most vulnerable citizens.

The most difficult *why* relates to the permanent holding of foreign slaves. The Bible doesn't say how these foreigners entered into slavery in the first place, so it's difficult to address possible reasons for this more stringent law. Several possibilities have been proposed, but there is no broad consensus (for example, these slaves may have been foreigners already in Israel who were hostile to God's purposes for His people; if they were released, it could have jeopardized national security).[5]

So how should we answer the skeptic who asks if it's ever moral to own another human as property? First, we must state that the same God who allowed these various forms of slavery created *all* humans in His image (Genesis 1:27). *God made no humans to be property.* Any institution that treats humans as property is clearly not a reflection of God's *ideal*.

Second, we should acknowledge that ancient Israel adopted various social structures that were not consistent with God's ideal—for example, polygamy and slavery. From our modern perspective, we might assume God's best moral course of action would have been to more swiftly (if not immediately) abolish such arrangements. However, we must recognize that civil laws are often not the same as moral laws; not everything that is immoral is illegal (for example, lying), and not everything that is illegal is immoral (for example, traffic violations). We see that same distinction even in the theocracy of ancient Israel.

God used civil laws to regulate, rather than eliminate, certain culturally entrenched institutions that weren't necessarily His moral ideal.

Last, we should be very clear about what exactly God *did* allow. It wasn't what's in the minds of most people who ask questions on this topic. The laws pertaining to indentured servants and arranged marriages for young girls show these people *weren't* treated as property, but as humans with important rights (money was exchanged for their service, but that doesn't mean they were property). God did allow foreign slaves to be held indefinitely, but we know too little about this particular group to understand why a distinction may have been made. Given all else we more clearly know, we can be confident in saying that God never "supported" slavery in the sense that it was His ideal. Rather, it was something He *tolerated* in certain forms, at a particular time, and in a particular place (just as He did with polygamy—God tolerated it for a time, though we know from Genesis 2:24 that His ideal for marriage was one man and one woman).

31. Does the Bible support rape?

Most Christians are at least vaguely aware of allegations from skeptics that the Bible has passages that are said to support slavery (see chapter 30). But far fewer are aware of the passages skeptics claim support rape.

The website EvilBible.com that I introduced you to in the last chapter has a page devoted to this topic. The author begins by saying,

> Few people know that the Bible often condones and even approves of rape. How anyone can get their moral guidance from a book that allows rape escapes me. Perhaps they have been lied to about the Bible and carefully detoured around all the nasty stuff in the Bible.[1]

While it's absolutely untrue that God approves of rape (as we'll see in this chapter), I would agree that many Christians have "detoured" around "nasty stuff" in the Bible. There are a *lot* of difficult passages in the Old Testament that never make their way into a Sunday school lesson or sermon topic, much less a children's Bible. In fact, I'm quite certain I've never heard any of the passages in this chapter discussed in church. But because of their jarring nature, skeptics love to highlight them whenever possible. We need to know how to respond, and how to help our kids navigate these shocking claims.

In this chapter we'll look at the Old Testament laws on rape, then consider three difficult passages skeptics often cite to support their claims.

Biblical Laws Pertaining to Rape

Deuteronomy 22:23-29 is the key passage that details God's laws for the Israelites on sexual encounters outside of marriage. We'll look at these verses in three parts. Each part corresponds to a different legal case. First, verses 23-24 say:

> If there is a betrothed virgin, and a man meets her in the city and lies with her, then you shall bring them both out to the gate of that city, and you shall stone them to death with stones, the young woman because she did not cry for help though she was in the city, and the man because he violated his neighbor's wife. So you shall purge the evil from your midst.

The situation described here is between two *consenting* adults—a man and an engaged woman.[2] Many skeptics erroneously assume the passage is talking about rape and say God wanted to stone the victim for not crying loudly enough (a horrible thought, to be sure). However, the passage doesn't say anything about rape. It assumes that if the encounter happened where people were nearby ("in the city"), the woman could cry for help; if she didn't, it assumes that means she consented. The penalty for this consensual sex between a married man and an engaged woman was death—just as it was for adultery between two married adults (Leviticus 20:10).

Of course, the modern reader wonders, *What if a woman was being raped in a city but wasn't able to cry for help?* The passage doesn't address that. Old Testament laws don't address every possible case, which can sometimes leave us hanging on the details. But the fact that this scenario wasn't specifically addressed doesn't make what *was* addressed less clear. This law had two consenting adults in mind. God didn't suggest *rape victims* should be stoned.

The next three verses (25-27) further make this clear, by comparison:

> But if in the open country a man meets a young woman
> who is betrothed, and the man seizes her and lies with her,
> then only the man who lay with her shall die. But you shall
> do nothing to the young woman; she has committed no
> offense punishable by death. For this case is like that of
> a man attacking and murdering his neighbor, because he
> met her in the open country, and though the betrothed
> young woman cried for help there was no one to rescue her.

This is the clearest condemnation of rape in the Bible. The passage says that, in this case, the woman was *not* consenting; the man seized her in a location where she couldn't get help ("open country"). If that happened, the rape victim was considered innocent and the rapist received the death penalty. *Obviously, God did not approve of rape.*

Note that both of these passages address what happened when an *engaged* ("betrothed") woman had sex with a man other than her future husband—in the first case, when it was consensual, in the second case, when it was not. The last two verses (28-29) in the passage address what happened when an *unengaged* woman was raped:

> If a man meets a virgin who is not betrothed, and seizes her
> and lies with her, and they are found, then the man who lay
> with her shall give to the father of the young woman fifty
> shekels of silver, and she shall be his wife, because he has
> violated her. He may not divorce her all his days.

As many people have pointed out, this law sounds horrendous. Why would the victim have to marry the man who raped her?[3] Here we need some context.

In the culture of the time, an unengaged woman who had lost her virginity was undesirable for marriage. Without the support of a husband, she would face a life of poverty and social isolation. *This law spared the rapist's life in order to ensure the victim's future economic security.* In the previous case, where the rape victim was engaged, the rapist could be executed because the woman *already had* the security of a future husband. The law sounds bad at first, but it was actually for the victim's protection.

You may have noticed that one scenario wasn't covered in this passage. What if a man had *consensual* sex with an *unengaged* woman? The answer to that can be found in Exodus 22:16-17: The man had to marry the woman in that case as well. Those verses include an additional note that the father didn't *have* to allow his daughter to marry the man if the father was able to provide for her on his own. Although the passage in Deuteronomy doesn't explicitly include this "opt-out" clause in the case of rape, the same precedent likely applied.

Now that we've looked at the relevant passages, we can state the bottom line on rape laws. If a man raped a married or engaged woman, he got the death penalty. The woman was innocent. If a man raped *or* had consensual sex with an unmarried/unengaged woman, he was required to marry her because he had substantially decreased her prospects for marriage. Ultimately, however, the girl's father could refuse the marriage if it wasn't in her best interest.[4]

Biblical laws clearly don't condone rape. However, a few Old Testament passages that describe the handling of female war captives have generated additional concerns. We'll look at the three most important ones.

Approval to Rape Female War Captives?

In Deuteronomy 20:10-14, God gave the Israelites wartime instructions for any battles that happen outside the boundaries of the Promised Land. Skeptics claim this passage shows God approved of raping female war captives:

> If [a city] makes no peace with you, but makes war against
> you, then you shall besiege it. And when the LORD your
> God gives it into your hand, you shall put all its males to
> the sword, but the women and the little ones, the livestock,
> and everything else in the city, all its spoil, you shall take

as plunder for yourselves. And you shall enjoy the spoil of your enemies, which the LORD your God has given you (verses 11-14).

As you can see, rape isn't mentioned here at all. God only says the Israelites shouldn't *kill* women and children, even when a city refuses to surrender. Far from encouraging rape, this law *protected* the women. Skeptics read into the text what they assume soldiers would do with their captives, but, as it turns out, the Bible doesn't leave that to the imagination. The next chapter in Deuteronomy clarifies that female prisoners of war could either fully integrate into Israelite society through marriage or be set free:

> When you go out to war against your enemies, and the LORD your God gives them into your hand and you take them captive, and you see among the captives a beautiful woman, and you desire to take her to be your wife, and you bring her home to your house, she shall shave her head and pare her nails. And she shall take off the clothes in which she was captured and shall remain in your house and lament her father and her mother a full month. After that you may go in to her and be her husband, and she shall be your wife. But if you no longer delight in her, you shall let her go where she wants. But you shall not sell her for money, nor shall you treat her as a slave, since you have humiliated her (Deuteronomy 21:10-14).

These verses show God wouldn't let the soldiers immediately marry—let alone have sex with—their war captives. A woman was to be given a month-long adjustment period before a marriage could even take place. If the soldier decided *not* to marry her, she was to go free.

Admittedly, in our culture today, we don't like the idea of anyone being obligated to marry. However, in the aftermath of ancient war, this was the best possible scenario for a woman. Her life was spared and, instead of facing a future with no economic means in a foreign land, she had the opportunity to fully integrate into Israelite society through marriage.

To say these passages demonstrate God's approval of rape grossly misconstrues the text. When you consider the biblical and cultural context, it becomes clear that these laws were in place to help *protect* women who were caught in the difficult aftermath of war.

Approval to Rape Midianite Virgins?

The Midianites were a group of nomadic tribes who lived in the deserts on the edges of the Promised Land. One group of Midianites, related to the Moabites, physically seduced the Israelites into worshiping their god Baal at Peor (the Israelites "whored" with their women; see Numbers 25). Because they had led the Israelites astray, God commanded Moses to wage war against them.

The Israelites proceeded to kill every male from this group and returned to Moses with the women and children. But Moses became angry when he saw that the women had been spared. He commanded all but the virgins to be killed: "Kill every male among the little ones, and kill every woman who has known man by lying with him. But all the young girls who have not known man by lying with him keep alive for yourselves" (Numbers 31:17-18).

If you read this passage out of context, it could sound like God was interested in keeping virgins alive for the Israelites' indiscriminate pleasure. However, such a reading completely ignores surrounding facts.

As we discussed, women were normally spared in wars outside of the Promised Land (Deuteronomy 20:10-14). But in this specific case, the women were guilty of seducing the Israelites, so God's judgment was upon them. The girls who were virgins obviously didn't participate in the incident, so they were allowed to live because they were *innocent*— not because God wanted to save them for the soldiers' sexual pleasure. They would have been treated according to the laws we already discussed in our look at Deuteronomy 21:10-14.

Approval to Rape the Women of Jabesh-gilead?

Judges 19 tells the strange story of a man from the tribe of Levi who was passing through the land of the tribe of Benjamin with his concubine one day. They were taken in for the night by a man in the

Benjaminite town of Gibeah. The inhabitants of Gibeah surrounded the house, demanding to have sexual relations with the Levite. The master of the house instead gave them the concubine and his own virgin daughter. The people of Gibeah left the concubine dead on the doorstep the next morning.

The Levite rallied the other tribes of Israel against Benjamin because the Benjaminites refused to punish the people of Gibeah for the incident. A civil war ensued, and all but 600 Benjaminite men were killed. The Israelites took a foolish oath and said, "No one of us shall give his daughter in marriage to Benjamin" (Judges 21:1). Yet they soon became concerned that the tribe of Benjamin might be lost forever. In order to prevent the tribe's extinction, they decided to wage war on the settlement of Jabesh-gilead and gave the 400 virgins they found to the Benjaminite men. They soon discovered, however, that there weren't enough women for all the men, so the Israelites hatched a plan for the Benjaminites to kidnap the rest of the women they needed from a place called Shiloh. They did, the tribe lived on, and the rest was history.

Sounds pretty awful, right? Wiping out a town to take 400 virgin inhabitants, then kidnapping hundreds more? How could God command such a thing?

He didn't. This passage *describes* a historical incident but never indicates this is something God *commanded* or *approved* of. In fact, the concluding verse of the passage—one skeptics conveniently omit when quoting this story—says, "In those days there was no king in Israel. Everyone did what was right in his own eyes" (Judges 21:25). Clearly, this story was an example of the chaos that reigned when the people did *not* follow God.

It's dishonest for skeptics to pull this purely descriptive passage out of the Bible and suggest that it demonstrates God's approval of rape—especially given the clear indictment that follows in verse 25.

The Bible Clearly Does Not Support Rape

It's often not easy to understand the Old Testament, given how far removed it is from our culture today. Correct interpretation depends on making the effort to understand the biblical and cultural context involved. Unfortunately, however, skeptics often isolate difficult passages without such consideration and use them to make a case that isn't accurate—like the accusation that the Bible supports rape. As we've seen, a closer look at the rape laws and specific events in question shows this is in no way true.

32. Does the Bible support human sacrifice?

In this final stop on our tour of moral outrage against the Bible, we'll look at the question of whether or not the Bible supports human sacrifice.

The nations that surrounded Israel practiced human sacrifice as part of their worship of false gods, and much is said in the Bible about that practice. Most importantly, God explicitly, repeatedly, and clearly condemned such activity. For example, Deuteronomy 12:31 states, "You shall not worship the LORD your God in that way, for every abominable thing that the LORD hates they have done for their gods, for they even burn their sons and their daughters in the fire to their gods" (see also Deuteronomy 18:10). Of course, just because God forbade something doesn't mean the Israelites listened. The prevalence of human sacrifice in their nation was one reason God exiled them from their land (see Ezekiel 16:20-21 and 20:31).

Even skeptics acknowledge that God condemns human sacrifice in the Bible. But there are also several accounts where they claim God violates His own prohibition. Ultimately, many have concluded the Bible supports such activity, or at a minimum is contradictory on the matter.[1]

We can't cover every questionable passage in this chapter, but we'll look at the most commonly cited ones. First, we'll look in detail at a unique and important "human sacrifice" story in the Bible—God's command for Abraham to sacrifice Isaac. Then we'll look at a category of passages that *describe* but don't *prescribe* human sacrifice. Last, we'll look at several examples where the passages in question are being misinterpreted and aren't about human sacrifice at all.

God's Command for Abraham to Sacrifice Isaac

Genesis 22:1-2 describes the famously difficult request God made of Abraham to sacrifice his son Isaac:

> God tested Abraham and said to him, "Abraham!" And he said, "Here I am." He said, "Take your son, your only son Isaac, whom you love, and go to the land of Moriah, and offer him there as a burnt offering on one of the mountains of which I shall tell you."

You might have a pretty good guess as to why skeptics go straight to this passage as Exhibit A of biblical support for human sacrifice. *God Himself asked Abraham to sacrifice his son.* To make sense of this, we have to understand the backstory.

In Genesis 12:1-2, God called Abraham to leave his family and go to a land He would show him. God promised that through Abraham's descendants all the families of the Earth would be blessed (as we later learn, Abraham would become the ancestral father of God's chosen people, the Israelites, and ultimately of Jesus Himself). Abraham obeyed and left his homeland. However, he later questioned God's promise because his wife, Sarah, had not become pregnant. God reiterated His promise, saying that Abraham *would* have an heir.

Meanwhile, Sarah took matters into her own hands by offering her Egyptian servant, Hagar, to Abraham as a second wife who could bear a child. Hagar gave birth to a son, Ishmael, but God made it clear to Abraham that this wasn't the heir He had promised. The heir through whom God would bless the nations would be *Sarah's* son, and his name would be *Isaac* (Genesis 17:19). God fulfilled that promise, and Isaac was later born.

Some years pass, and we now arrive at the episode where God asked Abraham to sacrifice Isaac. Having read the backstory, you should quickly spot a problem: God promised that Abraham would bless the nations through the descendants of Isaac, but now God is asking Abraham to *kill* Isaac. We'll come back to this tension—*the key to understanding the whole passage*—after seeing how the story ends.

Despite the difficulty of the request, Abraham dutifully obeyed. He took two men and Isaac with him to the requested location. Abraham told the men to wait while he and Isaac went to "worship," and said *they* would return. When Isaac asked his father where the lamb was for the sacrifice, Abraham responded that God would provide it Himself. Upon arrival at the chosen location, Abraham laid Isaac on an altar he had built and took out his knife to kill his son. At that moment, an angel of the Lord called him to stop, saying, "Now I know that you fear God, seeing you have not withheld your son, your only son, from me" (Genesis 22:12). A ram appeared in a thicket nearby, and Abraham sacrificed the animal instead of Isaac.

Now we have the background needed to look at three key things we should take away from this admittedly difficult story. First, *Isaac was never actually sacrificed.* Obviously, God knew when He made the initial request that He would eventually provide a ram and would not allow Abraham to actually kill Isaac. If a human sacrifice was never God's intent, no one can claim this story shows God *approves* of such actions (especially given the prohibitions elsewhere). The most a person could suggest is that God was cruel to ask something so difficult when He had no intention of letting Abraham do it. But there *was* a good reason, as we'll see.

Second, God's purpose in this event was to *test Abraham's faith* (Genesis 22:1). As the ancestral father to the Israelites and, eventually, the Savior of the world, Abraham was to become one of the most important figures in God's plan for mankind. God wanted the man in this incredible position to demonstrate great faith. *The ultimate test of Abraham's faith in God's promises was to ask him to eliminate the only apparent possibility of those promises ever being fulfilled: Isaac.* If Abraham followed through, he would demonstrate his faith that God wouldn't break His promises—even if their fulfillment sounded impossible given what God was asking.

Last, Abraham passed the test with flying colors. Recall that Abraham told the men that both he *and* Isaac would return. The text doesn't say how Abraham thought that would happen, but clearly he believed

God would make a way. Also, when Isaac asked about the sacrifice, Abraham told Him God would provide it. Given the other details, there's no reason to believe he was simply lying to Isaac. Abraham believed God would provide a way. And God did.

The story of Abraham and Isaac in no way demonstrates that God condones human sacrifice—God never actually let the sacrifice happen. *Why* God would make the request can be hard to understand, but the answer becomes clearer when we consider the theological context of God's desire to test Abraham's faith in a major way.

Passages That Are *Descriptive* but Not *Prescriptive*

Much of the Bible is purely descriptive; it records events that happened historically, but not necessarily because God *approved* of them. That's why it's such poor scholarship when skeptics simply pluck a verse out of the Bible and suggest that God must support whatever the text describes. We'll look at two example cases in this category.

Child Sacrifices of Kings and the People

We are told King Ahaz of Judah "burned his son as an offering" (2 Kings 16:3). The Bible, however, in no way *condones* that action; to the contrary, the rest of the verse compares his sacrifice to the "despicable practices of the nations whom the LORD drove out before the people of Israel." Second Kings 21:6 says King Manasseh of Judah sacrificed his son as well. The text then states, "He did much evil in the sight of the Lord, provoking him to anger."

There are several other references to both Israelites and non-Israelites sacrificing children, but never with God's approval, and usually with an explicit condemnation (see 2 Kings 3:26-27; 17:17; 23:10; Psalm 106:37; Isaiah 57:5; Jeremiah 7:31). There's no doubt the practice was common in biblical times, but the fact that the Bible *describes* what happened says nothing about God *approving* of it.

Jepthah's Vow

Jepthah was one of Israel's judges (Judges 11:29-40). Prior to a battle with the Ammonites, Jepthah vowed that if God gave him victory, he would sacrifice the first thing to come out of his house when he returned. Jepthah won the battle, and when he arrived home, the first "thing" to come out was his own daughter. Jepthah was devastated, and sadly informed her that he could not take back his vow. His daughter only asked that she be allowed to go away with friends for two months to weep for her virginity. She then returned to her father and he "did with her according to his vow that he had made" (verse 39).

Christians have interpreted this passage in two different ways. Some believe that Jepthah only offered his daughter as a *living* sacrifice by dedicating her as a virgin for service at the sanctuary. If true, that would explain why she was mourning her (permanent) virginity and not the loss of her *life*. In this case, no human sacrifice was even made. Others, however, believe that Jepthah really did sacrifice his daughter, as the vow suggested. If true, this would be an example of human sacrifice in the Bible. However, the text never suggests that God *approved* of the vow. The passage simply describes what happened. In light of other verses clearly condemning human sacrifice, there's no reason to believe that this case was an exception.

Misinterpretations: No Human Sacrifice at All

Many of the passages skeptics use to demonstrate God's support of human sacrifice aren't about human sacrifice at all. They're misinterpretations. Let's look at three of them.

Consecration of Firstborn Males

In Exodus 13:2, God says, "Consecrate to me all the firstborn. Whatever is the first to open the womb among the people of Israel, both of man and of beast, is mine."

Skeptics assume this verse means God wanted the firstborn to be killed. The verse obviously doesn't say that, but if there was any question about the meaning of "consecrate," we can refer to God's further instructions in Exodus 13:12-13: "You shall set apart to the LORD all that first opens the womb. All the firstborn of your animals that are males shall be the LORD's...Every firstborn of man among your sons you shall redeem." Note the distinction here. Firstborn animals are to be the *Lord's* (sacrificed), but firstborn humans are to be *redeemed* (paid a fee for instead of physically sacrificed). Numbers 18:16 specifies the price: "Their redemption price (at a month old you shall redeem them) you shall fix at five shekels in silver." When you look at the full context of Exodus 13:2, it's evident God wasn't requesting human sacrifice.

A Judicial Execution

In Joshua 7:15, God said, "He who is taken with the devoted things shall be burned with fire, he and all that he has, because he has transgressed the covenant of the LORD, and because he has done an outrageous thing in Israel." The context for this was the destruction of Jericho in Joshua 6 (see chapter 3). God told the Israelites to keep nothing that had been "devoted to destruction" (verse 18). But one man, Achan, disobeyed and kept some of the plunder. In accordance with God's warning, Achan was put to death. Importantly, Joshua 7:25-26 makes clear what God meant when He said a person would be "burned with fire"—Achan was stoned to death, then his body was burned. This was a judicial execution, not a human sacrifice.

Jesus' Death on the Cross

Jesus' death on the cross is frequently cited as a prime example of how God violated His commandments by sacrificing His own Son. Because Jesus' death was addressed in chapter 20, I won't repeat the discussion here. But the most important takeaway for this subject is that God, Jesus, and the Holy Spirit are three persons in one. God didn't sacrifice a "third party" human; He sacrificed *Himself.* This is not comparable to the types of human sacrifice seen in the Bible.

The Bible Clearly Condemns Human Sacrifice

There's no question the Bible explicitly condemns human sacrifice. When skeptics point to verses that supposedly contradict that condemnation, they're either looking at passages that are only *descriptive* of human sacrifice or are misinterpreting passages that don't speak to human sacrifice at all. In the unique case of God asking Abraham to sacrifice Isaac, God knew He wouldn't allow it to happen, so it can't be suggested that this event shows God approves of human sacrifice. The question of *why* God would ask such a thing in the first place is technically irrelevant for this particular discussion, but can be understood theologically in light of God's desire to test Abraham's faith.

PART 5:

Conversations About
SCIENCE

33. Why do Christians have varying views on how and when God created the world?

When our twins were three, my husband and I decided it was time to start working on developing their faith beyond singing "Jesus Loves Me" each night. We had no idea what to do, so we started like most Christian parents: We proceeded to the local bookstore and returned home proudly wielding our first children's Bible, complete with all the drawings of happy children and fuzzy sheep you could ever want.

That night, I dutifully opened their Bible to the creation account. I began to read.

"...God created the world in seven days. On the first day..."

I was interrupted by an outbreak of giggles from my daughter.

"MOMMY! God didn't *really* create the world in seven days, did He?"

Pause. I replied, "Well, um, the Bible says God created the world in seven days. Days may have been longer for Him than for us. We're not sure."

That was the best I could do. The extent of my knowledge on the topic was that the Bible said God created the world in seven days, and that some people think those days may have been longer than a twenty-four-hour period.

My daughter's response planted a small "to do" note in the back of my mind: Get up to speed on all that creation and evolution stuff.

Later that year, my husband and I joined a small group at our church. In one of the sessions, we were discussing the co-existence of faith and doubt. Our group leader admitted, "I have doubts too some-times—like what about the dinosaurs?" I chuckled and nodded as if I totally understood, taking the cues from everyone else in the room. In reality, I was thinking, *What* about *the dinosaurs?* I knew there was something controversial about them as it related to the Bible, but only from vague allusions I had heard over time.

I updated my mental note: Get up to speed on all that creation and evolution stuff...and find out what the dinosaur issue is.

A couple months later, I was pondering what reading material to take on a family vacation. My mental note suddenly surfaced and I somewhat grudgingly decided it was time to read a book on creation and evolution views. Doing that at a hotel pool somehow made the task seem more palatable.

One book. That was the plan.

In the weeks that followed, I ended up reading 16 books and countless articles on creation and evolution—literally thousands of pages.

The Heated Debate…Amongst Christians

When I set out on my reading journey, I thought I was going to learn about two views: the Christian view (based on Genesis) and the non-Christian view (based on evolution). I ended up on a reading spree after I learned that *Christians* have different views on how and when God created the world. I was surprised to learn it's actually a very heated debate.

So what are all those views? The one you're probably most familiar with is called *young-Earth creationism*—the belief that God created the Earth in six 24-hour periods about 6000-10,000 years ago. (You may not have associated a specific age of the Earth with a belief in six 24-hour creation days, but the two beliefs go hand-in-hand for reasons I'll explain in the next chapter.) Some Christians reject the young-Earth view because mainstream scientists from multiple fields estimate that the Earth is far older: 4.5 *billion* years older.[1] *Old-Earth creationism* is the belief that the scientific evidence for an Earth that is billions (not thousands) of years old is overwhelming and should be accepted by Christians. Old-Earth creationists say that a closer analysis of Scripture demonstrates that the Bible does not require a young-Earth interpretation.

While old-Earth and young-Earth creationists disagree about the age of the Earth, they agree that God created humans directly, rather than through evolution. There is a third view amongst Christians, however, that accepts evolution as God's creative process: *theistic evolution*. Theistic evolutionists differ on how they reconcile evolution with the Bible, but they often believe that the Holy Spirit accommodated the ancient biblical writers by working within their limited scientific understanding to communicate spiritual truths.

Finally, there is the theory of intelligent design. Christians often mistakenly assume intelligent design refers to a belief that the Christian God created the universe as described in Genesis. The theory of intelligent design, however, only says that "life, or the universe, cannot have arisen by chance and was designed and created by some intelligent entity."[2] Scientists who advocate intelligent design don't specify who or what the intelligent agent is, but state that some features of the universe and of living things are better explained by an intelligent cause than by the undirected natural process of evolution. That means intelligent design is *compatible* with Christianity, but it's not a comprehensive Christian view because it doesn't address the identity of the designer or how that identity relates to any particular religious book.

I know that's a lot to keep straight! On the next page is a diagram I created to help you visualize how all these views relate to one another. In the remaining chapters of the book, we'll look at young-Earth and old-Earth creationism in order to understand the scriptural and scientific case for each view. In addition, we'll look at naturalistic evolution to understand what exactly it is, the scientific evidence for it, and the scientific challenges against it. We'll end with a look at intelligent design.

As you read these chapters, it's important to not lose sight of the big picture. While Christians do disagree over questions of the Earth's age and God's method of creation, they agree on the most important question of all: that the universe is the work of a personal God. This is in stark contrast to the view of naturalistic evolutionists, who claim that the universe is the result of blind and undirected natural causes. That's really the heart of the origins battle: *Is the universe the product of an intelligent mind or of noncognitive forces?* Framing the debate in this way can give your kids a much-needed clarifying lens through which to explore all of these views.

Views on Origins

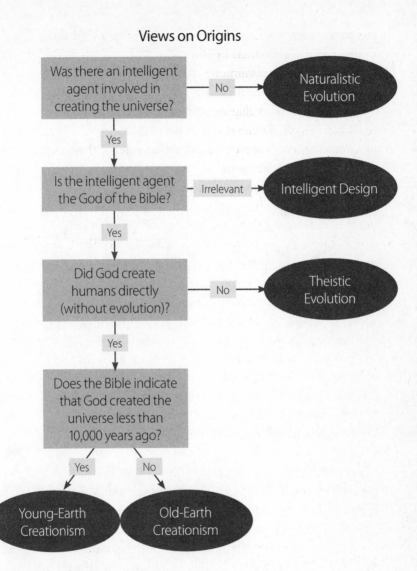

Why Should You Care?

Perhaps right now you're like I was when my daughter first asked me about Genesis: vaguely aware there are differences in beliefs but frankly pretty uninterested in the topic. Or perhaps you've studied the different views and aren't sure what to make of them all. Or perhaps you passionately hold to one particular view already. Whatever you're thinking as you arrive here, I want to assure you of this: Your kids desperately need you to invest time in understanding and discussing *all* of these views. *Don't skip this section.*

I very often receive emails from blog readers whose teenage children recently announced they no longer believe in God. And I can't think of a *single one* that did not cite scientific arguments as the primary reason. Here's a recent example:

> My son is 18 and just announced that he no longer believes in God. We brought both of our children up in church, and he alone made the choice to be saved and baptized. When he got older, he started hanging out with several kids who were atheists. He started changing his views on religion. I fought back with truth but felt like I was in a fight I couldn't win. I was defeated by all the scientific arguments I couldn't answer. I need stronger knowledge for the fight yet before me.

The science involved in the origins debate is very frequently the sole dividing line between Christian faith and atheism—for kids and adults alike. Whether in a public middle/high school, a secular university, or everyday life as an adult, our kids *will* eventually hear that evolution is simply a fact and that the Earth is unquestionably billions of years old. Our kids will also hear that those statements are irreconcilable with the Bible (in reality, some Christians would agree and some would not). Therein lies the question of the day: What will *your* kids do when they encounter these claims?

If you never take the opportunity to guide your kids through detailed views on creation and evolution, they'll eventually be entering some of the most difficult waters of Christianity without knowing how to swim—and when that happens, they'll likely be hit by tidal waves of challenges before they even realize their faith is struggling for air.

If you oversimplify the issue by teaching your kids that "you either believe the Bible or you don't," it's like suggesting that swimming in the tidal wave is as easy as moving your arms in a few circles. None of us would risk our kids *physically* falling into turbulent waters with such inadequate instruction. Why would we risk the spiritual equivalent?

I don't say these things to create fear, but rather give a sense of purpose and urgency. You can be certain that your kids won't learn about Christian views in a secular educational environment. You can be equally certain that they won't learn much about them at church; it's estimated that only a third of pastors teach on the subject more than once a year.[3] If your kids are going to be equipped to swim with confidence, that preparation will need to come from *you*.

Though this topic can fill thousands of pages, the following chapters will briefly highlight the most critical points and implications of the debate. *I will not be advocating any one view; my objective is to present the case each view makes for itself.*

Are you ready for some fascinating scriptural and scientific discussion about the origins of our Earth? Of course you are! You might not think so, but you just might get sucked in like I did while I was on vacation. You'll see the discussion is actually quite interesting. Most of all, it's hugely important for Christians today. We'll start with young-Earth creationism, the view you're probably already most familiar with.

34. What is young-Earth creationism?

Young-Earth creationism is the view that God created the Earth over six 24-hour days about 6000-10,000 years ago. This view is labeled *young-Earth* to contrast it with the mainstream scientific consensus that the Earth is 4.5 billion years old.

Gallup polls show that the young-Earth creationism view is held by more Americans than any other (42 percent).[1] A key reason the majority of Christians believe in six 24-hour days of creation (whether they've studied the controversy or not) is that this is what the most *obvious* reading of Genesis points to; it's what a reader most naturally understands the text to mean. When you read the following chapters on other views, I won't be surprising you with little-known verses that scream, "This whole creation thing happened over billions of years!" Christians of every view acknowledge that there is one obvious way to read Genesis, but they disagree over whether the *obvious* reading is the *right* reading based on other scriptural and scientific considerations.

For Christian kids today, it's not as straightforward as it sounds to simply accept the most obvious reading and blithely continue on with faith. They will encounter scientific challenges to a young-Earth belief when studying multiple school subjects: The fields of astronomy, geology, paleontology, biology, and archaeology *all* assume an old Earth. Kids who simply have a "default" young-Earth belief without a deeper understanding of the scriptural and scientific points involved may well be headed for an eventual faith crisis when confronted with conflicting claims from multiple sides. A blog reader named Shannon found herself in exactly that situation and shared her experience with me:

> As a student in public high school, I took a course in anthropology. Our teacher decided we should have a debate on creationism versus evolution. Being an outspoken Christian, I was nominated to debate the [young-Earth] creationism side. Having little to no understanding of the subject myself (I had never put much thought into the topic other than accepting what I had been taught as a child), I attempted valiantly to argue for a literal six-day creation. The other side crushed me, and I felt the full brunt of shame for not being able to defend myself or my views, deeply held as they were. To me, this was more than disheartening. It was a seminal moment in my life. It led me to question many of my previously deeply held beliefs, and I nearly walked away from my faith entirely over the course of the next year.

In this chapter, we'll look at four key pillars of the *biblical* case made by young-Earth creationists: (1) Genesis clearly states that God created everything in six 24-hour periods; (2) the age of the Earth can and should be calculated based on biblical genealogies and chronologies; (3) Noah's flood was a global event and was responsible for creating the Earth's geological features; and (4) belief in an old Earth undermines the entire gospel message. In the next chapter, we'll consider the *scientific* implications of the young-Earth view.

1. Genesis clearly states that God created everything in six 24-hour periods.

The word translated "day" in the Old Testament Hebrew text is *yom*. Just like the English word *day*, *yom* can mean different things in different contexts. For example, it can refer to daylight, a 24-hour period, or an indefinite amount of time (as in the expression "back in the day"). *Yom* is used 1704 times in the Old Testament and overwhelmingly refers to a 24-hour period.[2] Even so, context must be considered when determining how to understand the term. Young-Earth creationists make the following key points to show why the specific context of Genesis 1 requires a literal 24-hour day reading:

- Genesis 1:5 says, "God called the light Day, and the darkness he called Night. And there was evening and there was morning, the first day." This seems to explicitly define the first day as a period of day and night—a normal 24-hour timeframe.

- After the description of each of the first six days in the creation week, Genesis says there was "evening and morning"—the first, second, etc. day. One evening and one morning implies a single day had passed.

- Whenever *yom* is used in the Old Testament with either a cardinal number ("day 1") or an ordinal number ("first day"), it always means a 24-hour period. *Yom* is used with a cardinal number on the first day of creation and with ordinal numbers on days two through six.

In addition, young-Earth creationists point to scriptures outside of Genesis that they say imply a creation week of 24-hour days:

- Exodus 20:11 says, "In six days the LORD made heaven and earth, the sea, and all that is in them, and rested on the seventh day. Therefore the LORD blessed the Sabbath day and made it holy." (Similarly, see Exodus 31:17.)

- In Mark 10:6, Jesus said, "From the beginning of creation, 'God made them male and female.'" Young-Earth creationists say this shows humans existed from the beginning of Earth's "creation," not starting billions of years later (mainstream science says that billions of years passed between the formation of the Earth and the appearance of humans).

- In Luke 11:45-52, Jesus rebuked the scribes of the Pharisees, saying that "the blood of all the prophets, shed from the foundation of the world, may be charged against this generation, from the blood of Abel to the blood of Zechariah" (verse 50). Young-Earth creationists say this places the murder of Abel near the foundation of the entire world (again, not billions of years after the world was formed).

Young-Earth creationists believe that these collective points make a definitive case for reading the days of Genesis as six 24-hour periods.

2. The age of the Earth can and should be calculated based on biblical genealogies and chronologies.

The Bible never explicitly gives a year when God created the Earth. However, young-Earth creationists calculate an estimated age of the Earth by pulling together information from various scriptures. Though Bible scholars arrive at different numbers depending on the method used, they typically calculate that the Earth is between 6000-10,000 years old.

Here's a very simplified overview of how one estimate was calculated.[3] Don't worry about memorizing the details; just get a feel for the nature of the approach.

Step 1—Dating to the Exodus: Archaeologists have dated the death of Israel's King Ahab to about 852 BC. King Solomon's reign can be backed into from that date based on 1 Kings 11:42. It was 480 years before Solomon's fourth year of reign that Moses brought the Israelites out of Egypt (1 Kings 6:1). This places the Exodus about 1446 BC.

Step 2—Dating from the Exodus back to Abraham: Using biblical information on the years the Israelites were in Egypt, and the ages of each of the patriarchs when their children were born, a birth date of 1951 BC can be calculated for Abraham.

Step 3—Dating from Abraham back to Adam: Genesis 5 provides a detailed genealogy and list of ages from Adam to Noah. Genesis 11 provides similar information from Noah's son Shem to Abraham's father Terah. Based on this information, there were 2130 total years between Adam and Abraham. Adding 2130 years to Abraham's estimated birth date (from Step 2) results in a creation date of about 4081 BC. That leads to the determination that the world was created about 6000 years ago (4081 plus the current year).

First and foremost, young-Earth creationists estimate the age of the Earth using a biblical analysis like the one described here. That said, there are several organizations dedicated to scientific research in support of a recent creation. This research is referred to as *creation science* or *scientific creationism*. We'll look at creation science further in the next chapter.

3. Noah's flood was a global event and was responsible for creating the Earth's geological features.

Young-Earth creationists say the Bible clearly describes a *global* flood in Genesis 6–9. The reason this requires mention is that mainstream scientists say there is no evidence of a worldwide flood, and most old-Earth creationists accept that consensus. They believe Noah's flood must have been local in nature and interpret the Bible's flood account accordingly.[4] However, belief in a global flood is a scientifically necessary part of the young-Earth view. Here's why.

When mainstream scientists date the Earth, they assume that the natural laws and processes we see at work today are the same ones that have always been in operation (this is called *uniformitarianism*). For example, we know that water can break down rock little by little. To break down enough rocks to create a whole canyon at that rate would take millions of years. The scientific consensus is that the sheer existence of formations like mountains and canyons—geological features that are believed to have formed from the very slow processes we see today—demonstrates that the Earth is at least millions of years old.

This requires young-Earth creationists to answer an important question: What, other than vast periods of time, could have shaped the Earth like this? Young-Earth creationists answer that the catastrophic consequences of a global flood from the time of Noah can and do account for most of the Earth's physical structure (this is called *catastrophism*). That's why belief in a global flood is a necessary part of the young-Earth view: Something more catastrophic than the processes we see today had to have happened in order for the Earth to have these geological features and at the same time be less than 10,000 years old. Young-Earth scientists dedicate much of their research to developing models accordingly.

4. Belief in an old Earth undermines the entire gospel message.

If Christians simply disagreed over the age of the Earth, with no theological implications, this debate would be far less heated. But here's where the temperature rises: Young-Earth creationists say the theological implications of believing in an old Earth are problematic enough to undermine *the entire gospel message*.

The heart of the issue is whether, theologically speaking, there could have been death before Adam and Eve first sinned. In Genesis 2:17, God told Adam that he would "surely die" if he ate from the tree of the knowledge of good and evil. In Genesis 3, Adam and Eve ate from that tree. Young-Earth creationists believe it was at that moment that all death entered the world. However, the mainstream scientific interpretation of fossil evidence says that animal death, disease, suffering, and carnivorous eating existed for millions of years *before* humans arrived on Earth. The implication of an old-Earth view is that *God allowed death, disease, and suffering before Adam sinned*.

To emphasize the biblical case for the belief that all death must have entered the world through sin, young-Earth creationists often point to Romans 5:12: "Just as sin came into the world through one man, and death through sin, and so death spread to all men because all sinned." They also cite Romans 8:19-20 to stress that it wasn't just *human* death that entered the world after Adam sinned: "The creation waits with eager longing for the revealing of the sons of God. For the creation was subjected to futility, not willingly, but because of him who subjected it." And, last, young-Earth creationists say both humans and animals were vegetarian before the flood (Genesis 1:29-30).[5] If so, animals couldn't have eaten each other for millions of years prior.

An article published by *Creation Ministries International* summarizes why young-Earth creationists believe this has such significant implications for the entire gospel message:

> A central part of the Gospel is that death is the last enemy to be destroyed (1 Corinthians 15:26). Death intruded into a perfect world because of sin, and it is so serious that Jesus' victory over death cannot be entirely manifested while there is a single believer in the grave. Are we expected to believe that something the Bible authors described as an enemy was used or overseen by God for millions of years and was called "very good"?[6]

Young-Earth creationists clearly answer that question, "No."

Age of the Earth: No Small Thing

Ken Ham, president of the young-Earth organization Answers in Genesis, says, "Not to take Genesis 1 through 11 literally is to do violence to the rest of Scripture."[7] With such significant potential implications, why are there Christians who reject the young-Earth view? They believe the scientific evidence for an old Earth is undeniable. Let's look at that evidence now.

35. How do mainstream scientists estimate the age of the Earth?

In the last chapter, we looked at the biblical case for young-Earth creationism. A core tenet of young-Earth creationism is that the Earth is thousands of years old—not billions, as the mainstream scientific consensus states. Since the mainstream scientific dating of the Earth is the heated dividing line between young-Earth and old-Earth creationism (and is what will be presented as fact when your kids study astronomy, anthropology, geology, paleontology, biology, and/or archaeology), it's important to understand the basics of it.

In this chapter, we'll look at six methods scientists use to date the Earth and universe. While there are additional dating methods, I've selected the ones that are most frequently discussed at a popular level. One important thing to note about these dating methods is that they aren't all used to estimate the actual age of the Earth. Rather, some methods produce *minimum* ages for the Earth. For example, you'll see that scientists have estimated some tree areas are more than 11,000 years old. This doesn't directly date the whole Earth, since the Earth isn't necessarily the same age as its trees. But mainstream scientists use that information to show that the Earth must be *at least* that old in order to have those trees on it.

All of the methods discussed in this chapter date the Earth to at least 10,000 years old according to the mainstream scientific interpretation. This is significant in the age of the Earth debate because young-Earth creationists usually say the Earth is *at most* 10,000 years old. Young-Earth creation organizations conduct scientific research to respond to the old-Earth claims and to demonstrate the scientific plausibility of a (relatively) recent creation. As such, I've also included a brief explanation of the young-Earth scientists' response to each dating method.

We'll start with an example that mainstream scientists say dates the Earth to at least 10,000 years old and work our way up to a method they say dates the Earth to 4.5 billion years old. Finally, we'll move beyond the Earth and look at how mainstream scientists date the entire *universe* to 13.8 billion years old.

Methods Used to Date the Earth
Tree-Ring Dating

You probably remember from childhood that if you cut down a tree and count the rings on the inside, you can figure out how old it is (each ring represents one year of growth). Some of the oldest trees in the world are the Bristlecone Pines that live in the White Mountains of California. *Methuselah* is a living tree there that's estimated to be nearly 4800 years old based on samples taken from it. The thickness of tree rings can vary depending on annual weather conditions, so scientists also match the unique ring patterns of living and dead trees in a given area to calculate combined ages.[1] Using this technique, scientists have created area timelines going back 11,000 years.

What young-Earth creationists say: Trees have been shown to sometimes grow more than one ring per year. Assigning just one ring to every year, therefore, can overestimate a tree's age. The fact that there are no *living* trees with rings showing a significantly greater age than the estimated young-Earth creationist flood date (4500 years ago) is evidence for a global flood that destroyed creation. God also may have created trees with the rings already in place, just as He created Adam as a mature adult. [2/3] (This is called the *Appearance of Age Theory*.) In that case, the rings already present at creation would not actually represent years in existence.

Ice-Core Dating

Similar to how trees add a ring layer for each year they live, there are other layering processes on Earth that scientists use to measure time. Because those processes are ongoing today, scientists measure how fast they happen in an attempt to calculate the implied amount of time that's passed since those processes began.

One example of this is counting the layers in the ice that has accumulated in the polar regions. Scientists drill deep into the ice to remove sections called *cores* and study the layers. Upper layers of ice are more easily distinguishable from one another than deeper layers because the deeper layers compress due to the weight of all the ice on top of them. Scientists can visually count the upper layers, but they have to estimate the (indistinguishable) number of deep layers by modeling accumulation rates and ice flow. Using these techniques, they've estimated there are as many as 800,000 continuous layers of ice in Antarctica (implying the Earth is at least a few hundred thousand years old if layers were formed at a constant rate).

What young-Earth creationists say: Geological models developed by young-Earth creationists place the Ice Age around 2250 BC—after Noah's flood.[4/5] They say a post-flood rapid Ice Age (about 700 years long) would cause very thick annual layers of ice to form, which is what we now see at the bottom of the cores. The thinner annual layers on top represent the lower levels of snowfall we see today.[6]

Varve Dating

The bottoms of some lakes have yearly layers as well, called *varves.* They appear as light and dark bands that are deposited during different seasons of the year. In the Green River geologic formation in the western United States, scientists have counted up to six million varves (implying the Earth is at least millions of years old if the layers formed at a constant rate).[7/8]

What young-Earth creationists say: Catastrophic events can cause multiple varve-like layers to form in a short time. Noah's flood and/or a rapid post-flood Ice Age could have resulted in the quick formation of such varve-like layers.[9]

Radiometric Dating

The most important method used for dating the Earth is something called *radiometric dating.* The details of this method are rather technical, but given its importance, it's worth understanding the following basics.

All physical matter is composed of atoms. Atoms are defined by the number of protons they have; for example, hydrogen is an atom with one proton, helium is an atom with two protons, etc. The number of neutrons in an atom is usually the same as the number of protons, but sometimes there are extra neutrons that add weight to the atom. Different weight versions of the same atom are called *isotopes.* For example, a carbon atom usually has six protons and six neutrons, but if it has two extra neutrons in the nucleus, it's an *isotope* called carbon-14. Some isotopes, like carbon-14, are *unstable* because of their extra weight and go through a *radioactive decay process* to stabilize. The end result is a stable atom, but a different chemical element—for example, carbon-14 decays into nitrogen.

This decay process happens at a fixed rate that acts like a clock. Scientists can use that clock—from isotopes found inside of things like rocks and fossils—to estimate an object's age based on how long the decay process has been underway. (It might help to think of a car: If you know where it started, where it is now, and the rate at which it's moving, you can figure out how much time has passed since it began traveling.)

Carbon-14 is one of the most well-known unstable isotopes (you may have heard of "carbon-14 dating"). It's of limited use for dating the Earth, however, because it decays relatively quickly and is only found in previously living things like animals or trees. Several other radioactive isotopes are more useful for dating the Earth because they can be used to date rocks and have much longer decay rates. Uranium-235 decaying into lead-207 is one example. Using this method, scientists have dated rocks on the Earth to be billions of years old. Nearly all meteorites—rocks from the solar system that have fallen to Earth—have a similar radiometric age of 4.56 billion years old.[10]

What young-Earth creationists say: Three critical assumptions affect radiometric dating: (1) That the initial conditions of the rock sample are accurately known; (2) that the amount of the original isotope and the element into which it's decaying haven't been changed by processes other than radioactive decay; and (3) that the decay rate has remained constant since the rock was formed.[11] It's assumption (3) that young-Earth science models most frequently challenge. Young-Earth scientists say that assuming a constant radioactive decay rate ignores the possible impact of God's curse (Genesis 3:17-18) or Noah's flood (young-Earth models often suggest God may have triggered the flood by causing a drastic change in radioactive decay rates). In addition, young-Earth scientists say radiometric dating on rocks of *known* ages has shown that this dating method doesn't always work, so it shouldn't be trusted as readily as it is.

Methods Used to Date Other Galaxies and the Universe

So far, this chapter has focused on calculating the age of the *Earth*. But astronomers also to calculate the ages of galaxies and the universe. Here are two key methods they use.

Distant Starlight

The sun is about 93 million miles from the Earth. Light travels at 186,000 miles per second, so it takes about 8 minutes for light from the sun to reach the Earth. In other words, the light we see right now left the sun 8 minutes ago. Because the distances in space are so great, scientists use the speed of light to measure them. For example, scientists say the sun is 8 light-minutes away. Distances to objects farther away, such as galaxies, are measured in light *years*. *We can see light from galaxies that are billions of light years away.* That implies enough time must have passed to allow light to travel that far—billions of years.

What young-Earth creationists say: The mainstream scientific measurements of distances to other galaxies are based on sound methodology. There is also good reason to believe the speed of light has not changed over time (this would impact many other areas of physics).[12] Young-Earth scientists therefore usually respond in one of two ways: (1) God could have created light already in transit (similar to how Adam was created as a mature adult); or (2) because the rate at which time itself flows is not constant (a fact called *time dilation*), light that would presumably take billions of years to reach the Earth, as measured by clocks in deep space, could reach the Earth in only thousands of years as measured by clocks here.[13]

Expansion of the Universe

Recall from chapter 1 that the universe is expanding. The rate of expansion and the average distance between galaxies can be used to estimate how long the universe has been expanding from its beginning to its current size. This methodology estimates that the universe is 13.8 billion years old.[14]

What young-Earth creationists say: The Bible suggests that God stretched out the heavens (Job 9:8; Isaiah 40:22), so it's reasonable to believe the universe could be larger now than when it was first created. If God supernaturally stretched out the heavens, we cannot assume the universe has always been expanding at the same rate.[15]

Be Sure to Know Both Sides of the Issue

It's important to understand that this exceedingly brief scientific overview barely scratches the surface of the discussion. For any one of these dating methods, you can find endless back-and-forth articles and books by young-Earth and old-Earth proponents.[16] So consider this a jumping-off point for your own research, and be sure to read both perspectives on a given subject. Your knowledge and ability to discuss the complexity of these issues with your kids will be infinitely more valuable when you have a well-rounded understanding of them.

The Christians who accept the mainstream scientific consensus on the age of the Earth go on to make a *biblical* case in support of it (again, this is called *old-Earth creationism*). To that case we now turn.

36. What is old-Earth creationism?

I love steak. (There's a reason I'm telling you this, I promise.) I can only eat steak, however, when it's cooked to the point of leathery perfection—totally brown and dry on the inside. This annoys my husband to no end. As the master of our grill, he prides himself on being able to deliver a moist piece of meat with a perfect layer of pink inside. For a long time, he refused to accept that I don't want a pink steak. He would grill a steak, I would find the pink, and he would solemnly return to the grill to cook it longer. My grilling requirements have caused their fair share of remarkably boring arguments in our house.

Then we discovered the amazing Thermapen—a professional meat thermometer. Oh, sure, we had tried thermometers before, but they had never been consistently reliable. With the Thermapen, however, my husband could simply wait for 170 degrees to register on the display and know I would be happy.

This worked for several months. Then one day I cut a steak open and it looked almost rare despite the 170-degree reading. I handed the steak back to my husband. He stuck the thermometer in again, demonstrated that it indeed said 170 degrees, and confidently replied, "Nope, it's well-done. Take it." (Insert one of those remarkably boring arguments here.)

There were only three possibilities that could explain what had happened: (1) The thermometer was in error and the steak *really was rare*; (2) the thermometer was *not* in error, but my husband was *using* it wrong and the steak really was rare; or (3) the thermometer was not in error, my husband was using it correctly, and the steak was actually well-done.

In a way, the disagreement between young-Earth and old-Earth creationists is like this steak debate—the thermometer is like the Bible and the steak is like the Earth. *Both young-Earth and old-Earth creationists agree that the thermometer—the Bible—is not in error.* But they disagree on whether you can use it in more than one way.

Old-Earth creationists believe the breadth and depth of scientific evidence introduced in the last chapter is sufficient for knowing the Earth is old. They're saying, in essence, "This steak is definitely rare! We know the thermometer is never *wrong*, but since it's saying 170-degrees when we use it like this, we know we're not using it the right way." Young-Earth creationists are saying, "The thermometer is never wrong, and there's one clear way to use it, so whatever the thermometer says is correct—regardless of what anyone thinks by looking at the steak alone."

In this chapter, we'll look at three key points old-Earth creationists make in developing a biblical case to support their view: (1) The most obvious reading of some biblical passages is not necessarily the right reading; (2) a more precise understanding of the biblical text points to many clues that Genesis was not intended to be read as an account of creation in six 24-hour days; and (3) accepting the mainstream scientific consensus that animals died for millions of years before humans existed poses no theological difficulties for Christians (see chapter 34 for context).

Now let's get to the meat of things (sorry, I couldn't resist).

1. The most obvious reading of some biblical passages is not necessarily the right reading.

While young-Earth creationists emphasize how clearly Genesis speaks of 24-hour creation days, old-Earth creationists emphasize that the most obvious reading is not necessarily the right reading. David Snoke, in his book *A Biblical Case for an Old Earth*, uses what Jesus said in Matthew 16:28 as an example of this point: "Truly, I say to you, there are some standing here who will not taste death until they see the Son of Man coming in his kingdom."[1] The most obvious reading of this passage suggests that Jesus was going to return to judge the world within that generation. Snoke notes that we don't believe that's what Jesus actually meant because our experience—that Jesus has not returned yet—tells us otherwise. We therefore accept a *possible* alternative reading over the more obvious one. (This verse has been most commonly interpreted as predicting Jesus' transfiguration, His resurrection, or the destruction of the temple in AD 70.) Snoke concludes:

> In the case of the early return of Christ, if we insist on a rigid rule of the "most obvious" interpretation, we can cause people, including our children, to give up on the Bible, or reject Christianity outright as they lay what seems to be the most obvious interpretation alongside their experience.

Old-Earth creationists say our scientific "experience" should lead Christians to an admittedly less obvious but reasonable interpretation of Genesis. They do, however, differ on how exactly they interpret what the Bible says. The most common two views are the *Day-Age Theory* (sometimes called *Progressive Creationism*) and the *Framework Theory*.[2] Proponents of the *Day-Age Theory* believe that each creation day in Genesis 1 represents long periods of time, but that the days are chronologically accurate. This is the view promoted by the leading old-Earth organization, Reasons to Believe.[3] Proponents of the *Framework Theory* believe Genesis 1 is poetic in nature and doesn't intend to present a chronology of creation. The cases for these specific interpretations are very different and won't be covered here. For purposes of this chapter, we're focusing on what unifies them under the old-Earth creationism umbrella.

2. A more precise understanding of the biblical text points to many clues that Genesis was not intended to be read as an account of creation in six 24-hour days.

It's one thing to point out that it's possible to interpret biblical passages in more than one way. It's another thing to actually provide a positive case for a specific interpretation. Old-Earth creationists say that a more precise understanding of the text (for example, word definitions in the original language, grammatical context, cultural context, theological context, and the intended audiences) shows Genesis was actually not meant to be read as an account of creation in six 24-hour days.[4] Here are their key points.

- As discussed in chapter 34, the Hebrew word translated "day" (*yom*) has several possible meanings—daylight, a 24-hour period, or an indefinite amount of time. Old-Earth creationists say days aren't *necessarily* 24-hour periods, so looking at other clues from the context and from other scriptures becomes the key to a correct understanding (read on).

- Recall that young-Earth creationists say the phrasing "there was evening and morning, the X day" implies that *yom* means 24-hour days. Old-Earth creationists reply that if the sun was not created until day four, there could not have been an actual sunrise and sunset on the first three days—yet Genesis speaks of evening and morning starting on day one. They conclude that the words for evening and morning only mark the beginning and ending of each creative *period*, and they point out that morning and evening are used figuratively in Psalm 30:5, Psalm 49:14-15, and Psalm 90:6.[5]

- Old-Earth creationists believe that several Bible verses suggest God's Sabbath rest (day seven of the creation week) has not ended (Psalm 95:7-11; John 5:16-18; Hebrews 4:1-11). If God's "day" of rest is ongoing, it suggests the other days of Genesis 1 aren't meant to be read as 24-hour periods either.

- Old-Earth creationists say there is too much activity implied in the events of creation day six for it to be a 24-hour day. They especially question how Adam could have named all the animals God brought to him in that time (Genesis 2:19). Even a very conservative estimate of 2500 "kinds" of animals at creation would mean naming more than 100 animals per hour.[6/7]

- Recall that young-Earth creationists say the fact we are to work six (24-hour) days and rest on the seventh is evidence that God's creative days must have been 24-hour periods too (Exodus 20:8-11). Old-Earth creationists reply that Sabbath rest was also required for the land in the seventh *year* (Leviticus 25). They say this shows God applied the *pattern* of the creation week to His laws, not the *duration* of the days in the creation week.

Finally, let's look at what old-Earth creationists say about the question of animal death before human sin (the heated issue discussed in chapter 34).

3. Accepting the mainstream scientific consensus that animals died for millions of years before humans existed poses no theological difficulties for Christians.

Recall that young-Earth creationists believe the Bible clearly says *all* death entered the world at the time of Adam's sin. They say the old-Earth view undermines the entire gospel message because the mainstream interpretation of the fossil record is that animals died for millions of years *before* Adam's sin took place.

Old-Earth creationists reply that the Bible only indicates *human* death entered the world due to sin, and therefore the theological difficulties with animals dying for millions of years prior to humans are eliminated. Here are the key points old-Earth creationists make:

- In Genesis 2:17, God said to Adam (regarding the tree of the knowledge of good and evil), "In the day that you eat of it you shall surely die." Old-Earth creationists say this suggests Adam already knew what death was (presumably from the animals around him).

- God created the "beasts of the earth" on day six of creation (Genesis 1:24-25). The Hebrew word used to describe them (*chayah*) most often refers to carnivores in other biblical contexts.[8] If God created carnivores on day six, that would mean God's design for animals included death.

- While young-Earth creationists don't believe God would have called his creation "very good" if it included millions of years of animal death, old-Earth creationists say that's an unnecessary conclusion. An article published by Reasons to Believe explains:

  > We must be careful not to put too much weight on our ideas of what "good" means. The Bible does not tell us the creation was perfect. The Hebrew word for good, *towb*, connotes a practical or economic benefit. Thus, the creation was "very good" for achieving God's goals for mankind—namely, to allow rational, morally free agents to come into existence and make free choices to love, obey and be in relationship with Him. Animal death in no way conflicts with that goal.[9]

- Recall that young-Earth creationists say Romans 5:12 shows all death entered the world because of sin ("Just as sin came into the world through one man, and death through sin, and so death spread to all men because all sinned"). Old-Earth creationists use this same verse to say the Bible makes it clear that death spread specifically *to all men* (not all men and animals) because of sin.

- First Corinthians 15:21-22 says, "As by a man came death, by a man has come also the resurrection of the dead. For as in Adam all die, so also in Christ shall all be made alive." Old-Earth creationists say that because the "all" who will be made alive are humans, the corresponding "all" who die in Adam must be humans too.

Old-Earth creationists say these points show the Bible never says animal death entered the world due to sin. Therefore, they believe that accepting the mainstream scientific interpretation of the fossil record poses no theological difficulties for Christians.

Everyone Is Concerned for the Gospel

Just as young-Earth creationists believe that unnecessarily accepting an *old* Earth has dire consequences for the gospel, old-Earth creationists believe that unnecessarily accepting a *young* Earth has dire consequences for the gospel. Old-Earth creationists believe the scientific evidence is so undeniable that promoting a young-Earth view unnecessarily subjects Christianity to ridicule. In *Seven Days that Divide the World: The Beginning According to Genesis and Science*, old-Earth creationist John C. Lennox comments (regarding the young-Earth view):

> …If my views on something not fundamental to the gospel, on which equally convinced Christians disagree, attract ridicule and therefore disincline my hearers to listen to anything I have to say about the Christian message, then I should be prepared to entertain the possibility that it might be my interpretation that is at fault.[10]

While much separates their interpretation of science and the Bible, there is one major thing young-Earth and old-Earth creationists agree on: God created humans directly, *not* as the end result of evolution. Let's now look at what exactly *evolution* is.

37. What is evolution?

My son and I were sitting at the car wash one day when he started to get impatient with the long wait. I'm not one of those parents who can easily come up with 101 ways to entertain a child at any location, so I usually go with the standard, "Sit still and it won't be much longer." On that fateful Saturday, however, I attempted to be more like the creative moms I was reading about in the waiting room copy of *Parenting* magazine.

"Hey, buddy. What's that thing over there?" He turned around.

"Made you look!" I called out, totally pleased with myself. (Yes, unfortunately, this is as creative as I get.)

This took a minute to register, then a grin swept over my son's face.

"Hey, Mommy. Look over there. They're done with our car."

I fell for it, much to my son's delight. This launched a multiday made-you-look battle between the two of us. At first it was fun. But after a few days, my son was so determined to never, ever get tricked that every time I opened my mouth to say something, he would yell, "I'M NOT LOOKING!" We literally couldn't even have a conversation. He wanted to be sure he was *never* going to be fooled again. I finally had to ban the game from our house completely.

Fortunately, this was just a game, so I was able to end it when it got out of hand. But it's an apt analogy for what happens when we lose spiritual credibility with our kids. If what we teach them on an important subject turns out to be incomplete or inaccurate, it can cast a shadow of doubt on *everything* we've taught them. As in the made-you-look game, they won't want to hear a word more about faith from us for fear of being fooled again. Case in point: the subject of evolution. Many Christian parents downplay (if not trivialize) evolutionary theory with their children in favor of emphasizing God's direct creation. Kids are often shocked when they eventually study the evidence for evolution in detail and find it extremely convincing. This is exactly what happened to the following reviewer of Jerry Coyne's book *Why Evolution Is True*:

I was raised in a very conservative Christian environment and taught Young-Earth Creationism (anti-evolution, anti-Big Bang, etc.). I bought into it for a long time. In college, I finally began to investigate some of the claims for myself—reading what was *really* being said by "the other side," rather than what I was being told was being said. The disparity I discovered can hardly be exaggerated: what I had been taught bore essentially zero resemblance to the real thing. Genuine evolutionary theory was virtually unrecognizable in the creationists' caricatures of it. I learned that I had been lied to—intentionally, or not, I do not know—and that the quantity, diversity, and quality of evidence in support of evolution was simply crushing.[1]

We owe it to our kids to discuss evolution in an honest and *accurate* way so they aren't later shocked like this reviewer was when she got to college. In this chapter, we'll look at the basics you need to understand.

What Exactly Is Evolution?

The word *evolution*, in its most basic sense, simply means that a species has undergone genetic change over time (a *species* is a group of organisms capable of interbreeding—for example, humans are a species and dogs are a species). This basic concept of evolution isn't controversial at all. Genetic change within species is a well-documented fact that scientists can observe within a human lifetime. For example, evolutionary biologist Dr. Richard Lenski has tracked an array of genetic changes in 12 initially identical populations of E. coli bacteria since 1988 (60,000 generations have been studied to date).[2]

Evolutionary theory, however, encompasses much more than the basic idea of genetic change over time. The theory of evolution is a group of propositions that seek to explain how all life on Earth evolved from a single primitive species that lived roughly 3.5 billion years ago.[3] This is where the controversy lies: Can the same mechanisms that we know facilitate genetic change *within* a species actually create *new* species—and more specifically, every species on Earth? Most scientists say yes; the process is one and the same. Many Christians say no; species change, but variation has clear limits.

People sometimes use the terms *microevolution* and *macroevolution* to describe this distinction (*micro*evolution refers to variation within species and *macro*evolution refers to large-scale changes above the species level). For biologists, however, there is no functional difference between microevolution and macroevolution. Evolutionary theory says the mechanism that drives change within a species today is the same one that's driven change from one species into another over the last 3.5 billion years—from fish to amphibians, amphibians to reptiles, and reptiles to birds and mammals. When we look at the evidence for evolution in the next chapter, we'll focus on the evidence for this species-to-species evolution specifically, since that's where the controversy lies. In the remainder of this chapter, we'll look at how evolution (theoretically) works on any scale.

How Evolution Works

Modern evolutionary theory says the development of new species over time is made possible by random mutations that happen in DNA. Recall from chapter 1 that DNA is the complex molecule in cells that carries all the information needed to build and maintain an organism. It's like a detailed blueprint for how each living thing works. The information in DNA is stored as a code made up of four chemical bases represented by the letters A, G, C, and T: adenine (A), guanine (G), cytosine (C), and thymine (T). Human DNA has about three *billion* of these bases. Just as sequences of letters from our alphabet determine words, sequences of these bases determine genetic functions.

When organisms reproduce, a portion of their DNA is transmitted to their offspring. If DNA never changed from generation to generation, there would be no evolution. The same species would simply reproduce over and over. However, DNA does change. When cells divide, DNA copies itself and accidental changes in the sequence of the bases—called *mutations*—can occur. For example, a section of DNA can be lost (CAT can become CT), one base can be substituted for another (CAT can become CTT), or extra bases can be inserted (CAT can become CAAAT).

When individuals within a species differ genetically from one another due to these mutations, some of those differences can impact an individual's ability to survive and reproduce in a given environment. In the next generation, there will be relatively more organisms with the genes that led to better survival and reproduction. This process, where organisms better adapted to their environment tend to survive and produce more offspring, is called *natural selection*. As natural selection continues, evolutionary theory says the evolving population can eventually accumulate enough genetic changes that it can no longer produce fertile offspring with members of the original population. At that point, a new species has formed. It is through this process that evolutionary biologists say all life on Earth developed, starting from a single ancestral species.

The Galapagos Finches: Evolution in Action

It may help to picture all of this with an example of evolution in action today. One of the most well-known studies on the evolution of natural populations was conducted on the finches of the Galapagos Islands (finches are seed-eating songbirds).[4]

Researchers Peter and Rosemary Grant made their first trip to the Galapagos Islands in 1973. They began by catching and banding finches on seven of the islands, but soon focused their research on one of the smaller islands, Daphne Major. By focusing on a single environment, they were able to measure and band every individual in one particular species: the medium ground finch. Over four decades, the Grants studied in detail how this species genetically adapted to significant changes in its environment.

The most important factor influencing the medium ground finch's survival is the weather, and the resulting availability of seeds (their primary food). The first event the Grants saw that affected the food supply was a drought in 1977. The islands received no rain for 551 days. The very small seeds the finches normally ate became hard to find. The birds with larger beaks managed to survive by taking advantage of alternative food sources with less preferable larger seeds. Many of the birds with smaller beaks couldn't crack the big seeds open and died of starvation. In 1978, the Grants returned to the island to document the effects of the drought on the next generation of finches. They found the beaks of the offspring to be 3-4 percent larger than those of their grandparents. *The finch population had adapted to a change in its environment.*

In the winter of 1982–1983, the Galapagos Islands received more than ten times their normal rainfall. Plants grew in abundance and the finch population exploded. After that, the average beak size in the medium ground finch population returned to its previous value. Once again, the finches had adapted to a change in their environment.

This study of the Galapagos finches is often used to demonstrate how natural selection works. Consider what happened. First, there was genetic variation within the medium ground finch species (size of the birds and beaks). Second, there were environmental factors that favored the reproduction of birds with certain genetic traits over the others (the birds with larger beaks were better able to survive the drought). Third, the genetic makeup of the population's next generation was altered accordingly (average beak size increased by 3-4 percent). While that doesn't sound like a big change in beak size, it was the difference between life and death for many of the birds.

Scientists point to the Galapagos finches as an important case study of evolution in action today. Those who reject *macroevolution* (young-Earth and old-Earth creationists) agree that this is an example of *microevolution*, but deny that it demonstrates anything more; they emphasize it was a minor adaptation that simply allowed finches to *stay finches* under adverse conditions.

Next Stop: Evidence for Macroevolution

In this chapter, we defined evolutionary theory and saw that it seeks to explain how all life on Earth evolved from a single primitive species that lived roughly 3.5 billion years ago. We identified that it is species-to-species evolution—or *macroevolution*—that is controversial for many Christians; no one denies that evolution within species—or *microevolution*—occurs regularly. So what *is* the evidence for species-to-species evolution? That's the subject for our next chapter.

I didn't learn about the evidence for evolution until I was in my 30s. When I did, it rocked my lifelong faith in a matter of hours.

When I was growing up, evolution wasn't yet a subject taught in most public schools; I never encountered it academically. The only time I heard it mentioned was when my church youth group leader once laughed it off, saying, "Yeah, like we all really came from apes!"[1] I remember thinking that *was* a pretty far-fetched idea. In college, I studied economics, so I came no closer to evolutionary theory as a young adult. It was very much off my radar until I had kids and decided I should learn about it for their sake (see chapter 33).

I started studying evolution by reading an online series of introductory articles published by Biologos.org.[2] After studying just eight lessons one day, I numbly shut down my computer, pulled a blanket over my head, and felt years of faith sheepishly slink into the shadows of my newfound knowledge. The evidence was shockingly vast—far more extensive than I had ever imagined. The details were fascinating and compelling. This wasn't some half-baked idea about how fossils fit together, as I had previously imagined. This was...completely *scientific*. As scientific as any other science I had ever studied and assumed to be valid. It was hardly a leap to ask myself, *Why shouldn't I accept this science if I accept all other science I've been taught?* I felt like I couldn't breathe for hours as I lay pondering what life would look like without the God I had always believed in.

It's important to know that this *one night* when evolution floored me came after I had attended church for 30-plus years, served as a youth group leader, taken numerous Sunday school classes, read the Bible regularly, and engaged in an active prayer life. *None of those things prepared me to figure out what I should do with the evidence for evolution.* If evolution was true, I had no idea how Christianity could be true at the same time. If evolution was not true, I had no idea how there could be so much evidence for it.

It was devastating.

How much more is learning about the evidence for evolution

potentially devastating to young people with a relatively *inexperienced* faith? How much more will they "have no idea what to do with" compelling information that immediately seems to contradict the Bible? Recall from the introduction that we actually know that answer: At least 60 percent of young adults are turning away from Christianity today, and the evidence for evolution is one of the biggest reasons.

In my experience, many Christian parents have a limited understanding of the evidence for evolution. They often see evolution like a simple arrow being shot at their kids' faith and believe they can easily deflect it with the Bible. But I can tell you from personal experience that it can feel more like a *million* arrows. A million arrows that need answers before you can get up and march on with your faith. Our kids need us to be their guides.

This chapter will introduce you to some of the most important categories of evidence that evolutionists say support evolutionary theory—the evidence that your kids will undoubtedly study and will likely have questions about. Obviously, this chapter can only skim the surface of this complex subject. As with the other chapters in this section, consider it a topical guide you can use as a springboard for further reading.

To start, let's look at the most discussed evidence of all: evidence from the fossil record.

Evidence from the Fossil Record

Fossils are remains or traces of prehistoric organisms. Paleontologists (scientists who study fossils) refer to all the fossils discovered to date as the *fossil record*. Analyzing what the fossil record can tell us about the history of life requires three things: finding fossils, ordering fossils from oldest to youngest, and dating fossils. Before we can look at what evolutionists say is evidence for evolution from the fossil record, it's necessary to understand the basics of these three processes.

First, *finding fossils* is a difficult task. The vast majority of living things die and decay without leaving a trace. In order to become a fossil, the remains of an animal or plant must end up in water, sink to the bottom, and quickly get covered by sediment before they decay or get eaten. As you might imagine, that doesn't happen very often, and it isn't as likely to happen to some organisms as others. Even when it does happen, the fossils may never be discovered. For these reasons, the fossil record is very incomplete. Only about 250,000 different fossil species have been discovered out of an estimated 17 million to 4 billion species that mainstream scientists say have lived on Earth (a mere 0.1 to 1 percent of life's history).[3]

Second, *ordering fossils* requires scientists to determine the relationship of fossil-bearing rock layers found throughout the world. Generally speaking, it's assumed that rock layers are deposited in a time sequence, with the oldest on the bottom and the youngest on top. The ordering of the world's rock layers is well established and is generally accepted even by scientists who reject evolution and/or the idea of an old Earth.[4]

Third, *dating the fossils* assigns actual ages to the fossils found in a given rock layer. Scientists use radiometric dating to do this (see chapter 35 for details on this process). Because radiometric dating can't be used on the type of rock layers in which fossils are generally found, scientists look for layers of dateable rock above and below the fossils. By dating these surrounding layers, they determine the oldest and youngest possible ages the fossils can be.

Evolutionists say the fossil record provides evidence of evolution for many reasons. We'll look at two of the most important ones here: (1) There is an overall progression from simple to complex organisms, and (2) transitional fossils have been found, and found where predicted.

Overall Progression from Simple to Complex Organisms

If evolutionary theory is correct, and all life descended from a simple molecule, the fossil record should show a progression from very simple organisms in the bottom rock layers to very complex organisms in the top ones. That is the precisely the pattern found.[5] Fossils generally appear in the following order: simple bacteria, simple but multicelled organisms, four-legged animals, amphibians, reptiles, mammals, and finally humans. The fossilized species in the top layers are also the most similar to living species, which would be expected if evolutionary theory is true. The fact that the order of the fossil record is consistent with the predictions of evolutionary theory doesn't mean evolution must be true, but it's generally considered to be one of the strongest pieces of evidence for it.

Transitional Fossils Found, and Found Where Predicted

Transitional fossils are fossils that show the intermediate states between an ancestral species and its descendant species. For example, if whales really evolved from land animals (as claimed by evolutionists), transitional animals must have existed with a mixture of both whale and land animal traits. Evidence of those transitional animals should also be found at the right *time* in the fossil record (between the land animal ancestor and whale descendant). Evolutionists say transitional fossils abound, and in the predicted places. A booklet published by the National Academy of Sciences called *Science and Creationism: A View from the National Academy of Sciences* says:

> So many intermediate forms have been discovered between fish and amphibians, between amphibians and reptiles, between reptiles and mammals, and along the primate lines of descent that it often is difficult to identify categorically when the transition occurs from one to another particular species.[6]

Some of the most important fossils considered to be transitional include *Tiktaalik roseae* (a possible fish-to-four-legged-animal transitional animal), *Archaeopteryx* (a possible dinosaur-to-bird transitional animal), and *Ambulocetus* (a possible land-animal-to-whale transitional animal). If you're interested in learning more about the extensive discussion surrounding transitional fossils, I encourage you to start by searching for information on these well-known examples online.[7]

Evidence from Biogeography

Biogeography is the study of the distribution of species on Earth. Evolutionists say that many facts about biogeography only make sense in light of evolutionary theory. Two key topics in this category are *convergent evolution* and the distribution of species on islands.

Convergent Evolution

There are many cases where two distant areas of the Earth have a similar climate and terrain, yet very different types of life. This pattern seems odd because it might be assumed that the same environments would host the same forms of life—for example, you might think that all deserts would have the same plants. But they don't.

Many desert plants are succulents (plants with fleshy leaves or stems that can store water), but the types of succulent plants found vary from desert to desert. In the Americas, for example, deserts have cacti. In Asia, Australia, and Africa, deserts have succulents called euphorbs. Cacti and euphorbs have very similar traits that enable them to flourish in their harsh environment, but they're not (closely) related.

Evolutionists say this pattern can readily be explained by evolutionary theory. When different species live in similar habitats and experience similar natural selection pressures from their environment, they are likely to evolve similar adaptations (fleshy stems that can store water, in the case of succulents). The result is that they look and behave alike but are not actually (closely) related. This process is called *convergent evolution*. Evolutionists cite hundreds of such examples as evidence for an evolutionary history of life.

Distribution of Species on Islands

There are two types of islands on Earth. *Continental islands* are those that were once connected to a continent but later separated (for example, the British Isles). *Oceanic islands* are those that were never connected to a continent and instead arose from the seafloor as volcanoes or coral reefs (for example, the Hawaiian Islands).

Oceanic islands surprisingly lack many of the same groups of native species that exist on continents and continental islands: land mammals, reptiles, amphibians, and freshwater fish. The native species on oceanic islands—including plants, birds, and insects—are notably all species that can transport themselves or be transported from a distance over water. In addition, almost all animals and plants found on oceanic islands are similar to the species found on the nearest mainland, even when the terrain is quite different.

Once again, evolutionists say this all paints a picture consistent with evolutionary theory: Species on oceanic islands descend from the few ancestors that were physically able to colonize from the nearest mainland. Meanwhile, continental islands have the animal groups that are missing from oceanic islands because they broke off from the mainland with those species already in place. Evolutionists say this unexpected distinction between island types only makes sense in light of evolution.

Evidence from Vestigial Traits

Vestigial traits are parts of animals that evolutionists say were evolutionary adaptations in the past, but that have lost their usefulness or are now being used in other ways. Ostrich wings are the classic example. Wings are very complex structures that normally enable birds to fly, but ostriches have flightless wings. Ostriches can use their wings for simple functions like balancing, but those functions don't seem to be commensurate with their complexity. Evolutionists say this would be predicted by evolutionary theory, since traits constantly adapt from what is already available rather than immediately appear in a perfectly suited form.

Evidence from Atavisms

Atavisms are believed to be sporadic reappearances of an ancestral trait. They're different from vestigial traits because they occur only occasionally rather than in every individual. Evolutionists say this happens because traits that physically disappear do not necessarily disappear from an organism's DNA. Occasionally, something can trigger those gene sequences to become active again, resulting in the physical appearance of an ancestral trait. Frequently cited examples of atavisms include humans born with tails, horses born with extra toes, and whales born with legs.

Evidence from Pseudogenes

Pseudogenes are DNA sequences similar to normal genes but are believed to be nonfunctional. Evolutionary theory predicts that many such pseudogenes should exist in DNA as inactive "leftovers" from past evolutionary traits. Evolutionists say this is indeed the case (though the exact percent of DNA that is truly nonfunctional remains controversial—see chapter 39).

Evolutionists say the *comparison* of pseudogenes between species especially provides evidence for evolution. For example, humans have a pseudogene called GLO. GLO produces an enzyme that is used to make vitamin C. Almost all mammals have the ability to make their own vitamin C, but primates (a biological order of animals in which scientists include humans) must get it from food. Primates can't make their own vitamin C because GLO has been inactivated by a mutation—and humans have the same mutation as chimpanzees and other primates (the animals evolutionists say we are most closely related to). Evolutionists say the fact that humans and chimpanzees have the same broken gene only makes sense in light of a shared ancestry.

Two Sides to Every Story

When I first was blown away by the evidence given for evolution, my initial thought was not, *Let me now go research the challenges to evolution.* The case for evolution, as very briefly highlighted here, seemed clear-cut. But after some time of reflection, I picked myself up and got to work researching what skeptics of evolution had to say from a scientific perspective. I soon learned there are two sides to this story, even though many people only hear the one presented in this chapter. Let's look now at that other side.

39. What are the major challenges to evolution?

Atheist Richard Dawkins once said that people who refuse to accept evolution are "ignorant, stupid, or insane." To that statement he eventually added,

> I don't withdraw a word of my initial statement. But I do now think it may have been incomplete. There is perhaps a

fifth category, which may belong under "insane" but which can be more sympathetically characterized by a word like tormented, bullied, or brainwashed. Sincere people who are not ignorant, not stupid, and not wicked can be cruelly torn, almost in two, between the massive evidence of science on the one hand, and their understanding of what their holy book tells them on the other.[1]

While there is significant scientific evidence that is consistent with evolutionary theory (see chapter 38), that evidence is not without scientific challenges. You'd never know it, however, given the nature of widespread comments made by passionate atheists like Dawkins. Their general message is that anyone who hasn't accepted evolution is living in the Dark Ages. Similarly, Bill Nye, in *Undeniable: Evolution and the Science of Creation* (note the claim about evolution in the title itself—*undeniable*), says, "Here's hoping we can work together to bring the children of the creationists' preachers' flocks to a more *enlightened*, boundless way of thinking about the world around us"[2] (emphasis mine).

If your kids are in a secular academic environment, that is the picture of evolution they'll get: It's an undeniable fact that can't reasonably be questioned. There *are* significant scientific challenges to evolutionary theory, but your kids almost certainly won't hear about them if you don't proactively take the time to introduce the discussion. This isn't to say that there aren't Christians who believe evolution can be reconciled with the Bible (this is the position of *theistic evolutionists*), but rather that all kids should be given the opportunity to hear both sides of the story so they can develop an informed viewpoint—both theologically and scientifically.

In this chapter, we'll look at a few of the biggest scientific challenges to evolutionary theory: challenges from the fossil record, challenges from DNA, challenges from natural selection, and challenges from the origin of life. It should be noted that young-Earth creationists also challenge evolutionists on the age of the Earth. If the Earth is 6000-10,000 years old, as young-Earth creationists believe, there wouldn't have been enough time for evolution to produce the diversity of life we see today. However, because we already discussed the age of the Earth debate in chapter 35, this chapter will focus on other challenges (challenges that remain after granting a timescale of billions of years).

You'll note that the following challenges aren't point-by-point rebuttals to the evidence discussed in the last chapter. That's because the rebuttals to those points aren't necessarily the biggest challenges to evolution. I've chosen to focus here on the challenges that matter most. If you're interested in point-specific rebuttals to chapter 38, I've listed some recommended websites in the following endnote.[3]

Challenges from the Fossil Record

While evolutionists point to the fossil record as prime evidence in support of evolution, skeptics of evolution point to the same record as prime evidence *against* it. Here we'll look at two of the most important challenges: (1) Limited transitional fossils, and (2) the Cambrian Explosion.

Limited Transitional Fossils

Recall from the last chapter that *transitional fossils* are fossils that show intermediate states between an ancestor and its descendant species. Evolutionists consider transitional fossils to be some of the strongest evidence for evolution because they demonstrate the progression of form that evolutionary theory predicts. However, skeptics of evolution say the fact that there aren't *more* transitional fossils poses a serious problem for evolutionists.

Dr. William Dembski, Senior Fellow at the Center for Science and Culture, explains the issue this way:

> Yes, the fossil record contains organisms that can be placed in a progression suggesting gradual change. But most of these progressions result from arbitrary picking and choosing among the totality of fossils. With millions of fossils to choose from, it is likely that some gradual progressions will be found. Also, such progressions invariably come from organisms with the same basic body plan. In the "evolution" of the horse, we are always dealing with horse-like

organisms. And even with the "evolution" of reptiles into mammals, we are dealing with land-dwelling vertebrates sharing many common structures. What we don't see in the fossil record is animals with fundamentally different body plans evolving from a common ancestor. For instance, there is no fossil evidence whatsoever that insects and vertebrates share a common evolutionary ancestor. [4]

In other words, skeptics of evolution say there is a lot of room for interpretation when it comes to lining up and classifying fossils. It's not that *no* possible transitional fossils have been found. However, for any given fossil, there can be extensive debate as to its place in the history of life (search online for the transitional fossils mentioned in chapter 38 to see the discussion firsthand).

Cambrian Explosion

In evolutionary theory, species arise from other species in small steps over long periods of time. As we discussed in the last chapter, that means the fossil record should show a gradual progression from simple organisms in the bottom rock layers to complex organisms in the top ones. And, indeed, nearly everyone agrees that this is the *overall pattern* of the fossil record. However, there is one particularly significant time period during which the fossils jump surprisingly quickly from simple to complex, and skeptics say it defies evolutionary explanations. This famous finding is called the *Cambrian Explosion* and is thought to have happened between 570 and 530 million years ago.

Over a geologically brief period of 20-40 million years, most major animal body plans suddenly appear in the fossil record. Body plans (called *phyla* in biology) are the unique types of body structures found in the animal kingdom. Examples of body plans include cnidarians (corals and jellyfish), arthropods (crustaceans and insects), and chordates (all vertebrates, including human beings). Based on the fossil record, it appears that body plans of animals living before the Cambrian period remained relatively constant. Then, in the Cambrian period, there is a surprising "explosion" of fossils with new body plans.

Skeptics of evolution say that evolutionary theory cannot sufficiently account for this finding. First, they say Precambrian fossils are too different from Cambrian fossils to suggest a clear ancestor-descendant relationship.[5] Evolutionists typically respond that the Precambrian organisms were soft-bodied, so they would only rarely turn into fossils which we might find today (fossilization usually requires hard body parts like skeletons). However, Precambrian fossils of bacteria and microscopic animal embryos *have* been found, so skeptics of evolution say it's reasonable to assume at least some larger animals—ancestral to the Cambrian animals—would have been found if they existed.

Second, skeptics of evolution point out that the body plans from the Cambrian Explosion are very unique from one another, yet they've exhibited remarkable stability since that time. They say this is significant because it would be surprising if such vastly different creatures evolved quickly from a common ancestor, then maintained the same body plans for millions of years.[6]

Third, skeptics of evolution say the sudden emergence of Cambrian animals represents an enormous jump in the complexity of DNA found in the biological world.[7] The more complex Cambrian animals would have required more cell types to direct their increased functions. Each of those cell types would have required new and specialized proteins, and those proteins would have required significant amounts of new information to develop in the animals' DNA. Skeptics question how evolution could have generated this sudden steep increase in information.[8]

While theories abound, there is no widespread scientific consensus on what may have triggered the Cambrian Explosion or why so much change appears to have occurred at that time. For skeptics, it remains one of the key scientific challenges to evolutionary theory.

Challenges from DNA

Skeptics of evolution say the structure and nature of DNA pose at least two major challenges to evolutionary theory: (1) There is limited "junk" in DNA, and (2) most DNA mutations are harmful or neutral.

Limited "Junk" DNA

Evolutionary theory predicts that nonfunctional DNA should accumulate in the genomes of organisms over time (a *genome* is all of an organism's DNA). That's because DNA sequences don't just disappear from an organism when genes stop working or are no longer expressed. Organisms carry them forward like baggage from their past history. After millions of years of evolution, the human genome should theoretically show an extensive build-up of this nonfunctional DNA (popularly called "junk" DNA).

In 2003, scientists first completed the mapping of the human genome. Based on their research, they estimated that just 2 percent of DNA was functional. This was a boon to evolutionists, who said it was exactly what evolutionary theory predicted: Our DNA is 98 percent "junk" left over from our evolutionary past. Since 2003, however, further research significantly changed our understanding of the genome's functionality.

After the genome was mapped, the National Human Genome Research Institute launched a public research consortium called ENCODE to identify all of its *functional* elements (what the various parts of the mapped genome actually *do*).[9] In 2012, a series of papers published in the science journal *Nature* reported that the project had found evidence of function for at least *80 percent* of the human genome—not 2 percent, as previously thought.[10] They discovered that much of the DNA previously believed to be "junk" actually performs critical functions such as determining *which* genes are expressed and directing *when* and *where* genes are expressed. Research is ongoing and new functions continue to be found. Skeptics of evolution say the fact that the vast majority of our DNA is functional defies evolutionary predictions.

Harmful or Neutral Nature of Most Mutations

Recall from chapter 37 that it is DNA mutations (random changes to the genetic code) that create variations between organisms. If mutations never happened, organisms would only have limited ways of responding to their environment and evolution could not produce the diversity of life we see today. Mutations are a major key to evolutionary theory.

Skeptics of evolution, however, question whether DNA mutations really can produce the new information needed to develop advantageous traits. They say mutations usually reshuffle or delete existing information—not add *new* information. For example, cystic fibrosis, sickle-cell anemia, and colorblindness are all caused by the harmful mutation of a single gene. Skeptics argue that while some cases of information-gaining mutations have been found, in order for evolution to be true, there would need to be billions of them—far more than we see. [11]

Challenges from Natural Selection

Skeptics of evolution acknowledge that natural selection is adequate for explaining small-scale changes in organisms, but say that it fails to be a powerful enough mechanism to have driven the entire history of life. This is a concern even amongst some evolutionists. For example, a group of scientists committed to evolution have developed a website called "The Third Way of Evolution" to provide "a vehicle for new voices to be heard in evolution debates." More specifically, these scientists question the power of natural selection:

> Some Neo-Darwinists have elevated Natural Selection into a unique creative force that solves all the difficult evolutionary problems without a real empirical basis. Many scientists today see the need for a deeper and more complete exploration of all aspects of the evolutionary process. [12]

This group is quick to point out that they don't support any explanation that "resorts to inscrutable divine forces." However, the group's existence demonstrates the problems that both skeptics of evolution and some evolutionists have with the theoretical role of natural selection in the current ("neo-Darwinian") theory of evolution.

Challenges from the Origin of Life

Technically speaking, evolutionary theory deals only with the manner in which life has changed *after* it began. It doesn't claim to explain the origin of the *first* life. However, a purely naturalistic account of the world (one with no supernatural involvement) must address both evolution *and* the origin of the first life, so these topics are often discussed together.

Evolutionists believe that the first life emerged from nonliving matter. This process is called *abiogenesis*. Scientific research to date has failed to provide a generally accepted explanation as to how abiogenesis could have occurred on Earth, though many experiments have been conducted. Physicist and evolutionist Paul Davies once commented, "Many investigators feel uneasy about stating in public that the origin of life is a mystery, even though behind closed doors they freely admit that they are baffled."[13] This present lack of an explanation for the origin of life doesn't necessarily invalidate evolution, but skeptics of evolution say it's a significant challenge to the purely naturalistic worldview of which evolution is a part.

From Scientific Challenges to a Positive Case

This chapter presents key, basic scientific challenges to the validity of evolutionary theory. These challenges are important to understand. But it's one thing to challenge a theory and another thing to build a case for *another* theory. Even if evolutionary theory were proven wrong tomorrow, it wouldn't mean the only alternative is a divine creator. It's important, therefore, to ask one final question on this topic: Is there any scientific evidence in biology *for* a supreme intelligence? Enter the world of *intelligent design theory*, the subject of the next chapter.

40. What is intelligent design?

One afternoon, my four-year-old proudly showed me a card she had just finished "writing." It had lines and lines of haphazardly strewn-together letters.

"Mommy, what does it say?" she asked with great anticipation.

"Well, it doesn't *say* anything because you haven't learned to write words yet. But it looks very pretty. Good job with your letters!" I replied.

Big tears of disappointment fell down her cheeks. "But it must say *something*! What does it say?" she pleaded again.

My husband walked by and quickly chimed in, "It says, 'I love my daddy so, so much and I will never date anyone until he says they are okay, and not before age thirty.'"

Her eyes got huge. "REALLY? It says that?"

We couldn't help but laugh that she thought it was possible to accidentally write such an elaborate sentence when she couldn't even read or spell yet. If the card really said what my husband told her, we wouldn't have thought for a second that she was the one who wrote it. There's simply no way she could have put the letters in the right combinations to make meaningful words and put the words in the right order to make a meaningful sentence all by chance.

People subconsciously make these kinds of assessments of what can and cannot happen by chance all the time. Think of the carved stone faces on Mount Rushmore, for example. When you see their fine details and their likeness to known presidents, you immediately assume they're the result of someone's *design*—not the result of millions of pieces of rock falling into the right places by *chance*.

This distinction between *chance* and *design* has become an important and controversial topic in the evolution debate. Recall from chapter 37 that the DNA mutations underlying evolutionary theory are random; that is, they happen by chance. Natural selection is the undirected process that theoretically acts on those random mutations to produce evolutionary adaptations and, ultimately, new species. In a purely naturalistic worldview, all of this happens without intelligent input or guidance. But scientists have long noted that many of the complexities in biology at least *appear* to be the product of design— they look like Mount Rushmore rather than millions of pieces of rock falling into the right places by chance.

While many scientists acknowledge the *appearance* of design in biology, they usually reject the *reality* of design. This should lead us to ask: Is there an objective way to determine whether apparent design in nature is truly the product of an intelligent cause or if it's simply the product of an undirected process like natural selection? That's precisely the question *intelligent design theory* seeks to answer.

Intelligent design is the scientific theory that says some features of the universe and living things are best explained by an intelligent cause. To this end, intelligent design proponents attempt to find objective ways to detect any *actual* design in nature. In this chapter, we'll look at how they do that.

Before we move on, however, it's important to clarify that the theory of intelligent design has no religious commitments. It doesn't attempt to identify or describe the intelligent cause that might be responsible for any scientifically detected design. The conclusion of design is strictly based on an inference from data. That doesn't mean there are no theological implications, of course. If scientific evidence of intelligent design can be discovered, that's clearly consistent with the possibility that God might be the designer.

Detecting Design in Biology

From a scientific perspective, it's not enough to "eyeball" something and say a designer must be behind it, even if that's what intuition suggests. For example, astronomer Johannes Kepler (1571–1630) thought the craters on the moon were designed by moon dwellers.[1] Of course, we now know they were formed by purely natural processes. To avoid intuition-based mistakes like this, scientists have formulated objective models to detect design. More specifically, intelligent design theorists say that design can be detected when information—such as the information contained in DNA—exhibits what is called *specified complexity*.

The term *specified complexity* sounds very technical, but it's not overly difficult to understand. To exhibit specified complexity—the theoretical mark of design—information must be *contingent, complex*, and *specified*. Let's look briefly at each of those criteria, then we'll apply them to DNA in the context of the creation-evolution debate.

Contingent

To determine whether something is designed, scientists must first eliminate the possibility that it's actually the result of a necessary event. For example, star-shaped ice crystals have a very ordered structure that might look like a design, but they're only shaped that way as a result of natural laws; they *necessarily* take that form given the properties of water. Things that *aren't* necessary are *contingent*. Contingency is the first qualifier of design.

Complex

The *complexity* in *specified complexity* refers to improbability. If my daughter's card had only two scribbles, and they happened to form the word *hi*, I would have laughed in surprise at the coincidence, but I wouldn't have been blown away. On the other hand, a much longer note that "happened" to suggest she wouldn't date until she had her daddy's approval (and not before age 30!) would have been utterly shocking. Too shocking. It would have been so improbable that I would have assumed someone else wrote it for her. The more words her card had, the more complex the information would have been, and the less likely she could have written it by chance. Complexity is an important design qualifier because scientists want to make sure they aren't attributing every somewhat improbable event to design when many of those events are possible by chance (events like my daughter writing *hi*).

Specified

Even if something is *extremely* improbable, that doesn't mean it didn't happen by chance. For example, if you flip a coin 1000 times, you'll witness a highly improbable event. Whatever exact sequence of heads and tails you get has less than a one in 10^{100} chance of occurring![2] Obviously, however, that sequence wasn't by design despite its improbability. One last qualifier is therefore necessary: The information must be *specified*.

The *specified* in *specified complexity* means that the information matches a known pattern. Let's revisit that coin-flipping example. What if you flipped the coin 1000 times and got a sequence of 1000 heads in a row? The probability of that result would be the same as in the prior example, but you'd be much more likely to assume it wasn't due to chance because you would note a pattern. The existence of a meaningful pattern in complex information is therefore an important consideration for determining design.

Applying Specified Complexity to DNA

So far we've seen that intelligent design theorists say design can be detected when information is *contingent, complex,* and *specified.* The reason they claim this is the mark of design is that *all known examples* of information meeting these criteria are the product of intelligent agents—not material processes. A computer programming code is one example that meets these criteria and is clearly the product of a mind. No one argues that computer languages have come into existence through natural forces.

As we saw in chapter 37, DNA is very much like a computer code. It's made up of about 3 *billion* chemical bases (represented by the letters A, G, C, and T) and the sequences of those bases determine genetic functions. Recall from chapter 1 that the volume of information carried by those bases is roughly equivalent to 12 sets of *The Encyclopedia Britannica*—384 volumes of information!

Given that DNA exhibits specified complexity, and that all other known examples of specified complexity originate from an intelligent source, intelligent design theorists say we can also infer that intelligence is the best explanation for the biological origin of DNA.[3]

Leading intelligent design proponent Dr. Stephen C. Meyer concludes,

> Because we know intelligent agents can (and do) produce complex and functionally specified sequences of symbols and arrangements of matter, intelligent agency qualifies as an adequate causal explanation for the origin of this effect. Since, in addition, materialistic theories have proven universally inadequate for explaining the origin of such information, intelligent design now stands as the only entity

with the causal power known to produce this feature of living systems. Therefore, the presence of this feature in living systems points to intelligent design as the best explanation of it, whether such systems resemble human artifacts in other ways or not.[4]

Intelligent Design: Exciting But Controversial

Rather than merely challenging evolution, intelligent design makes a positive case *for* a designer.[5] It doesn't suggest that every aspect of biology is designed, however. Recall from the beginning of this chapter that intelligent design theory only states that *some* features of the universe and living things are best explained by an intelligent cause. Intelligent design theorists see the history of life as the result of both intelligent and natural forces. William Dembski, another leading intelligent design proponent, explains:

> Naturally occurring systems can exhibit specified complexity, and nature operating without intelligent direction can take preexisting specified complexity and shuffle it around. That is not the point. The point is whether nature (conceived as a closed system of blind, unbroken natural causes) can *generate* specified complexity in the sense of originating it when previously there was none.[6]

Intelligent design theory has been the target of attacks from all sides. Evolutionists regularly reject it as illegitimate science.[7] Some theistic evolutionists express skepticism that God's supernatural activity in the world would be scientifically detectable.[8] Other Christians criticize intelligent design proponents for not going to the next level of making a case for the biblical God.[9] For these reasons, the idea and value of intelligent design theory have remained controversial despite its potentially exciting contributions to the conversation of faith and science. For more information on intelligent design theory and to stay up-to-date on new findings, visit the Center for Science and Culture at http://www.discovery.org/id/.

10 TIPS
for Having Deeper
Faith Conversations
with Your Kids

10 Tips for Having Deeper
Faith Conversations with Your Kids

Wow. We've covered a lot of ground!

My hope is that you've arrived at this point feeling inspired, energized, and better equipped as a Christian parent—ready and raring to put all this into action.

But I also know you might be feeling a bit overwhelmed.

Even with all this material now rummaging around in your mind, you may be wondering how to *do* something with it in your own home. That's actually a perfect question to have!

As we talked about in the introduction, it's not possible to outline a definitive one-size-fits-all conversation plan. Every family has a unique group of personalities, ages, interests, relationships, and spiritual histories to work with. All of those factors affect how to best engage with your kids. That means it will take some intentional thought on your part to figure out how you're going to deepen your kids' faith with these (and other) conversations. If the answer isn't immediately obvious to you, don't worry. It isn't for most people. We're *all* learning as we go.

That said, there are some things that will facilitate deeper faith conversations in *any* family. Below are ten tips you can put into action no matter what your family situation is.

1. Commit to continually deepening your understanding of Christianity.

As I mentioned before, I've received many emails from parents who are panicking because their child no longer believes in God. Invariably, the parent asks what book or other resource they should give their child to convince them that God is real and the Bible is true. The unstated problem is this: The parents don't know how to make that case themselves.

Don't get me wrong. There is absolutely a time and place for giving your kids third-party resources to aid in their spiritual development. But there is no replacement for *you*. If *you're* not prepared to be the number one representative of Jesus in your kids' lives, you'll lose spiritual credibility. When you can't answer their big questions, you'll leave them wondering if all this really matters, given that you seemingly haven't given your faith as much thought as they have.

By reading this book, you've taken a great step toward deepening your understanding of Christianity. But please don't stop here. Make continual study a way of life.

For further reading on the topics covered in this book, I've created a list of recommended resources at www.NatashaCrain.com/ReadingList. The list is continually updated as books become available in the marketplace.

2. Make spiritual space in your home.

Let's assume that you take tip number one to heart. Fantastic! But now you need to *transfer* that understanding to your kids. It won't happen magically. Most families are incredibly busy, trying to stay afloat between school, homework, and after-school activities—not to mention the parents' jobs! These kinds of conversations simply won't happen on any meaningful level unless you make *spiritual space* for them.

By spiritual space I mean dedicated time for your family to engage together in growing your understanding of and relationship with God. There's no reason such a time shouldn't be scheduled just like all the other (less important) activities in your life. Start with 30 minutes once per week—a feasible goal for virtually any family. Then add time as you are able. *Making spiritual space will completely change your family's spiritual life.*

3. Study the Bible with your kids. Really.

I know that sounds like Christian parenting 101. But there are two reasons I'm including the seemingly obvious here. First, even if you know it's important, statistics show you're probably not doing it (recall from the introduction that fewer than 1 in 10 Christian families read the Bible together in a given week). If your kids perceive that you've relegated the Bible to the back burner of relevancy, they'll have little reason to see it as the authoritative book Christians claim it to be.

Second, I want to point out the difference between *reading* the Bible and *studying* it. Simply reading the Bible helps kids learn key stories and events. But *studying* the Bible helps them learn what it all means and introduces them to the importance of interpretation. When we study the Bible, we look at questions like, Who wrote this book? Who were they writing to? Why were they writing it? What does this verse mean in the context of the verses before and after it? How does this apply to my own life?

These Bible study skills are a foundation for many years of faith conversations.

4. Proactively and regularly ask your kids what questions they have.

Parents often believe their kids *will* ask questions about faith because they've been told they *can*. Those same parents are later shocked when their kids suddenly announce they don't believe in God. They wonder why their kids never voiced their questions and concerns.

It's undoubtedly important to let your kids know you're an open door for their faith questions. But there are many reasons they may never walk through that door, even when they know it's open—such as too many other things going on, fear of your reaction, or simple disinterest. You need to *proactively* pull your kids' questions to the forefront of conversation. You don't have to have all the answers, but you do need to provide the forum.

The good news is that's really easy to do once you've created your family's spiritual space (see my last tip). As I mentioned in chapter 20, our family dedicates a night each week to letting our kids ask any questions they have about God. In case you're wondering, they've *never* run out of things to ask. We almost always have to cut them off in order to get them to bed.

5. Ask your kids the tough questions they don't ask of you.

If you regularly encourage your kids to ask questions, you'll have a lot of great conversations—probably on many of the topics in this book. Some questions that are important for deepening a child's faith, however, might never cross their mind to ask.

For example, I don't think it ever occurred to me as a kid that it defies what we know from everyday experience to believe that Jesus rose from the dead. I never thought about it because, like many kids raised in Christian homes, I just grew up learning it as a fact. Yet it takes about 30 seconds for an atheist to point out for the first time just how "crazy" and "unscientific" that actually sounds and make a kid question everything he believes.

If we want to help our kids develop a robust faith, we can't just react to the questions they happen to have. We need to proactively put *all* the questions we know are important (like the 40 in this book) right in front of them.

6. If your kids are struggling with faith, become a detective.

One day when I was getting my kids into the car to leave for church, my son (age four at the time) moaned, "I hate God." I literally gasped. Then I started yelling.

"That is a *terrible* thing to say! Don't ever say that again. What are you thinking?"

He looked at me blankly without an answer. We all spent the next ten minutes driving in that awkward state where there's a bunch of family tension despite the ironic fact you're headed to church (you know exactly what I'm talking about, right?).

Finally, I realized I needed to figure out what he really meant. I asked him a series of questions to find out when, where, and why he had those feelings. It turned out it was only on Sundays...because he didn't like church...because he didn't like dancing to the songs in kids' worship. Yes, it turned out that "I hate God" meant "I don't like dancing at church."

Obviously, not every faith difficulty is so easily remedied. But the point remains the same: When your kids are struggling with faith, don't panic, and don't immediately start dispensing answers. Instead, find out (1) what *exactly* they mean when they say what they say, and (2) *why* they've come to that conclusion. Then you'll be able to address the *real* concerns.

7. Emphasize critical thinking skills.

When your kids encounter challenges to their faith, chances are they won't be stated exactly like the questions in this book. Challenges often come wrapped in a pretty package of rhetoric and it can be difficult to isolate the underlying issue from the propaganda. In order to do this, kids need more than answers—they need *critical thinking skills*.

Teaching kids how to think critically means teaching them how to objectively evaluate the validity of what someone else is asserting and how to draw logically appropriate conclusions themselves. For example, if your kids hear someone say, "There can't be one right religion because there are billions of people and they have many different beliefs," they should be able to detect the *logical* problem of such thinking right away (just because people disagree doesn't mean there isn't a correct answer). That has nothing to do with the truth of Christianity. It has everything to do with *good thinking*.

One way you can help your kids learn critical thinking skills is in how you facilitate conversations. Instead of imagining your conversations as some kind of lecture, think of them as you coming alongside your kids to discover the truths of Christianity. To do that, encourage them to talk through the answers to your (or their) questions before you offer your own knowledge. This allows you to directly observe their thought process and challenge the validity of their conclusions in a safe environment.

For resources on developing your kids' critical thinking skills, please see the following endnotes.[1/2]

8. Work with your kids on how to seek answers to faith questions online.

When you help your kids with homework, you don't give them all the answers. You know they need to learn how to figure out the answers themselves because you won't be their lifelong sidekick. It's the same with their spiritual lives. They need practice finding answers on their own.

A great way to do this with older kids is by giving them a question and asking them to research the answer online. As we all know, the Internet is a web of information and misinformation tangled together in often indistinguishable strands. A research project gives kids excellent practice in exercising critical thinking, research skills, and spiritual discernment.

For example, you could ask your kids, "How do we know Jesus existed?" Ask them to find both Christian and non-Christian answers online. Also ask them to keep track of their process: What did they do first? What kinds of sites did they end up visiting (blogs? ministries? discussion forums? news articles?)? What differences in information and views did they find between these sources? Which source(s) did they end up trusting for their answer, and why?

Giving your kids research challenges and discussing their process of finding answers can lead to enormously valuable conversations that will benefit them for life.

9. Teach your kids about religions and worldviews other than Christianity.

When my twins were toddlers, I started teaching them the letters of the alphabet using an easel we had. I put up one magnetic letter at a time and they had to tell me what it was. Months later, I bought them a preschool alphabet workbook so they could learn writing too. The letter *c* page had a tree with several *c*'s and *o*'s hanging on it. I was dumbfounded when my son, who had known his letters for months, couldn't distinguish the *c*'s from the *o*'s. He had always seen and identified *c* and *o* individually on the easel. But now he couldn't tell them apart when next to each other.

Similarly, our kids can easily get confused by competing worldviews that have roughly the same contours. Sure, we can broadly tell them that those religions are completely different in their core claims (see chapter 10), but it's a lot more meaningful when you study and compare the actual beliefs.

In addition to other religions, be sure to study the atheist worldview in-depth, given its significance today. I've included a resource in the following endnote to give you 14 ways of doing that.[3]

10. Start today.

Writing "start today" makes me laugh. It sounds like the final 30 seconds of a horrible late-night infomercial for a fitness program. But there's a reason that phrase is often used by marketers—they want to create a sense of urgency because people are so busy that procrastination is the default on anything not deemed truly vital.

Similarly, it will be tempting to do absolutely nothing with what you've read in this book. The spiritual status quo in your family is probably quite comfortable, particularly if your kids are still young. But please don't get into the mind-set that you have an indefinite amount of time to impact your kids' faith. You don't. In fact, Barna Group research has shown that many people form a significant portion of their eventual adult faith by the time they are just 13.[4]

So don't put it off. You really *should* start today in transforming your family's spiritual life.

A Final Thought

I want to leave you with one final thought that has helped me tremendously to remain motivated in my Christian parenting efforts: *The time and consideration we give to our kids' faith development is an investment, not a purchase.*

With a purchase, a person gives with the expectation of a certain and specific return.

With an investment, a person makes contributions, knowing that there is also a risk of that investment not resulting in the desired outcome.

Make no mistake: It's an *investment* of our training efforts that God has asked us to make with our kids (Deuteronomy 6:6-7). There are no guaranteed outcomes, as with a purchase. For a long time, I didn't fully grasp that difference. I envisioned certain *outcomes* for my children based on the effort I was putting into their spiritual development. When they didn't live up to my expectations, it resulted in my frustration and even anger. It made me not want to do anything more because it didn't seem worth it.

Then I realized one day that I was pursuing results, as if I could *purchase* those outcomes with the currency of my efforts. I was immediately convicted of the error in that thinking and realized I needed to become an *investor*. I felt liberated—newly free to do the job God has given me without the burden and illusion of control.

So go be an investor. Put in all you've got. Then pray that *God* will take that and make it grow, all for His glory.

Notes

All websites last accessed March 31, 2015.

What Your Kids Need for a Confident Faith

1. See www.barna.org/barna-update/article/16-teensnext-gen/147-most-twentysomethings-put-christianity-on-the-shelf-following-spiritually-active-teen-years.

2. For a helpful summary of related research, see www.coldcasechristianity.com/2015/are-young-people-really-leaving-christianity.

3. Search Institute, *Effective Christian Education: A National Study of Protestant Congregations* (Minneapolis, MN: The Institute, 1990).

4. George Barna, *Revolutionary Parenting: Raising Your Kids to Become Spiritual Champions* (Carol Stream, IL: BarnaBooks, 2010).

5. See http://www.pewforum.org/2012/10/09/nones-on-the-rise/.

Chapter 1—What evidence is there for God's existence?

1. William Lane Craig and J.P. Moreland, *The Blackwell Companion to Natural Theology* (Oxford: John Wiley & Sons, 2009), p. 194.

2. Mario Seiglie, "DNA: The Tiny Code That's Toppling Evolution," *The Good News Magazine* (May-June 2005), at http://www.ucg.org/science/dna-tiny-code-thats-toppling-evolution/.

3. Sean McDowell, *77 FAQs About God and the Bible: Your Toughest Questions Answered* (Eugene, OR: Harvest House, 2012).

4. For a list of these, see Dr. Hugh Ross' article "Fine-Tuning for Life on Earth," at http://www.reasons.org/articles/fine-tuning-for-life-on-earth-june-2004.

5. If you're interested in reading more about the Christian response to moral relativism (the idea that there's no objective morality), I highly recommend Paul Copan's *True for You, But Not for Me* (Bloomington, MN: Bethany House, 2009).

6. Antony Flew is a famous example of this. Flew was a 20th-century philosopher who was a strong advocate of atheism. Toward the end of his life, he converted to deism (the belief in an inactive creator God) based on his acceptance of intelligent design arguments. Flew tells his story in the book *There Is a God: How the World's Most Notorious Atheist Changed His Mind* (New York: HarperOne, 2008).

Chapter 2—How could a good God allow evil and suffering?

1. Norman Geisler's book *If God, Why Evil?: A New Way to Think About the Question* (Minneapolis, MN: Bethany House, 2011), is an excellent introduction to the subject.

2. Christians interpret "the fall" in various ways, depending on their view of Genesis. See part 5 for a detailed discussion of Christian views on origins.

3. C.S. Lewis, *Mere Christianity* (New York: HarperCollins, 2009), p. 48.

4. Dinesh D'Souza, "Why We Need Earthquakes," *Christianity Today* (April 28, 2009), at http://www.christianitytoday.com/ct/2009/may/12.58.html?start=1.

Chapter 3—Why would God command the genocide of the Canaanites?

1. See http://dictionary.reference.com/browse/genocide.

2. Some have made the case that God didn't actually command the complete destruction of the Canaanites. There's evidence that much of the book of Joshua is written in the style of other ancient Near Eastern military narratives that exaggerate for the sake of emphasis (called *hyperbole*). The book of Judges makes clear that the "conquest" of Canaan wasn't nearly as successful as the book of Joshua makes it sound. If the language of "utter destruction" is hyperbole in Joshua, therefore, it's possible that the language in God's original command is hyperbole as well. On this view, the main purpose of the conquest was not to kill all the Canaanites, but to expel them from the land. For a detailed book that covers this hypothesis, see Paul Copan and Matthew Flannagan's *Did God Really Command Genocide?: Coming to Terms with the Justice of God* (Grand Rapids, MI: Baker, 2014).

3. For two excellent articles that respond to various critical claims, see Paul Copan's "Yahweh Wars and the Canaanites: Divinely-Mandated Genocide or Corporate Capital Punishment" and Clay Jones' "We Don't Hate Sin So We Don't Understand What Happened to the Canaanites: An Addendum to 'Divine Genocide' Arguments," both in *Philosophia Christi* 11, no. 1 (2009).

Chapter 4—How can a loving God send people to hell?

1. John F. Walvoord, William Crockett, Zachary J. Hayes, and Clark H. Pinnock, *Four Views on Hell* (Counterpoints: Bible and Theology Series), eds. William Crockett and Stanley N. Gundry (Grand Rapids, MI: Zondervan, 1996).

2. C.S. Lewis, *The Problem of Pain* (New York: Macmillan, 1961), p. 116.

Chapter 6—Why would God need people to worship Him?

1. Daniel C. Dennett, *Breaking the Spell: Religion as a Natural Phenomenon* (New York: Penguin, 2006), p. 265.

2. John Piper, *Desiring God: Meditations of a Christian Hedonist* (Colorado Springs: Multnomah, 2011), pp. 81-82.

Chapter 7—Why is God so hidden?

1. Quoted by philosopher Dr. Michael J. Murray in his paper at https://edisk.fandm.edu/michael .murray/Hiddenness.pdf.

2. Paper by Murray at https://edisk.fandm.edu/michael.murray/Hiddenness.pdf.

Chapter 8—Is faith in God the opposite of reason?

1. Tom Gilson and Carson Weitnauer, eds., *True Reason: Confronting the Irrationality of the New Atheism* (Grand Rapids, MI: Kregel, 2013), p. 121.

2. Sam Harris, *The End of Faith: Religion, Terror, and the Future of Reason* (New York: W.W. Norton, 2005), p. 19.

3. A lecture by Richard Dawkins extracted from *The Nullifidian* (December 1994).

4. William Harwood, *Dictionary of Contemporary Mythology* (NP: Independent Custom Press, 2013), Kindle edition, under definition for the word *faith*.

5. Al Seckel, ed., *Bertrand Russell on God and Religion* (Amherst, NY: Prometheus Books, 1986), p. 10.

Chapter 9—What is the difference between objective and subjective truth?

1. See https://answers.yahoo.com/question/index?qid=20100203025742AAczstG.

2. See http://www.debate.org/opinions/is-teaching-children-religion-brainwashing.

Chapter 10—Do all religions point to the same truth?

1. See http://www.jainworld.com/education/stories25.asp.

2. Floyd and Mary Beth Brown, "Oprah's Evolution," *Townhall* (March 13, 2008), at http://townhall.com/columnists/floydandmarybethbrown/2008/03/13/oprahs_evolution/page/full.

3. Adelle M. Banks, "Oprah's 'gospel,' influence concerns some Christians," *USA Today* (July 9, 2008), at http://usatoday30.usatoday.com/news/religion/2008-07-07-oprah-christian_N.htm.

4. Ann Oldenburg, "The divine Miss Winfrey?" *USA Today* (May 11, 2006), at http://usatoday30.usatoday.com/life/people/2006-05-10-oprah_x.htm.

5. See http://www.jainworld.com/education/stories25.asp.

6. See http://www.debate.org/opinions/can-all-religions-be-true.

Chapter 12—How can personal experience help determine what is true?

1. Mark Webb, "Religious Experience," *The Stanford Encyclopedia of Philosophy* (Winter 2011 edition), at http://plato.stanford.edu/archives/win2011/entries/religious-experience/.

2. Alan White, "These Christians Hope to Spread the Word of God by Having Swinger Sessions," *BuzzFeed* (September 25, 2014), at http://www.buzzfeed.com/alanwhite/pumping-iron-and-possibly-other-things.

Chapter 13—How can common sense help determine what is true?

1. James Hervey Johnson, *Superior Men* (1949), at http://www.positiveatheism.org/hist/johnson6.htm.

2. See http://www.merriam-webster.com/dictionary/common%20sense.

3. See http://dictionary.cambridge.org/us/dictionary/american-english/weird.

4. Jeffery DelViscio, "A Fight for the Young Creationist Mind," *The New York Times* (November 3, 2014), at http://www.nytimes.com/2014/11/04/science/in-undeniable-bill-nye-speaks-evolution-directly-to-creationists.html?_r=0.

5. See http://dictionary.reference.com/browse/make+sense.

6. Neal Stone, "Does this make sense to you? It makes sense to Christians!" ExChristian.Net (July 12, 2009), at http://articles.exchristian.net/2009/07/does-this-make-sense-to-you-it-makes.html.

Chapter 14—If Christianity is true, why are there so many denominations?

1. See http://en.wikipedia.org/wiki/List_of_Christian_denominations.

2. See http://www.religioustolerance.org/chr_defn3.htm.

3. Additional essential doctrines are sometimes included in this list, such as human depravity, Christ's virgin birth, Christ's sinlessness, and Christ's second coming. For a more detailed discussion of this topic, see http://www.equip.org/articles/the-essential-doctrines-of-the-christian-faith-part-one/#christian-books-3.

Chapter 15—Is Christianity responsible for millions of deaths in history?

1. See these sites as typical examples: http://truthbeknown.com/ and http://markhumphrys.com/christianity.killings.html.

2. This chapter looks at deaths attributable to Christianity and not to religion in general because, unlike Harris implies, religion as an entire category can't be meaningfully evaluated for this purpose; every religion is based on a different set of "instructions." Every set of teachings must be looked at individually to determine if they can rightfully be blamed for resulting human actions.

That said, it's worth an endnote to briefly comment on Harris' claim that religion is our world's most prolific source of violence. The 1502-page *Encyclopedia of Wars* compiled by Charles Phillips and Alan Axelrod (New York: Facts on File, 2004) describes 1763 conflicts, representing every major war, rebellion, and revolution from 3500 BC to the present. Of the 1763 documented wars, these historians categorized 123 as religious—just 6.9 percent of the total. Clearly, religion is not the most prolific source of violence in our history. That statement is demonstrably false.

3. See this time series of maps for an overview of Muslim expansion from AD 600 to 1091: http://www.reclaimingthemind.org/blog/2013/01/four-misconceptions-about-the-crusades-1-the-crusades-were-not-provoked/.

4. Rodney Stark, *God's Battalions: The Case for the Crusades* (New York: HarperCollins, 2009).

5. See http://en.wikipedia.org/wiki/List_of_wars_and_anthropogenic_disasters_by_death_toll.

6. See http://catholicbridge.com/catholic/inquisition.php.

7. Much has been written to demonstrate that torture was used far less frequently than people popularly claim, but for purposes of this chapter, that's neither here nor there. The question remains: Is there biblical warrant for *any* of the abuses committed during the Inquisition?

8. Bob Chaundy, "The burning times," *BBC News Magazine* (October 30, 2009), at http://news.bbc.co.uk/2/hi/uk_news/magazine/8334055.stm.

9. See http://en.wikipedia.org/wiki/Mao_Zedong.

10. Palash Ghosh, "How Many People did Joseph Stalin Kill?" *International Business Times* (March 5, 2013), at http://www.ibtimes.com/how-many-people-did-joseph-stalin-kill-1111789.

11. Atheists sometimes claim that Hitler was a Christian, and that the Holocaust was actually caused by Christian fundamentalism. While Hitler did make several public statements that appear to show he was a Christian, most historians conclude those statements were used for political gain. Biographer Laurence Rees concluded, "Hitler's relationship in public to Christianity—indeed his relationship to religion in general—was opportunistic. There is no evidence that Hitler himself, in his personal life, ever expressed any individual belief in the basic tenets of the Christian church." (See http://en.wikipedia.org/wiki/Religious_views_of_Adolf_Hitler for more historical background on this topic.)

12. See http://www.history.com/topics/pol-pot.

Chapter 16—Are Christians less intelligent than atheists?

1. Kaitlyn Schallhorn, "Ohio State core class teaches Christians are dumber than atheists," *Campus Reform* (July 24, 2014), at http://www.campusreform.org/?ID=5789.

2. Richard Lynn, John Harvey, and Helmuth Nyborg, "Average intelligence predicts atheism rates across 137 nations" (April 29, 2008), at http://www.sciencedirect.com/science/article/pii/S0160289608000238.

3. If you're interested in the statistical details, the exact correlation between the measures was 0.60.

4. See this article for further details on relevant studies: http://en.wikipedia.org/wiki/Nations_and_intelligence.

5. Miron Zuckerman, Jordan Silberman, and Judith A. Hall, "The Relation Between Intelligence and Religiosity: A Meta-Analysis and Some Proposed Explanations" (November 2013), at http://psr.sagepub.com/content/17/4/325.

6. This can be determined by calculating the correlation between IQ and atheism on each subset of data discussed. The correlation between these measures for nations with an IQ less than 85 and greater than 95 is not statistically different from zero.

7. Zuckerman, Silberman, and Hall, "The Relation Between Intelligence and Religiosity."

8. Zuckerman, Silberman, and Hall, "The Relation Between Intelligence and Religiosity."

9. All past studies were included as long as they reported "intelligence and religiosity at the individual level, and if the effect size (Pearson r) of that relation was provided directly or could be computed from other statistics."

10. William M. Briggs, "Do Atheists Really Have Higher IQs than Believers?" *Strange Notions* at http://www.strangenotions.com/atheists-higher-iqs/.

11. See Table 4 for weighted mean correlations in Zuckerman, Silberman, and Hall, "The Relation Between Intelligence and Religiosity."

12. The weak relationship is a -0.17 correlation between intelligence and religious beliefs for the college studies and a -0.20 correlation for the noncollege studies.

Chapter 17—How do we know Jesus existed?

1. See https://answers.yahoo.com/question/index?qid=20130930232302AA178kU.

2. Randy Dotinga, "Biblical scholar Bart Ehrman supports the historic existence of Jesus," *The Christian Science Monitor* (July 3, 2012), at http://www.csmonitor.com/Books/chapter-and-verse/2012/0703/Biblical-scholar-Bart-Ehrman-supports-the-historic-existence-of-Jesus.

3. William Lane Craig discusses the quality of this reference at length in this article: http://www.reasonablefaith.org/thallus-on-the-darkness-at-noon.

Chapter 18—Did Jesus really claim to be God?

1. Christian Smith and Melinda Lundquist Denton, *Soul Searching: The Religious and Spiritual Lives of American Teenagers* (New York: Oxford University Press, 2009).

2. Smith and Denton, *Soul Searching*, pp. 162-63.

3. Bart Ehrman, *How Jesus Became God: The Exaltation of a Jewish Preacher from Galilee* (New York: HarperOne, 2014), p. 127. If you want to better understand how skeptics often interpret Jesus' life, Ehrman's book is a good, accessible overview. I recommend you then read the Christian rebuttal to Ehrman's book, called *How God Became Jesus*, by Michael F. Bird, Craig A. Evans, Simon Gathercole, Charles E. Hill, and Chris Tilling (Grand Rapids, MI: Zondervan), 2014.

4. Norman L. Geisler and Ronald M. Brooks, *When Skeptics Ask: A Handbook on Christian Evidences* (Grand Rapids, MI: Baker, 2013), pp. 110-13.

5. See Geisler and Brooks' book *When Skeptics Ask*, pp. 110-11, for several additional ways Jesus referenced His equality with the Yahweh of the Old Testament.

6. If you're interested in learning more about messianic prophecies and their fulfillment (and why Jews reject Jesus), here is an excellent index of online articles on the subject: https://chab123.wordpress.com/answering-jewish-objections-to-jesus/.

7. See more examples at http://www.tektonics.org/jesusclaims/miscclaims.php.

Chapter 19—Did Jesus' followers really believe He was God?

1. See Bart Ehrman's book, *How God Became Jesus: The Exaltation of a Jewish Preacher from Galilee* (New York: HarperOne, 2014) for an example of this.

Chapter 20—Why did Jesus need to die on the cross for our sins?

1. See https://www.youtube.com/watch?v=ZX8I2aTuoNw.

2. See http://www.oxforddictionaries.com/us/definition/american_english/sin.

3. Richard Dawkins, *The God Delusion* (New York: Mariner, 2008), p. 287.

Chapter 21—What are the historical facts of the resurrection that nearly every scholar agrees on?

1. Gary Habermas and Michael Licona, *The Case for the Resurrection of Jesus* (Grand Rapids, MI: Kregel, 2004), Kindle edition, Introduction to Part 2.

2. Habermas and Licona, *The Case for the Resurrection of Jesus,* chapter 3.

3. Habermas and Licona, *The Case for the Resurrection of Jesus,* chapter 3.

4. Habermas and Licona, *The Case for the Resurrection of Jesus,* chapter 4.

Chapter 22—What are the major theories people use to explain those facts?

1. William D. Edwards, Wesley J. Gabel, and Floyd E. Hosmer, "On the Physical Death of Jesus Christ," *Journal of the American Medical Association* 255, no. 11 (March 21, 1986): 1463.

2. John M. Grohol, "Grief Brings Out Hallucinations, Illusions," *PsychCentral* at http://psychcentral.com/blog/archives/2008/12/03/grief-brings-out-hallucinations-illusions/.

3. Two additional and similar psychological theories—that people were deluded or had visions—are discussed in detail in chapter 6 of Gary Habermas and Michael Licona's book *The Case for the Resurrection of Jesus* (Grand Rapids, MI: Kregel, 2004). Space prohibits me from discussing them here.

4. Here's one popular website that promotes the parallels between Jesus and Mithra (amongst other similar claims): http://www.truthbeknown.com/mithra.htm.

5. See http://tektonics.org/copycat/mithra.php.

6. This is the case with the popularly discussed figure Apollonius. See Tekton Apologetics' article "Apollonius of Tyana and Jesus" at http://www.tektonics.org/copycat/apollonius.php for more.

7. The apologetics website Tektonics.org offers a wealth of information on each myth, with a list of popular claims and scholarly references to evaluate them. See http://www.tektonics.org/copycathub.html.

8. For more information on how scholars determine this, see Ryan Turner's article, "An Analysis of the Pre-Pauline Creed in 1 Corinthians 15:1-11," at http://carm.org/analysis-pre-pauline-creed-1-corinthians-151-11.

9. J. Warner Wallace's article "What Were the Disciples Saying About Jesus Prior to Writing the Gospels?" gives valuable additional background context on this passage: http://coldcasechristianity.com/2014/what-were-the-disciples-saying-about-jesus-prior-to-writing-the-gospels/.

10. Some scholars claim that this was an "interpolation"—text added many years later. Christopher Price's article "Is 1 Corinthians 15:3-11 an Interpolation?" offers a response and analysis: http://www.christiancadre.org/member_contrib/cp_interpolation.html.

11. For additional theories, see Gary Habermas and Michael Licona's *The Case for the Resurrection of Jesus* (Grand Rapids, MI: Kregel, 2004).

Chapter 23—Why do Christians believe a supernatural resurrection best explains the facts?

1. Michael Licona, *The Resurrection of Jesus: A New Historiographical Approach* (Downers Grove, IL: IVP Academic, 2010), Kindle edition, chapter 1.

2. As cited in John Ankerberg and John Weldon, *Handbook of Biblical Evidences: The Facts on Jesus, Creation, the Bible* (Eugene, OR: Harvest House, 2008), pp. 133-34.

Chapter 24—How can Christians believe miracles are even possible?

1. See http://www.cdc.gov/reproductivehealth/maternalinfanthealth/pretermbirth.htm.

2. See http://www.merriam-webster.com/dictionary/miracle.

3. John Lennox, *Miracles: Is Belief in the Supernatural Irrational?* (Harvard: The Veritas Forum, 2013), p. 22.

4. Lennox, *Miracles*, p.22.

Chapter 25—How were the books in the Bible selected?

1. The Roman Catholic canon includes seven Old Testament books that the Protestant canon does not: 1 and 2 Maccabees, Sirach, Wisdom, Baruch, Tobit, and Judith.

2. I highly recommend F.F. Bruce's classic work *The Canon of Scripture* (Downers Grove, IL: Inter-Varsity, 1988) for more detailed reading on the canonization of both the Old and New Testaments. If you're looking for a higher-level resource, I recommend Craig Blomberg's *Can We Still Believe the Bible?: An Evangelical Engagement with Contemporary Questions* (Grand Rapids, MI: Brazos, 2014) and Norman L. Geisler and William E. Nix's *From God to Us: How We Got Our Bible* (Chicago, IL: Moody, 2012).

3. Bart D. Ehrman, *Lost Scriptures: Books That Did Not Make It into the New Testament* (Oxford: Oxford University Press, 2003), p. 2.

4. Geisler and Nix, *From God to Us*, p. 144.

5. Blomberg, *Can We Still Believe the Bible?*, Kindle edition, chapter 2.

6. Bruce, *The Canon of Scripture*, chapter 11.

7. Blomberg. *Can We Still Believe the Bible?*, chapter 2.

8. Bruce, *The Canon of Scripture*, chapter 19.

9. Geisler and Nix, *From God to Us*, p. 143.

10. See Geisler and Nix's *From God to Us* for more detail on these individual books.

11. F.F. Bruce, *The New Testament Documents: Are They Reliable?* (Downers Grove, IL: InterVarsity and Grand Rapids, MI: Wm. B. Eerdmans, 2003), p. 22.

Chapter 26—Why were books left out of the Bible?

1. Craig Blomberg, *Can We Still Believe the Bible?: An Evangelical Engagement with Contemporary Questions* (Grand Rapids, MI: Brazos, 2014), Kindle edition, chapter 2.

2. Darrell L. Bock, *The Missing Gospels: Unearthing the Truth Behind Alternative Christianities* (Nashville, TN: Thomas Nelson, 2006), Kindle edition, chapter 1. This fantastic book takes an in-depth look at Gnosticism and the current scholarly interest in the "missing gospels." I highly recommend it for further reading on this topic.

3. Norman L. Geisler and William E. Nix, *From God to Us: How We Got Our Bible* (Chicago, IL: Moody, 2012), p. 156.

4. Bock, *The Missing Gospels*, chapter 3.

5. Conservative scholars date Matthew, Mark, and Luke to the 60s and John to the 90s. Liberal scholars often date Mark to the 70s, Matthew and Luke to the 80s, and John to the 90s. Paul wrote at least 7 books (Galatians, 1 Thessalonians, 1 and 2 Corinthians, Romans, Philippians, and Philemon), and scholars date them to between the late 40s and early 60s (many scholars believe Paul wrote at least 13 books).

6. See Bock's *The Missing Gospels*, chapter 4, for an extended discussion on the *Gospel of Thomas*.

7. Bock, *The Missing Gospels*, chapter 14.

8. F.F. Bruce, *The Canon of Scripture* (Downers Grove, IL: InterVarsity, 1988), Kindle edition, chapter 21.

9. Bock, *The Missing Gospels*, chapter 14.

Chapter 27—How do we know we can trust the Bible's authors?

1. J. Warner Wallace, *Cold-Case Christianity: A Homicide Detective Investigates the Claims of the Gospels* (Colorado Springs, CO: David C. Cook, 2013). I really can't say enough good things about this book. It's engaging and packed full of information. Det. Wallace also writes an excellent daily blog to which you can subscribe via email at http://coldcasechristianity.com/.

2. Det. Wallace provides a great summary of evidence that Mark's Gospel is based on Peter's account here: http://coldcasechristianity.com/2014/good-reasons-to-believe-peter-is-the-source-of-ma rks-gospel/. This evidence is highly important since Mark himself was not an eyewitness.

3. Wallace, *Cold-Case Christianity*, p. 183.

4. Wallace, *Cold-Case Christianity*, p. 239.

Chapter 28—How do we know the Bible we have today says what the authors originally wrote?

1. Robert B. Stewart, ed., *The Reliability of the New Testament: Bart D. Ehrman and Daniel B. Wallace in Dialogue* (Minneapolis, MN: Fortress, 2011), p. 27.

2. Stewart, *The Reliability of the New Testament*, p. 32.

3. Stewart, *The Reliability of the New Testament*, p. 33.

4. Stewart, *The Reliability of the New Testament*, pp. 38-46.

5. Stewart, *The Reliability of the New Testament*, p. 40.

6. Bart Ehrman, *Misquoting Jesus: The Story Behind Who Changed the Bible and Why* (New York: HarperCollins, 2005), p. 252.

Chapter 29—Does the Bible have errors and contradictions?

1. See http://bibviz.com/blog/going-viral-again/.

2. A fuller discussion of the bat and other biological "errors" in the Bible can be found in Eric Lyons' article, "Did the Bible Writers Commit Biological Blunders?" *Apologetics Press* (2009), at http://www.apologeticspress.org/apcontent.aspx?category=13&article=2731.

3. See Article X of the "Chicago Statement on Biblical Inerrancy" at http://www.etsjets.org/files/documents/Chicago_Statement.pdf.

4. See http://www.tektonics.org/harmonize/greenharmony.htm as one example.

Chapter 30—Does the Bible support slavery?

1. See http://www.evilbible.com/.

2. See http://www.evilbible.com/.

3. See http://rationalwiki.org/wiki/Slavery_in_the_Bible.

4. Space prohibits me from addressing every slave law. For an excellent in-depth article that breaks down what various scholars say about each verse on slavery, please see http://christianthinktank.com/qnoslave.html.

5. See Paul Copan's *Is God a Moral Monster?: Making Sense of the Old Testament God* (Grand Rapids, MI: Baker, 2011), pp. 140-47 for a discussion of several possibilities.

Chapter 31—Does the Bible support rape?

1. See http://www.evilbible.com/Rape.htm.

2. See Paul Copan's *Is God a Moral Monster?: Making Sense of the Old Testament God* (Grand Rapids, MI: Baker, 2011), pp. 118-19.

3. Some commentators believe consensual sex, rather than rape, is in view here. If that's the case, there's no controversial rape question in these verses. However, many commentators do treat this as a rape law, so I've addressed this more challenging interpretation for reference.

4. Space prohibits me from addressing the exchange of money, or *bride-price*, these verses mention. I highly recommend Copan's *Is God a Moral Monster?* for further reading on the topic.

Chapter 32—Does the Bible support human sacrifice?

1. See http://www.evilbible.com/Ritual_Human_Sacrifice.htm.

Chapter 33—Why do Christians have varying views on how and when God created the world?

1. See this article from the US Geological Survey for more information on the generally accepted age of the Earth: http://geomaps.wr.usgs.gov/parks/gtime/ageofearth.html.

2. See http://www.oxforddictionaries.com/us/definition/american_english/intelligent-design.

3. David Roach, "Pastors Oppose Evolution, Split on Earth's Age," *LifeWay* (January 9, 2012), at http://www.lifeway.com/Article/Research-Poll-Pastors-oppose-evolution-split-on-earths-age.

Chapter 34—What is young-Earth creationism?

1. Gallup, "Evolution, Creationism, Intelligent Design," *Gallup.Com* at http://www.gallup.com/poll/21814/evolution-creationism-intelligent-design.aspx. Interestingly, researchers left out any answer option that would identify someone as an old-Earth creationist; choices only included young-Earth creationism, theistic evolution, and atheistic evolution.

2. Dr. Kenneth L. Gentry, Jr., "The Length of the Days of Genesis 1," *Covenant Media Foundation* at http://www.cmfnow.com/articles/pt555.htm.

3. Dr. Bert Thompson, "The Bible and the Age of the Earth" (Montgomery, AL: Apologetics Press, 2003), pp. 7-8. Available as a free ebook at http://apologeticspress.org/pdfs/e-books_pdf/BibleAge.pdf.

4. For one example explanation, see Greg Nyman's article "Old Earth Creation Science," *Old Earth Ministries* (May 29, 2003), at http://www.oldearth.org/flood.htm.

5. For a detailed discussion of the vegetarian question, see Jim Stambaugh's article "Creation's Original Diet and the Changes at the Fall," *Answers in Genesis* (August 1, 1991), at https://answersingenesis.org/animal-behavior/what-animals-eat/creations-original-diet-and-the-changes-at-the-fall/.

6. Gary Bates and Lita Cosner, "Did God create over billions of years?" *Creation Ministries International* (October 6, 2011), at http://creation.com/Did-god-create-over-billions-of-years/.

7. Ken Ham, *The Lie: Evolution/Millions of Years* (Green Forest, AR: Master, 2012), Kindle edition, chapter 5.

Chapter 35—How do mainstream scientists estimate the age of the Earth?

1. Scientists work to confirm that each ring corresponds to a year based on carbon-14 dating of each one. This method has been used in several cases to support biblical archaeology. See Dr. Jeff Zweerink's article "Multiple Lines of Evidence Support an Ancient Earth," *Reasons to Believe* (December 17, 2010), athttp://www.reasons.org/articles/multiple-lines-of-evidence-support-an-ancient-earth.

2. Gary Bates, "Patriarchs of the Forest," *Creation Ministries International* at http://creation.com/patriarchs-of-the-forest.

3. Frank Lorey, "Tree Rings and Biblical Chronology," *Institute for Creation Research* at http://www.icr.org/article/tree-rings-biblical-chronology/.

4. Dr. Andrew Snelling and Mike Matthews, "When Was the Ice Age in Biblical History?" *Answers in Genesis* (February 26, 2013), at https://answersingenesis.org/environmental-science/ice-age/when-was-the-ice-age-in-biblical-history/.

5. Michael Oard, "The Ice Age and the Genesis Flood," *Institute for Creation Research* at http://www.icr.org/article/ice-age-genesis-flood/.

6. Michael Oard, Larry Vardiman, and Carl Wieland, "Cold comfort for long-agers," *Creation Ministries International* (August 31, 2005), at http://creation.com/cold-comfort-for-long-agers.

7. See http://en.wikipedia.org/wiki/Green_River_Formation.

8. Greg Neyman, "The Truth About Varves," *Old Earth Ministries* (November 1, 2004), at http://www.oldearth.org/varves.htm.

9. Dr. John D. Morris, "Varves: Proof for an Old Earth?" *Institute for Creation Research* at http://www.icr.org/article/varves-proof-for-old-earth/.

10. "How are the ages of the Earth and universe calculated?" *BioLogos* (April 16, 2012), at http://biologos.org/questions/ages-of-the-earth-and-universe.

11. Mike Riddle, "Does Radiometric Dating Prove the Earth Is Old?" *Answers in Genesis* (October 4, 2007), at https://answersingenesis.org/geology/radiometric-dating/does-radiometric-dating-prove-the-earth-is-old/.

12. Tim Chaffey and Jason Lisle, *Old-Earth Creationism on Trial: The Verdict Is In* (Green Forest, AR: Master, 2010), p. 141.

13. Jason Lisle, "Does Distant Starlight Prove the Universe Is Old?" *Answers in Genesis* (December 13, 2007), at https://answersingenesis.org/astronomy/starlight/does-distant-starlight-prove-the-universe-is-old/.

14. See http://hubblesite.org/the_telescope/hubble_essentials/.

15. Chaffey and Lisle, *Old-Earth Creationism on Trial*, p. 143.

16. As one example, you can read an online article entitled "101 evidences for a young age of the earth and the universe" at http://creation.com/age-of-the-earth#20110326, then read a point-by-point rebuttal at http://rationalwiki.org/wiki/101_evidences_for_a_young_age_of_the_Earth_and_the_universe.

Chapter 36—What is old-Earth creationism?

1. David Snoke, *A Biblical Case for an Old Earth* (Grand Rapids, MI: Baker, 2006), p. 18.

2. If you research the old-Earth creationism view further, you may come across a less popular idea called the Gap Theory. The Gap Theory, more popular in decades past, proposes that there was a gap of indefinite time implied between Genesis 1:1 and 1:2. It says that God created a perfect world (Genesis 1:1) but then it *became* formless and void (Genesis 1:2). Gap theorists believe that scientists are measuring the age of the ruined creation, and that Genesis records the six-day restoration.

3. See http://www.reasons.org/.

4. Hugh Ross, *Navigating Genesis: A Scientist's Journey through Genesis 1-11* (Covina, CA: Reasons to Believe, 2014), chapter 1.

5. For a fuller discussion, see Greg Neyman's article "Word Study: Yom," *Old Earth Ministries* (March 16, 2005), at http://www.oldearth.org/word_study_yom.htm.

6. Andrew Kulikovsky, "How could Adam have named all the animals in a single day?" *Creation Ministries International* at http://creation.com/how-could-adam-have-named-all-the-ani mals-in-a-single-day.

7. For a more detailed discussion of the day six activities, see Travis Campbell's article, "The Sixth Creation Day: Biblical Support for Old-Earth Creationism," *Reasons to Believe* (February 19, 2014), at http://www.reasons.org/articles/the-sixth-creation-day-biblical-support -for-old-earth-creationism.

8. Rich Deem, "Did God Create Carnivores on the Sixth Day?" *Evidence for God from Science* (October 29, 2013), at http://www.godandscience.org/youngearth/carnivores.html.

9. Greg Moore, "Does Old-Earth Creationism Contradict Genesis 1?" *Reasons to Believe* (March 1, 2007), at http://www.reasons.org/articles/does-old-earth-creationism-contradict-genesis-1-2.

10. John C. Lennox, *Seven Days that Divide the World: The Beginning According to Genesis and Science* (Grand Rapids, MI: Zondervan, 2011), p. 32.

Chapter 37—What is evolution?

1. See http://www.amazon.com/Why-Evolution-True-Jerry-Coyne-ebook/dp/B001QEQRJW/ ref=sr_1_1?ie=UTF8&qid=1407125415&sr=8-1&keywords=jerry+coyne.

2. See http://en.wikipedia.org/wiki/E._coli_long-term_evolution_experiment.

3. Ker Than, "All Species Evolved From Single Cell, Study Finds," *National Geographic News* (May 14, 2010), at http://news.nationalgeographic.com/news/2010/05/100513-science -evolution-darwin-single-ancestor/.

4. A detailed account of this research is in Jonathan Weiner's Pulitzer Prize winning book *The Beak of the Finch* (New York: Vintage, 1995).

Chapter 38—What are the major pieces of evidence for evolution?

1. For the record, this is a common misunderstanding of evolution. Evolutionists do not suggest that humans descend from modern apes; rather, they say that humans share a *common ancestor* with modern apes.

2. Biologos.org is the website of an organization committed to theistic evolution (or "evolutionary creation," as they prefer to call it). They publish a wealth of articles on science and faith. If you're interested in learning more about theistic evolution, this is the place to start.

3. Jerry A. Coyne, *Why Evolution Is True* (New York: Viking, 2009), p. 22.

4. For a young-Earth creationism view on the ordering of the fossil record, see Andrew Snelling's article "Doesn't the Order of Fossils in the Rock Record Favor Long Ages?" *Answers in Genesis* (September 9, 2010), at https://answersingenesis.org/fossils/fossil-record/doesnt-order -of-fossils-in-rock-favor-long-ages/. While young-Earth creationists generally accept the mainstream consensus on the order of the fossil record, they reject the assigned ages of the layers.

5. Here is a helpful visual of how the fossils change from the bottom to top rock layers: http://www.britannica.com/EBchecked/media/1650/The-geologic-time-scale-from-650 -million-years-ago-to.

6. National Academy of Sciences, *Science and Creationism: A View from the National Academy of Sciences* (Washington, DC: National Academy Press, 1999), p. 14.

7. This website catalogs several of the major fossils evolutionists classify as transitional and includes links to more information: http://www.transitionalfossils.com/.

Chapter 39—What are the major challenges to evolution?

1. Richard Dawkins, "Ignorance Is No Crime," *Council for Secular Humanism* (February 13, 2004), at http://www.secularhumanism.org/library/fi/dawkins_21_3.html.

2. Bill Nye, *Undeniable: Evolution and the Science of Creation* (New York: St. Martin's, 2014), p. 18.

3. Websiteswithextensivearticlesrebuttingevolutionincludewww.answersingenesis.org,www.icr.org, and www.creation.com (young-Earth creationist sites); www.reasons.org and www.godand science.org (old-Earth creationist sites); and www.evolutionnews.org (intelligent design site).

4. William A. Dembski, "Five Questions Evolutionists Would Rather Dodge," designinference.com (April 2004), at http://www.designinference.com/documents/2004.04.Five_Questions_Ev.pdf.

5. Stephen C. Meyer, P.A. Nelson, and Paul Chien, "The Cambrian Explosion: Biology's Big Bang," *Discovery Institute* (2001), at http://www.discovery.org/articleFiles/PDFs/Cambrian.pdf. This document discusses the Cambrian Explosion in detail.

6. Meyer, Nelson, and Chien, "The Cambrian Explosion."

7. Meyer, Nelson, and Chien, "The Cambrian Explosion."

8. Stephen C. Meyer's book *Darwin's Doubt: The Explosive Origin of Animal Life and the Case for Intelligent Design* (New York: HarperOne, 2014) is an excellent and detailed resource for more information on the topic of the Cambrian Explosion.

9. See http://www.genome.gov/10005107.

10. The ENCODE Project Consortium, "An integrated encyclopedia of DNA elements in the human genome," *Nature* 489 (September 6, 2012), at http://www.nature.com/nature/journal/ v489/n7414/pdf/nature11247.pdf.

11. Bodie Hodge, "Are Mutations Part of the 'Engine' of Evolution?" *Answers in Genesis* (February 18, 2010), at https://answersingenesis.org/genetics/mutations/are-mutations-part-of -the-engine-of-evolution/.

12. See http://www.thethirdwayofevolution.com/.

13. Paul Davies, *The Fifth Miracle: The Search for the Origin and Meaning of Life* (New York: Touch- stone, 1999), pp. 17-18.

Chapter 40—What is intelligent design?

1. William A. Dembski, *The Design Revolution: Answering the Toughest Questions About Intelligent Design* (Downers Grove, IL: InterVarsity, 2004), Kindle edition, chapter 1. This is an excellent (though somewhat advanced) resource for understanding the goals of and challenges to intel- ligent design theory.

2. Dembski, *The Design Revolution*, chapter 8.

3. Space prohibits me from discussing applications of specified complexity in nonbiological areas, but an excellent overview can be found in this article (along with answers to common chal- lenges): Casey Luskin, "Straw Men Aside, What Is the Theory of Intelligent Design, Really?" *Evolution News and Views* (August 10, 2013), at http://www.evolutionnews.org/2013/08/what_ is_the_the075281.html.

4. Stephen C. Meyer, *Signature in the Cell: DNA and the Evidence for Intelligent Design* (New York: HarperCollins, 2009), pp. 385-86.

5. The applications of intelligent design theory also reach into physics, cosmology, and astronomy. I've focused on the application of intelligent design theory to biology since that's the subject for this section of the book (and it's probably the most commonly discussed application).

6. Dembski, *The Design Revolution*, chapter 1.

7. See http://www.ucsusa.org/scientific_integrity/what_you_can_do/evolution-and-id-footnotes.html#4-2.

8. See http://biologos.org/questions/biologos-id-creationism.

9. Mark Looy, "It's Intelligent, but Is That Good Enough?" *Answers in Genesis* (March 29, 2000), at https://answersingenesis.org/intelligent-design/its-intelligent-but-is-that-good-enough/.

10 Tips for Having Deeper Faith Conversations with Your Kids

1. I've written a blog post that explains how I've been teaching my kids critical thinking at home. This activity has fundamentally changed the way my kids think. I highly recommend it for kids of any age! See http://NatashaCrain.com/how-im-teaching-my-6-year-olds-to-be-critical-thinkers/.

2. *The Fallacy Detective: Thirty-Eight Lessons on How to Recognize Bad Reasoning* (Muscatine, IA: Christian Logic, 2009) is a great little book by Nathaniel Bluedorn and Hans Bluedorn. Each chapter has a short lesson on a logical fallacy (an error in thinking) with several exercises to give your kids. Answers are included. See my review for more information: http://NatashaCrain.com/how-to-teach-your-kids-critical-thinking-skills-a-great-resource/.

3. See http://NatashaCrain.com/14-ways-for-christian-parents-to-teach-kids-about-atheism/.

4. Barna Group, "Research Shows That Spiritual Maturity Process Should Start at a Young Age," *Barna Group* (November 17, 2003), at https://www.barna.org/barna-update/article/5-barna-update/130-research-shows-that-spiritual-maturity-process-should-start-at-a-young-age#.VQPCEo54pcQ.